Practitioner Research in Counsel

Practitioner Research in Counselling and Psychotherapy

The Power of Examples

EDITED BY
LIZ BONDI AND JUDITH FEWELL

 palgrave

First published 2016 by
PALGRAVE

Palgrave in the UK is an imprint of Macmillan Publishers Limited,
registered in England, company number 785998, of 4 Crinan Street,
London, N1 9XW.

Palgrave Macmillan in the US is a division of St Martin's Press LLC,
175 Fifth Avenue, New York, NY 10010.

Palgrave is a global imprint of the above companies and is represented
throughout the world.

Palgrave® and Macmillan® are registered trademarks in the United States,
the United Kingdom, Europe and other countries.

ISBN 978–1–137–39029–5 paperback

This book is printed on paper suitable for recycling and made from fully
managed and sustained forest sources. Logging, pulping and manufacturing
processes are expected to conform to the environmental regulations of the
country of origin.

A catalogue record for this book is available from the British Library.

A catalog record for this book is available from the Library of Congress.

Printed and bound by CPI Group (UK) Ltd, Croydon, CR0 4YY

Contents

Notes on the Contributors

Liz Bondi is Professor of Social Geography at the University of Edinburgh, where she contributes to professional education in Counselling and Psychotherapy, and a psychodynamic counsellor accredited by COSCA (Counselling and Psychotherapy in Scotland). Liz began her academic career in human geography, which she continued while training part-time in counselling. Combining her academic background in human geography (and the social sciences more generally) with her interest in counselling and psychotherapy, she has led or contributed to a series of research projects about the cultural shaping of counselling and psychotherapy in Scotland. She also applies ideas from counselling and psychotherapy to the developing field of 'emotional geographies'. She is founding editor of the journal *Emotion, Space and Society* and author of numerous academic papers as well as coeditor or coauthor of several books.

Siobhan Canavan recently retired from a post as Lecturer in Counselling and Psychotherapy at the University of Edinburgh where she worked for 14 years. She is an accredited counsellor, clinical supervisor, and trainer. She has taught at all levels of undergraduate and postgraduate study, has supervised master's and doctoral students, and been involved in post-qualification training. She has also been responsible for the mentoring and support of new master's supervisors. Among many other jobs, she has managed a counselling centre in higher education, has maintained a small private practice, and continues to supervise counsellors.

Patrick Fegan began his counselling journey in 1996 as a consequence of his experience working on a telephone helpline. This led to his formal counselling training at the University of Edinburgh and a career in the addictions field, managing community and residential drug services across Scotland. He is an integrative counsellor, the foundations of his orientation being born out of a dialogue between the person-centred approach and psychodynamic perspectives. He manages a school-based counselling service, works with supervisees, and designs and teaches courses for counsellors and therapists working with children and young people. Patrick works clinically with all age groups.

Judith Fewell is a psychoanalytic psychotherapist in private practice in Edinburgh and an Honorary Fellow at the University of Edinburgh. For many years she worked as a freelance trainer within the statutory and voluntary sectors in Scotland, delivering workshops and courses based on psychodynamic thinking for professionals and volunteers. At the University of Edinburgh, in Counselling and Psychotherapy, she contributed to the development and delivery of the Postgraduate Diploma in Counselling, supervised master's and doctoral students, and participated in the research programme. Judith has a long-term interest in, and commitment to, the single case study as a legitimate form of research into psychotherapeutic practices and understandings. This has led her to explore and write about how personal and professional narratives of the psychotherapist can help illustrate and illuminate psychoanalytic theory and practice.

Linda Gardner, originally from a nursing background, is now a BACP (British Association for Counselling and Psychotherapy)-accredited counsellor who has worked for many years as a counsellor in the field of substance misuse, working with both adults and young people. She is also a trained relationship counsellor and works both as a volunteer counsellor and in private practice with couples and individuals. She has a keen interest in mindfulness practice.

Connie Johnson has been a practising counsellor for 25 years and has worked in a variety of settings including voluntary and community sectors as well as in further and higher education. She is a senior teaching fellow at the University of Edinburgh, where she teaches postgraduate students on professional programmes. She is currently engaged in studying for a PhD for which she is researching aspects of the client/counsellor relationship where the client is disabled.

Janette Masterton is a BACP-accredited counsellor and holds an MSc in Counselling from Edinburgh University. Over a period of 16 years on a voluntary basis, she set up and developed a bereavement counselling service in Edinburgh Prison under the auspices of Cruse Bereavement Care Scotland. Janette's research explored the lived experience of bereavement in prison through telling the stories of imprisoned clients whose grief was shared with her during counselling. As such, it was a qualitative case-based practitioner research study, which was grounded in practice. Its findings and recommendations have been used to inform the Scottish Prison Service (SPS) strategy framework for bereavement care in Scottish prisons. The SPS has worked in partnership with Cruse to replicate in other Scottish prisons the counselling service Janette set up in Edinburgh Prison.

April Parkins is a music therapist and psychodynamic counsellor, accredited by BACP. She teaches at Queen Margaret University in Edinburgh on the MSc Music Therapy course and contributes to the Counselling and Psychotherapy Postgraduate Diploma training at the University of Edinburgh. She works as a counsellor and supervisor and is a registered supervisor for the British Association for Music Therapy. She also practises Guided Imagery and Music.

Seamus Prior is a Senior Lecturer in Counselling and Psychotherapy at the University of Edinburgh and a practising psychodynamic counsellor. He teaches on professional training programmes and research programmes in counselling and psychotherapy and supervises master's and doctoral students. He also contributes to the development of ethical research practice among social science doctoral students across the university.

Lynne Rollo works as a counsellor in the east of Scotland, and her practice is mainly rooted in the dialogue between the person-centred approach and psychodynamic perspectives. Before training to be a counsellor, Lynne's professional background was in social work, and she continues to work in this field. Her social work experience includes working with people who have learning difficulties and with vulnerable homeless adults. Since 2006 Lynne has worked as a social worker within specialist mental health services and has qualified as a mental health officer. Lynne completed the Postgraduate Diploma and Master of Counselling at the University of Edinburgh and has a particular interest in issues of gender and power in the counselling relationship.

Chris Scott is a psychodynamic counsellor working in primary care as part of an NHS Lothian psychological therapies team. Chris initially studied human relations and counselling with the Scottish Institute of Human Relations before undertaking a Master of Counselling training with the University of Edinburgh. Chris has combined this learning with studies in cognitive and behavioural psychotherapy at the University of Dundee. Chris's principal area of interest is in attachment theory, in particular its application in short-term counselling contracts.

Diana Sim works as a counsellor in a university counselling service. She holds an MSc in Counselling. She has also worked in statutory and voluntary settings doing both long- and short-term counselling. Prior to becoming a counsellor Diana worked as a primary school teacher for many years. Her interest in child development extends into her work as a counsellor where she remains particularly interested in the impact of early childhood on later life. Diana's journey from teacher to counsellor has also enabled her to explore the concept of knowledge. She is interested in the difference between the type of knowledge that is acquired through the education system and the learning that comes through counselling, which often means paying attention to what is not known.

Anna St Clair began her career in the arts as a professional dancer before gaining her teaching qualifications with the Royal Academy of Dance. She mentored and supervised teachers in training and entered students for examinations within her dance school. A change in career led her to complete a Master's in Counselling at the University of Edinburgh and go into practice working with children, young people, and adults. Anna is a co-developer and deliverer of a communication programme that centres its approach on the quality of the interaction between physician and patient.

Linda Talbert works as a counsellor and human resources consultant for a Christian charity. She is a PhD candidate at the University of Edinburgh where she holds an MSc in Counselling and Psychotherapy. She earned a BA in English Literature from the University of Maryland and a Diploma in Biblical Studies from the International School of Theology. Her academic work reflects an interest in textual interpretation and the interfaces between literature, theology, and therapy.

Mags Turner is a psychodynamic counsellor working in private practice in Edinburgh. She began her counselling training at the University of Edinburgh in 2007 and graduated in 2011 with a Master of Counselling. She has over this time worked with adults, young people, and children and has a particular interest in group therapy. The relational aspect and the idea of connection are pivotal in her work. In the past Mags gained a BSc in Management, and she has worked in many areas, most notably in publishing. She draws on both her professional and personal experiences to inform her counselling practice. Her Irish heritage of originating from a large Catholic family is a constant source of inspiration and exploration and validates the central message of the importance of the single case study as a legitimate form of research.

Acknowledgements

This book has been in the making for many years. In 2004 we began working together on a new dedicated research course for master's students who had completed Postgraduate Diplomas in Counselling. Our approach was influenced by our immersion in critical social science and feminist studies, as well as by our experience as practitioners and counselling educators. Since then, we have had the privilege of working with numerous students, a small selection of whom became contributors to this book. They have all helped us to develop our thinking. So too have the wide range of colleagues in university and practice settings with whom we have had the good fortune to discuss and reflect on the work that we do. Along the way we have worked with many clients, learning anew in each and every therapeutic relationship. We would like to thank all of these people who have helped to shape our thinking and practice in myriad ways.

Liz Bondi and Judith Fewell

Part I

Reclaiming the Wisdom of Practice in Counselling and Psychotherapy Research

1 Why Does Research So Often Alienate Practitioners and What Can Be Done About It?

LIZ BONDI AND JUDITH FEWELL

How do we develop knowledge in the field of counselling and psycho-therapy? There is a tendency for this question to be addressed in two rather different ways, depending upon whether the 'we' is taken to refer to individuals becoming practitioners or to researchers who are often understood to be the people who advance a body of knowledge about counselling and psychotherapy. In the first case, we might think of the question as being about how we acquire the capacity to become qualified and skilful practitioners through training and practice. In the second case, the question tends to become one about how we expand the knowledge base of the field through research. Of course the two are connected to one another in the sense that training has the potential to be informed by research and vice versa. But these connections are rather abstract and are not inevitable. In our experience, practitioners and those in training often express fear and anxiety or even antipathy towards what they understand research to be, viewing it as inherently alien when set alongside therapeutic practice. We also have a sense from our own experience in a variety of settings of considerable tension within the community of people who make up the field of counselling and psy-chotherapy, including practitioners and researchers, about what makes for truly knowledgeable, expert, and high-quality practitioners and about what makes for a valuable body of knowledge capable of giving the field weight, especially when compared to other, older disciplines.

These tensions do not seem to be addressed explicitly in the professional or research literature of counselling and psychotherapy. Instead, what we witness are efforts by professional bodies, including but not limited to the British Association for Counselling and Psychotherapy (BACP),

3

to promote research on the grounds that it will raise the prestige of the field as a whole. As well as sponsoring research projects and research events, through its journals BACP exhorts its members to enhance and update their practice-based knowledge by engaging with research, most obviously as readers of its research journal *Counselling and Psychotherapy Research*. This drive towards research has also been fostered by a shift in the location of training away from providers without any links to further or higher education (typically voluntary or private organisations) towards what is now the almost universal delivery of training with academic credentials attached, whether through validation or direct delivery by colleges and universities. The association of training with universities lends credence to the view that counselling has a knowledge base that has developed and is continually being enhanced through research.

We – the authors of this chapter and editors of this book – occupy peculiar positions in relation to this promotion of research within counselling and psychotherapy. We are experienced practitioners with long involvement in the training and education of counsellors and psychotherapists at the postgraduate level. We are also experienced researchers who came to the field of counselling and psychotherapy after spending several years involved in academic research in the social sciences. We might therefore appear to be natural advocates of the increasing value attached to research in counselling and psychotherapy. However, we have both been deeply troubled by *the form of research* that has swiftly acquired particular authority within counselling and psychotherapy, together with the accompanying assumptions about what constitutes valued knowledge and valuable ways of knowing in the field. We have been painfully disappointed and often alienated by many of the papers published in research journals, including *Counselling and Psychotherapy Research*, as well as by the policies of at least some of these journals, which, despite proclamations of openness, seem unable to comprehend critiques of, and alternatives to, the particular types of research they promote. So, although we are experienced researchers, we find ourselves just as doubtful about the value of much of what is presented as research in counselling and psychotherapy as numerous practitioners who have no such experience of research.

The core problem from our perspective is that the kind of research that is promoted via professional bodies and by many university researchers embodies the very antithesis of what we value most highly in our approach to training and practice. Research of the kind by which we are troubled claims to provide and to generate definitive, robust, and reliable forms of knowledge of a different and more authoritative form than the practice-based wisdom conveyed and cultivated through training. From this dominant perspective, research produces an objective 'evidence base' through which to validate counselling and psychotherapy in ways that funders – especially those who fund healthcare services – recognise. This kind of research, which dominates the medical and psychological sciences too, takes it for granted that valuable and reliable knowledge consists of generalisations, typically based on large numbers of instances, or on carefully controlled and replicable experiments, or on rule-based analysis of material by an objective and detached researcher. Generalisations are statements that are assumed to be capable of being applied across widely differing contexts and therefore also capable of being used to make predictions. The underlying methodologies on which such research is based are predominantly numerical or quantitative and often statistical, and they are intrinsically 'experience-far' in the sense that there is a considerable and intentional distance between the lived experience to which they ultimately refer and the evidence in which they deal. For example the misery of depression is turned into numerical scores, which stand as objective representations of the often barren despair and hopelessness that characterise the subjective experience of those living with depression and by which practitioners are likely to be touched.

When practitioners are exhorted to apply the findings generated by such research to their practice, we often find ourselves at a loss. How are practitioners to apply findings formulated in terms of generalisations of various kinds in their work with unique individuals in the context of unique therapeutic relationships? Staying with the example of depression, a crucial task for practitioners is likely to entail understanding and coming alongside the specificity of a client's experience, perhaps quietly holding hope but without expecting or pressuring the person to change. Faith in the possibility of predicting when and through what mechanisms or steps the person will feel 'better' is likely to be more of a hindrance than a help. Clearly, the translation or application of research findings that take the form of generalisations into practice is very far from straightforward, and it is not surprising that practitioners have little use for such research. To our dismay, even when different kinds of methodologies are used in counselling and psychotherapy research, including those that purport to work much more closely with qualities of subjective experience, the underlying model of knowledge through which they are framed often remains very close to this dominant image of research-based knowledge.

For example, evidence is often presented as thing-like, and researchers appear to remain at a distance from it in a way that is radically different from the experience of practitioners.

To introduce the idea of an approach to research that does not depend upon distance and objectification, we draw on a distinction attributed to the American psychoanalyst Heinz Kohut (1971) and taken up by the anthropologist Clifford Geertz (1983) between 'experience-near' and 'experience-far' or 'experience-distant'. By 'experience-near' we mean close to the feelings and subjective states of those involved in therapeutic practice as practitioners and clients, whereas we understand 'experience-far' to mean at a distance from such feelings and subjective states. Therapeutic work is based in relationships, which themselves depend upon lived experiences of selves and of others. Training in counselling and psychotherapy cultivates in practitioners the capacity to stay with, value, and process in an 'experience-near' mode, with beginners often discovering the need to give up attempts to apply 'experience-far' ways of working.

In this context we find very troubling the dominance of approaches to research that exclude, dismiss, objectify, reduce, or control the experience-near. We do not deny that objective, experience-far forms of knowledge may be useful in some circumstances, for example for instrumental purposes with funders and commissioners. However, we also argue that they are of limited relevance to practitioners in counselling and psychotherapy for whom sensitivity to the very particular context of each therapeutic relationship is paramount. Indeed, research that positions itself as remote from lived experience and capable of offering objective knowledge about it will tend to reinforce the feelings of alienation to which we have already referred. We wonder why the 'experience-near' ways of working associated with therapeutic practice tend to be so devalued in counselling and psychotherapy research, particularly given their prominence in other fields. And we are deeply perplexed about how experiences of doing or being involved in research of the kind that has come to dominate our field relate to the work practitioners actually do to make therapeutic relationships possible and to work effectively within them. If research and practice operate at such different poles, it is not surprising to find a gulf in comprehension between them.

This book offers a very different way of thinking about the relationship between research and practice in counselling and psychotherapy in which they remain closely connected through a shared emphasis on the experience-near. We argue that if we understand practice in terms of lived experiences, the research to which it relates needs itself to take a form that honours and fosters lived experiences of being and struggling to be in relationship to ourselves and others. More specifically this book makes the case for, and provides examples of, an approach to research that does not seek to generalise or objectify but, instead, stays close to therapeutic work and therapeutic relationships as they are experienced. The examples presented in Chapters 4 to 14 are all drawn from dissertations conducted by master's students, most of whom also completed their professional training in counselling at the University of Edinburgh, where one of us – Judith Fewell – played a major role in the development of counsellor training in Scotland and has worked as a counselling trainer for many years, and where the other of us – Liz Bondi – has led the development and delivery of master's and doctoral research training for students in counselling and psychotherapy. Our professional training programme is founded on a dialogue between the person-centred approach, located within the humanistic tradition, and psychodynamic perspectives, located in the psychoanalytic tradition.

The examples presented in the book all work at, or are close to, the boundaries between research and practice, and they seek to minimise the distinction between research and reflective practice in the field of counselling and psychotherapy. We hope that they will be relevant to and perhaps inspire practitioners in relation to their practice within and beyond counselling and psychotherapy, as well as students considering how to approach their own research and educators seeking to develop curricula for research.

Some commentators might view the examples this book offers as not conforming to what is meant by the term research, precisely because they are equally expressions of reflective practice. However, it is our intention to contest this point of view and, in chapter two, to put forward a way of thinking about and doing research characterised by rich, creative examples deeply informed by the values and principles of practice in the field of counselling and psychotherapy. We make our case by drawing on arguments developed in the social sciences about the limitations of approaches to research modelled on the natural sciences, about the importance of practical wisdom, and about the power of examples for developing knowledge about the human world. Our approach has been especially influenced by the contribution of feminist perspectives to debates in the social sciences. Our argument also builds on a long tradition of valuing sustained, deep, rigorous, and sometimes wide-ranging reflections on specific instances of therapeutic work and therapeutic relationships.

In order to be consistent with the approach to research we set out in this book, we give the majority of the space to examples of practitioner research of the kind we advocate. The opening three chapters set these examples in context by elaborating our argument for this approach to research, which is closely aligned to reflective practice. In the next section of this chapter we point to the early history of our field in which Sigmund Freud and his colleagues took for granted that reflection on clinical cases provided the route by which knowledge could and should be developed. We then consider two broad reasons why the clinical case study has fallen out of fashion as the favoured means for approaching research in counselling and psychotherapy: one concerned with changing fashions in what counts as authoritative knowledge and one concerned with questions of ethics and professional values. We finish the chapter by outlining the chapters that make up the rest of the book.

Knowledge, Research, and Practice

In the first issue of *Counselling and Psychotherapy Research,* its founding editor John McLeod explained the rationale for the creation of the journal. He argued that 'research and practice have become disconnected' in the field of counselling and psychotherapy and that it is crucial to develop 'a research tradition consistent with the practices and values of counselling and psychotherapy' in order to overcome this disconnection (McLeod, 2001, p. 3). While transformations in the relationship between research and practice are never likely to happen rapidly, there is little evidence to date to suggest that much has changed in the years since *Counselling and Psychotherapy Research* came into being. People studying and practising in counselling and psychotherapy continue to report being rather less than enthusiastic about research in the field. Researchers and professional organisations acknowledge the persistence of this view and, in some of the ways in which they seek to reach past it, even hint that it may be inevitable. One influential example is the primer *Essential Research Findings in Counselling and Psychotherapy,* written by Mick Cooper (2008) and endorsed by the British Association for Counselling and Psychotherapy, which is subtitled 'the facts are friendly' as if the expectation is that the term 'research findings' will put off the book's intended audience.

Our argument in this book is that instead of trying to persuade or cajole practitioners into agreeing that research is worth engaging with, we need to think more deeply about how knowledge develops in our field of practice and how practitioners themselves develop their competence at the beginning of their training and throughout their careers. We argue that the knowledge that is embodied in practitioners in their routine practice is the knowledge that makes a difference to how they work with those who consult them. So if engaging with research is to be valuable, it too needs to be embodied and it needs to take a form that is 'consistent with the practices and values of counselling and psychotherapy' (McLeod, 2001, p. 3).

As McLeod (2001) has noted, reflecting on, discussing, and writing clinical case studies based on specific examples of clinical practice were crucial activities for the originators of counselling and psychotherapy. Freud, and many of those who followed him, developed the body of knowledge that underpins counselling and psychotherapy through their case studies. In other words, specific examples of clinical work were used to build up a body of knowledge that has informed subsequent generations of practitioners. One early example of how clinical case studies generate knowledge is in the text *Studies in Hysteria* written jointly by Josef Breuer and Sigmund Freud (1955 [1893–1895]), which narrates and discusses five case studies, starting with Breuer's account of his treatment of Fraülein Anna O. That case study is widely credited as the point of origin for the method of free association and the term 'the talking cure' (Schwartz, 1999). A legend has also grown up about the termination of Breuer's work with Anna O, which endows it with a decisive role in the development of Freud's idea of the transference. Anna O came into treatment with Breuer because of painful and debilitating symptoms she suffered without apparent organic cause, which doctors including Breuer understood to be manifestations of hysteria. According to the legend, in what was to be the final session of work with Breuer, Anna complained of acute abdominal cramps, which she attributed to being in labour with Breuer's baby. In response to Anna's claim that he had impregnated her, Breuer promptly terminated the treatment. Looking back on the case (and perhaps having constructed this story of how it ended), Freud came to understand what had happened as providing a key enabling him to recognise the importance and the power of the transference. Freud viewed Anna's fantasy of being impregnated by Breuer as an expression of an unconscious transfer from her desire in relation to her father onto the man with whom she had worked therapeutically. Even if the story is more of a myth than an accurate description of how Breuer's work with Anna O came to an end, it illustrates what we mean by the power of example: one case, one of a kind, utterly distinct, can have a decisive influence on the development of theory and practice. Freud did not need hundreds of patients to imagine that they were pregnant by their therapists to formulate his idea.

Many other key principles of therapeutic practice also have their origins in careful reflections on particular examples (Rustin, 2001), not only within the psychoanalytic tradition but also within humanistic psychotherapies. For example, Carl Rogers' (1942) influential early text *Counseling and Psychotherapy: New Concepts in Practice*, in which he first set out his argument about the centrality of an empathic, accepting therapeutic relationship, includes numerous clinical vignettes as well as an extended case study of his work with Herbert Ryan. Two decades later, Virginia Axline (1964) published what has become a classic account of her work with a young boy called Dibs, through which she helped to shape the development of humanistic therapeutic practice with children and families.

Despite the enormous importance of clinical case studies in the development of psychoanalysis and other approaches to counselling and psychotherapy, their role has changed considerably, especially over the last 50 years or so. One indication of this is that journals that communicate primarily through the clinical examples, including for example the *British Journal of Psychotherapy*, have come to be regarded as practitioner journals as opposed to research journals. The occasional appearances of special issues devoted to case-study research in other journals, such as Volume 13, issue 2 of *Person-Centered and Experiential Psychotherapies* (2014), make clear their exceptional status and turn out to be concerned at least as much with how clinical case studies can be pressed into a format that makes them look more like the very forms of research that have come to dominate understandings of research than discussions of clinical examples found in practitioner journals or indeed classic texts. In the light of this, in the next two sections of this chapter we set out two broad reasons why clinical case studies have fallen out of favour as an approach to research, one concerned with assumptions about the nature of knowledge and one concerned with questions of ethics. In so doing we pave the way for considering how a return to case-study research might once more help to close the gap that has opened between practice and research.

Authoritative Knowledge

Education and training in counselling and psychotherapy continue to accord a central role to learning through reflection on practice, that is, on what happens in live examples of the clinical work of the learner. In other words, the careful study of particular cases continues to be seen as a crucial ingredient in the development of the capacity to work as a practitioner. But alongside the continuing centrality accorded to the clinical case study in the education and training of practitioners, the way research is thought about in fields that have been especially influential in counselling and psychotherapy, including psychology and medicine, has moved in a very different direction, which has eroded the value accorded to clinical case studies. Indeed, in discussions of research in counselling and psychotherapy, clinical case studies have come to be regarded as anecdotal and unduly subjective and thus as lacking the authority required to provide a robust knowledge base. Understandings of research in counselling and psychotherapy have therefore gravitated towards a model of knowledge development far removed from that which informs thinking and practice on how we develop ourselves as practitioners.

Freud thought of himself as a scientist and believed that he was contributing to the development of scientific theory through his and his colleagues' discussion of their clinical cases. However, since then, and especially during the second half of the twentieth century, views of reliable, trustworthy evidence within Western healthcare systems have changed a great deal. The dominant influence has come from approaches established in medical science, which are avowedly experience-far and which have been brought to bear on a wider range of arenas, including many in which publicly funded services are provided within and beyond healthcare settings.

While medical research has a long history, its norms and assumptions have changed over time. Beginning in the second half of the twentieth century, numerous major contributions to clinical practice have been achieved through the use of randomised controlled trials (RCTs), ideally 'double-blind' and prospective in format. Randomisation entails the random allocation of patients with particular conditions or symptoms (and excluding those who have conditions or symptoms additional to those on which the trial focuses) to receive a specific treatment or to receive a placebo, with the latter forming the 'control' group. A trial is 'double-blind' if neither the patients nor the clinicians in contact with them know whether any particular individual is receiving the treatment being tested or the placebo, something that is possible to achieve when the treatment is a medication but which is impossible for a whole range of interventions, including counselling and psychotherapy, which entail interpersonal interactions between the client and the practitioner. A trial is prospective if the research follows people from the beginning of the process rather than relying on retrospective analysis of what has happened in the past.

RCTs and related methods have greatly improved standards of treatment in many areas of medicine, especially where the treatment takes the form of medication. For people needing treatment for a specific medical condition, it is very reassuring to know that the treatment recommended has been subjected to rigorous investigation rather than being more vaguely based on what one doctor thinks might work. RCTs have also led to the development of robust systems for evaluating evidence in such fields, establishing a normative framework for medical research that includes the idea of a hierarchy of evidence. Clinicians have much more to draw upon in proposing treatment plans, and their decisions are increasingly informed by guidance developed and issued at a national level, for example in the United Kingdom by the National Institute for Health and Care Excellence (NICE; formerly, until 2013, National Institute for Health and Clinical Excellence) and the Scottish Intercollegiate Guidelines Network (SIGN). It is within the hierarchy of evidence that has developed as a result of RCTs that case studies reported directly by practitioners have come to occupy a very lowly position, viewed as anecdotes from which bias, confounding errors, and other reasons for scepticism cannot be excluded.

This hierarchy of evidence and the ensuing guidance, which drives decisions about funding and therefore the availability of treatments and services, applies just as much to mental health care as to physical health care. For example, NICE guideline 91, published in October 2009, addresses the treatment of depression in adults, and SIGN guideline 114, published in January 2010, sets out guidance on the non-pharmacological treatment of depression. These documents shape the commissioning of services across much of the UK, and both adhere strictly to a view of evidence that privileges statistical reliability and that treats clinical case reports as lacking sufficient credibility to inform decision-making. They therefore rely almost exclusively on evidence from trials conducted according to strict protocols about the diagnosis of depression, together with manualised approaches to therapeutic practice that specify in considerable detail how clinicians should work with their clients or patients. This evidence base is therefore remote from, and actively excludes consideration of, the great majority of the therapeutic work that counsellors and psychotherapists do with adults who experience the symptoms of depression.

Medicine is an extremely important and influential field. Discoveries and developments in medical science have made huge differences to the lives of people all over the world. Consequently, medical research is very highly regarded and has acquired great authority, which is hard to question or compete with. This has, inevitably, impacted on researchers in the field of counselling and psychotherapy, with some of them accepting without question the lowly place accorded to clinical case studies (Aveline, 2005; Rowland and Goss, 2000). Furthermore, given that counselling and psychotherapy services and practitioners often struggle for recognition from those commissioning healthcare services, it is not surprising that efforts have been made to demonstrate the effectiveness and value of counselling and psychotherapy (or particular forms thereof) using RCTs and related methods (e.g. King, Marston, and Bower, 2014; Pybis et al., 2014). Trials of counselling and psychotherapy as interventions cannot conform to the idea of a double-blind format; nor can counselling be offered in placebo form. Consequently these trials typically compare the effects (or outcomes) of counselling with those of medication, or with 'usual care', or they compare the effects of different kinds of counselling. Where it is not possible to set up trials, there has been much emphasis on gathering and analysing standardised, quantifiable forms of evidence, as in the use of Clinical Outcome and Routine Evaluation (CORE) questionnaires, whether to study outcomes or other aspects of counselling and psychotherapy within a quantitative framework (see Barkham et al., 2006, for a brief history).

So what is wrong with this? RCTs and other quantitative approaches designed to test the effectiveness and value of counselling and psychotherapy attempt to fit therapeutic practice to a framework designed for other purposes. Within the normative hierarchy of evidence that has become so influential within the governance of health services, they remain vulnerable to criticism because of the awkwardness of the fit. More fundamentally, it is important to consider whether methods designed to generate knowledge appropriate for decisions about medication and comparable treatments are suited to the development of knowledge in other fields, including counselling and psychotherapy. Important light on this question comes from within the field of medicine itself. For example, one influential commentator has expressed his view that 'the commitment to "evidence-based medicine" *of a particular sort*' has been transformed unhelpfully and inappropriately 'into an intellectual hegemony' (Berwick, 2005, p. 315, emphasis added). This commentator, Donald Berwick, is an eminent clinician and health improvement expert of international renown, influential in the United States of America and the United Kingdom. He draws attention to the way in which some kinds of knowledge can only be developed through practice when he asks:

> Did you learn Spanish by conducting experiments? Did you master your bicycle or your skis using randomized trails? Are you a better parent because you did a laboratory study of parenting? Of course not. And yet, do you doubt what you have learned? (Ibid., p. 315)

Berwick's concern about the dangers of over-valuing experience-far, objective forms of knowledge, and of under-valuing the testimony of patients themselves is echoed by other senior and highly regarded medical practitioners. We point to three recent such examples, each of which speaks to values that counsellors and psychotherapists hold dear. First, the American surgeon, public health expert, and 2014 Reith lecturer Atul Gawande (2014, p. 182) offers an impassioned plea to health workers to engage their terminally ill patients in conversations about death and dying and makes the point that 'this process requires as much listening as talking. If you [the clinician] are talking more than half the time...you're talking too much'. Second, the British neurosurgeon Henry Marsh (2014, p. ix) discusses his attempts 'to find a balance between the necessary detachment and compassion that a surgical career requires' and gently chides trainee surgeons who begin case reports by considering brain scans rather than the descriptions of symptoms relayed by their patients. Third, the American neurologist Allan Ropper and his coauthor Brian Burrell (2014) write movingly of the way, when something goes wrong with a person's brain, like Alice in Wonderland that person disappears down a rabbit hole. To help them, the neurologist needs to find a way to reach down the rabbit hole in order to begin the painstaking effort of trying to find a way to get them out. This task necessarily means working with the unique presentations of unique individuals in a way that shares some resemblance to psychotherapeutic practice.

All of these medical clinicians demonstrate how they acquired their expert knowledge as much through specific clinical examples as through mastery of the research findings consolidated in medical textbooks and updated via new RCTs and other experience-far forms of research. Alongside them, recent decades have witnessed the rise of 'narrative medicine', which insists on the importance of patients' subjective accounts of their suffering in the context of their lives and which also advocates experience-near approaches to practice, education, and research in medicine (Charon, 2006). So, while the authority of medical science of the kind associated with RCTs and a singular hierarchy of evidence may be immense, its reach is challenged and resisted within medicine. It is therefore surely possible to challenge and resist its overweaning extension into other fields.

Medicine may have great prestige and authority in modern societies, but it has not always been so highly regarded. Historians, philosophers, and others have traced the transfer of authority and power from clerics through lawyers to doctors, following where Western societies have tended to locate their hopes and fears about matters of life and death (Rieff, 1966; Taylor, 2007). In the context of this progressive transfer of authority to medicine, we might conjecture that prominent research methods associated with prestigious ways of knowing are themselves invested with power and therefore sponsor the kind of intellectual hegemony to which Berwick refers. We would add to this the fact – very far from coincidental – that rigorous methods, such as RCTs, are highly technical and that techniques can be controlled at a distance because they depend upon wholly explicit rules. To control things at a distance is crucial to modern governance (Miller and Rose, 1990). This goes some way to explain why publicly funded services within and beyond health care tend to be subject to forms of accountability that valorise technical ways of knowing. On this account, the rise and extension of the RCT and related methods expresses the power of medicine and technical mastery.

It is in this context that the value of clinical case studies has been eroded substantially, within medical science and elsewhere, including within approaches to research in counselling and psychotherapy. Although the careful, reflective study of particular examples remains important within the training of counsellors and psychotherapists and in their ongoing supervision, the kind of knowledge that practitioners come to embody through their training and experience has become disconnected from the dominant understandings of knowledge that inform and guide research. However, in the argument we have set out above, we have also begun to question the transfer of an approach to research about the effectiveness of medical treatment to other fields, as well as pointing to misgivings about its ascendancy even within medicine.

In this book we advance and illustrate an argument for a reformulated version and vision of the clinical case study as a robust and powerful approach to research in counselling and psychotherapy, based on a radically different understanding of the nature of knowledge and learning from that associated with the technical paraphernalia of the RCT, the associated hierarchy of evidence, and other experience-far, technically driven approaches to research. Our argument is also about what we mean by counselling and psychotherapy research and its role in the development of knowledge. We seek to reintegrate research and learning at all stages of professional development, a theme that we take forward in Chapter 2.

Ethics and Professional Values

One important feature of research is that it seeks to make knowledge widely available through publication and other forms of dissemination. As we have already noted, in the early days of psychoanalysis, Sigmund Freud and his colleagues published studies of their clinical work with individual patients. Although they took some precautions to protect the identities of the patients about whom they wrote, by modern standards these precautions were too limited and the identities of many of those written about became known, including, for example Bertha Pappenheim as the person behind the pseudonym Fraülein Anna O. The decline of the case study within the domain of public, freely circulating knowledge in counselling and psychotherapy is not solely the result of changing understandings of research; it has also been driven by changes in expectations around the responsibilities of practitioners to protect the privacy of their clients. Linked to this, the responsibilities of practitioners to minimise intrusions into the therapeutic process have also grown, rendering strategies such as seeking informed consent – which are widely used in other fields of research in the medical and social sciences – highly complex.

When Freud published 'Fragment of an analysis of a case of hysteria' (Freud, 1953 [1901–1905]) – his discussion of his work with Dora (a pseudonym) – he set out three steps that he had taken to protect his patient: he had delayed publication for several years; he published in a specialist journal aimed at a restricted readership; and he disguised some details (Polden, 1998). None of these steps is foolproof alone or together; none is without contention. How long is long enough? How, given the enormous interest in personal experience, can readership be predictably restricted? How much disguise is needed to ensure confidentiality and how much is possible before veracity is compromised? Freud's efforts did not prevent Dora's real identity as Ida Bauer becoming known. In an infamous example to which Jane Polden (1998) refers, a newspaper article written by a well-known psychotherapist, which included a brief case history, led swiftly to an angry letter from the client, saying that, despite the use of a pseudonym and alteration of some details about her, she had immediately recognised herself, as had her own mother, and that she had neither been asked nor had given her consent to be written about in this way. Freud had not considered seeking consent from his former patient, but this is another safeguard that requires consideration. However, consent does not provide a simple solution. Practitioners considering this possibility always need to ask how the act of seeking consent might impact upon the therapy, whether at outset, during, or after it has ended.

Thinking about these various questions provides an indication that sharing anything about clinical work in a way that moves it into a public or semi-public domain has become more complex in the years since Freud and his immediate colleagues were working. Several factors have made it increasingly difficult for counsellors and psychotherapists to discuss their work beyond very tightly defined confidential contexts. We identify three such factors here.

First, sensitivity to the power dynamics and the associated risks of abuse in therapeutic relationships has greatly increased. Freud's work with Dora has itself attracted much commentary on this account (Bernheimer and Kahane, 1985; Billig, 1997; Masson, 1985). Freud listened to what Dora had to say but has been extensively criticised for attempting to impose on her his own interpretation of her desires. In the century since then, the profession has become much more aware of the vulnerability of clients in the face of subtle or less subtle forms of persuasion or pressure exerted by practitioners. With this has come a heightened sense of the responsibility we assume as therapists to honour the trust that is placed in us. How can we do this if we seek to use the work for anything other than its primary, original purpose, which necessarily prizes the needs and experiences of the client?

Second, consideration of power dynamics and the possible abuse or exploitation of clients links to a more general intensification of concern about privacy, especially in relation to matters of mental health. Indeed, counsellors and psychotherapists themselves have argued strongly for the need for privacy, without which therapeutic work is impossible

(Bollas and Sundelson, 1996). In this context how can we also expect to be able to use this work in public domains? If we ask patients or clients for permission to use the work for research purposes, we may secure it, but we have also changed in subtle but potentially important ways the very nature of the therapeutic relationship and therefore the therapy we wish to discuss in our research and scholarship.

Third and moving to a still more general level, the rise of the so-called Risk Society (Beck, 1992) has created an environment of hyper-awareness of the risks of what might happen and the need for ever more robust arrangements to install safeguards. Practitioners are therefore much more closely governed than before by codes of conduct and/or frameworks for ethical practice. These are designed to prevent problems from arising, which might seem like an unalloyed good. However, the insistent orientation towards what might happen in the future across many aspects of modern life itself fuels an expectation that future – and therefore unknown – happenings can be guarded against. While anticipating what might happen and mitigating potential risks may be highly valued, there are attendant drawbacks for counselling and psychotherapy. Nick Totton (2011, p. 233) has argued that 'if therapy is going to be good, it can't also be safe', explaining that:

> [b]y 'good' I mean tending to increase the range of clients' relaxation, freedom, expression and self-acceptance; by 'safe', I mean free from pain, anxiety and risk of failure.

His point is that regulating in ways that attempt to prevent bad practice can have the unintended effect of squeezing out good practice too by avoiding risk. For practitioners contemplating drawing on their clinical work in research and publication there are enormous challenges to face about what is possible not only within the ethical frameworks to which they seek to adhere but also in terms of balancing the potential benefit against the risks in risk-averse and increasingly litigious cultural contexts.

Taking these points together, changes within the field of counselling and psychotherapy and in the cultural contexts in which it is embedded have contributed to the decline of the clinical case study in the production of published and publishable knowledge. These changes do not undermine the relevance of clinical examples for the production of knowledge but do greatly complicate and constrain the scope for practitioners to use case studies in scholarship and research. In Chapter 3 we consider these complexities in more depth. Then, Chapters 4 to 14 provide examples of some of the variety of ways in which the ethical challenges of experience-near research may be addressed in practice.

Where Next?

Having set out some of the reasons for the erosion of the clinical case study as an approach to developing knowledge in the field of counselling and psychotherapy, the next two chapters begin the work of reconstructing an approach to research closely aligned to clinical practice. In Chapter 2 we take forward questions about authoritative knowledge and set out an argument informed by debates in the social and human sciences about the power of examples. Our argument offers a radically different view of knowledge and research from that associated with dominant models and epitomised by the RCT. For reasons we explain along the way, we do not offer step-by-step instructions explaining how to do this kind of research. Instead we argue that, rather like therapeutic practice itself, this way of doing research can only be learned or developed in the doing of it. In Chapter 3 our colleagues Siobhan Canavan and Seamus Prior turn to ethical considerations in research that draws on clinical practice. As we have explained, researching experiences of counselling requires sustained reflection on the thoughts, feelings, and behaviours involved in the interpersonal relationship of client and counsellor. The firm commitment to confidentiality and respect, which enables therapeutic work to occur, presents significant ethical challenges to the practitioner researcher who is also committed to investigating and disclosing the complexity and richness of the therapeutic process and relationship and their practice experience. The chapter discusses these ethical dimensions and proposes ways to address the ethical complexity and dilemmas implicated in such research. Practitioner research is rarely undertaken in isolation, and most practitioner researchers first embark on this process while students in master's and doctoral programmes. Consequently supervisors are also deeply engaged in these ethical dimensions of research. The chapter therefore also explores the complexities of supervising research rooted in students' clinical practice.

Following the first part of this book, in which we establish the rationale and the underpinning values informing the approach to research that we advocate, the remainder of it is given over to a series of eleven examples. Each is written by a practitioner who has studied with us and taken up our approach to research. In the second part of the book we present three chapters which explore experiences of coming into the field of counselling. In each case, the author uses her own experience of struggling with aspects of training and practice to offer fresh resources for thinking about themes of concern to many beginning counsellors and those who support them, namely trusting the process, questions around touch, and personal motivations for working as a counsellor. The third part of book consists of four chapters that give priority to the voices of clients. One draws on the author's own experience as a client. Two provide illustrations of the possibility of case studies that draw directly on therapeutic work with individual clients, in both cases in the context of institutional settings. The fourth uses published stories to stage a dialogue between a practitioner and two imagined clients. The fourth and final part of the book illustrates how counsellors make use of theory personally and practically. The examples presented show how theory is lived in therapeutic work and how it animates therapeutic relationships. In each of the four chapters this part of the book includes, practitioners write about their embodied understanding of theory, and through the examples they explore they contribute to the development of the theories on which they draw. We return to all these examples at the end of Chapter 2, where we elaborate in more depth the form and character of their various contributions to knowledge.

References

Aveline, M. (2005) 'Clinical case studies: Their place in evidence-based practice', *Psychodynamic Practice*, 11, 133–152.

Axline, V.A. (1964) *Dibs: In Search of Self* (New York: Ballantine Books).

Barkham, M., Mellor-Clark, J., Connell, J., and Cahill, J. (2006) 'A core approach to practice-based evidence: A brief history of the origins and applications of the CORE-OM and the CORE System', *Counselling and Psychotherapy Research*, 6 (1), 3–15.

Beck, U. (1992) *Risk Society: Towards A New Modernity* (London: Sage).

Bernheimer, C., and Kahane, C. (1985) *In Dora's Case: Freud, Hysteria, Feminism* (London: Virago).

Berwick, D. M. (2005) 'Broadening the view of evidence-based medicine', *Quality and Safety in Health Care*, 14 (5), 315–316.

Billig, M. (1997) 'Freud and Dora: Repressing an oppressed identity', *Theory, Culture and Society*, 14, 29–55.

Bollas, C., and Sundelson, D. (1996) *The New Informants* (London: Karnac).

Breuer, J., and Freud, S. (1955 [1893–1895]) 'Studies in hysteria', *The Standard Edition of the Complete Psychological Works of Sigmund Freud,* Volume II, translated and edited by James Strachey (London: Hogarth Press) pp. ix–322.

Charon, R. (2006) *Narrative Medicine: Honoring the Stories of Illness* (Oxford and New York: Oxford University Press).

Cooper, M. (2008) *Essential Findings in Counselling and Psychotherapy* (London: Sage).

Freud, S. (1953 [1901–1905]) 'Fragment of an analysis of a case of hysteria', *The Standard Edition of the Complete Psychological Works of Sigmund Freud*, Volume VII, translated and edited by James Strachey (London: Hogarth Press) pp. 1–122.

Gawande, A. (2014) *Being Mortal: Illness, Medicine and What Matters in the End* (London: Profile Books).

Geertz, C. (1983) *Local Knowledge: Further Essays in Interpretive Anthropology* (New York: Basic Books).

King, M., Marston, L., and Bower, P. (2014) 'Comparison of non-directive counselling and cognitive behaviour therapy for patients presenting in general practice with an ICD-10 depressive episode: A randomized control trial', *Psychological Medicine*, 44 (9), 1835–1844.

Kohut, H. (1971) *The Analysis of the Self: A Systematic Approach to the Psychoanalytic Treatment of Narcissistic Personality Disorders* (New York: International Universities Press).

Marsh, H. (2014) *Do No Harm: Stories of Life, Death and Brain Surgery* (London: Weidenfeld and Nicolson).

Masson, J. (1989) *Against Therapy: Warning, Psychotherapy May be Dangerous to Your Mental Health* (London: Collins).

McLeod, J. (2001) 'Developing a research tradition consistent with the practices and values of counselling and psychotherapy: Why *Counselling and Psychotherapy Research* is necessary', *Counselling and Psychotherapy Research*, 1 (1), 3–11.

Miller, P and Rose. N. (1990) 'Governing economic life', *Economy and Society*, 19 (1), 1–31.

Polden, J. (1998) 'Publish and be damned', *British Journal of Psychotherapy*, 14, 337–347.

Pybis, J., Cooper, M., Hill, A., Cromarty, K., Levesley, R., Murdoch, J., and Turner, N. (2014) 'Pilot randomised controlled trial of school-based humanistic counselling for psychological distress in young people: Outcomes and methodological reflections', *Counselling and Psychotherapy Research* doi: 10.1080/14733145.2014.905614.

Rieff, P. (1966) *The Triumph of the Therapeutic: Uses of Faith after Freud* (New York: Harper Row).

Rogers, C. (1942) *Counseling and Psychotherapy: New Concepts in Practice* (Boston: Houghton Mifflin).

Ropper, A. H., and Burrell, B. D. (2014) *Reaching Down the Rabbit Hole: Extraordinary Journeys into the Human Brain* (New York: St. Martin's Press).

Rowland, N., and Goss, S. (eds) (2000) *Evidence-Based Counselling and Psychological Therapies: Research and Applications* (London: Routledge).

Rustin, M. (2001) *Reason and Unreason: Psychoanalysis, Science and Politics* (London: Continuum).

Schwartz, J. (1999) *Cassandra's Daughters: A History of Psychoanalysis* (London: Karnac).

Taylor, C. (2007) *A Secular Age* (Cambridge, MA: Harvard University Press).

Totton, N. (2011) 'Not a tame lion', in L. Bondi, D. Carr, C. Clark, and C. Clegg (eds) *Towards Professional Wisdom* (Farnham: Ashgate) pp. 233–246.

2

The Power of Examples

LIZ BONDI AND JUDITH FEWELL

In the opening chapter of this book we described how the authority of medical science has grown since the middle of the twentieth century, to a considerable extent because of the success of rigorous and highly technical ways of doing research such as the Randomised Controlled Trial (RCT). We also suggested that attempts to extend this kind of approach into the field of counselling and psychotherapy have contributed to the distance and disconnection between the forms of knowledge embodied by practitioners and those most commonly associated with research. In the first section of this chapter, we draw on debates about knowledge in the social sciences to explain in greater depth why an approach to research imported from medical science does not provide an adequate basis for the development of meaningful knowledge about the human world, including within counselling and psychotherapy. In the second section we elaborate further on the idea introduced in Chapter 1 that some kinds of knowledge can only be developed through practice. We emphasise the importance of this view for counselling and psychotherapy and explore the implications for how we think about knowledge and expertise in the field. Building on this analysis, the final section of the chapter begins the task of elaborating an alternative approach that is consistent with an understanding of counselling and psychotherapy as forms of knowledge integrally bound up with their status as practices. In this section we also provide an overview of how that task is carried through by the eleven chapters that make up parts two to four of the book.

Positivism and Its Discontents: Rethinking the Basis of Knowledge in the Social Sciences

In Chapter 1 we drew attention to the ascendancy and influence of a particular approach to medical science, epitomised by the RCT, that valorises objectivity and technical mastery in ways that render such research experience-far and therefore remote from the messy, imprecise, difficult-to-articulate quality of much of the work that happens in therapeutic practice. This approach to research is often given the epithet of 'positivist' and it has been enormously influential across the natural, medical, and social sciences.

The term 'positivism' comes from the work of the early nineteenth-century philosopher August Comte (1798–1857) who viewed science as having a central and positive role in human progress. He set out five methodological precepts through which he argued that the scientific status of knowledge could be guaranteed (Gregory, 1978; Habermas, 1972; Keat and Urry, 1975). Notwithstanding more than a century of criticism and contestation by scientists and philosophers, his precepts remain recognisable in many contemporary descriptions of scientific research, within and beyond medicine.

- *Le réel.* This refers to the principle that scientific knowledge is grounded in 'immediate reality' or evidence apprehended through the senses, hence the idea that science is grounded in direct empirical observations.
- *La certitude.* This refers to the principle that observations (or evidence) must be accessible to and replicable or verifiable by all scientists, which underpins the notion that evidence is objectively knowable and that observers are detached or separate from what they observe.
- *Le précis.* This refers to the logic of the scientific method in which theories are built upon and can be tested by evidence, according to explicitly formulated rules. The scientific method gives science its technical and analytical rationality and gives scientific theories their explanatory and predictive power.
- *L'utile.* This refers to the idea that science is concerned with means and not ends and is therefore wholly separate from consideration of values. It underpins claims about the neutrality of science.
- *Le relative.* This refers to science as a project that is unfinished and that progresses through the gradual development of theories that unify principles across more and more fields. It portrays science as an inherently progressive, singular, and coherent way of knowing.

Comte based his account on the study of the natural sciences (especially physics and chemistry, which have become fundamental to much medical science), and he is sometimes described as having been the first philosopher of science. However, his vision was not limited to the natural sciences: he argued that in the future the social (or human) sciences should and would develop the same characteristics as the natural sciences. To the extent that counselling and psychotherapy research, along with research in other fields within the social sciences, have adopted an approach to research modelled on a broadly Comtean understanding of the natural sciences, his predictions were correct. However, there has also been resistance to, disappointment with, and criticism of attempts to extend the precepts of Comtean positivism into research in counselling and psychotherapy as well as many other fields within the social sciences. In Chapter I we drew attention to criticisms of the dominance of technically driven, experience-far forms of research, including the RCT, that adhere to the precepts of positivism. In the remainder of this section we explain why positivism is so ill-suited as a basis for developing research in counselling and psychotherapy. We draw on arguments developed in the social sciences that emphasise the importance of attending to human experience and human meanings and that are therefore directly relevant to counselling and psychotherapy.

In an exploration of knowledge in the social sciences, the Danish social scientist Bent Flyvbjerg (2001) has argued that research in the social sciences cannot succeed or achieve respect if it seeks to emulate approaches to knowledge characteristic of the natural sciences. He makes the case that the social sciences and the natural sciences are fundamentally different kinds of enterprises with distinct areas and forms of expertise. Further, he argues that social science will inevitably be weak and found wanting if it is evaluated according to the criteria used to make judgements about the natural sciences. He does not accept this fate for the social sciences because, if understood to offer a fundamentally different form of knowledge, he considers their potential to be enormous. He writes that:

> the social sciences are strongest where the natural sciences are weakest: just as the social sciences have not contributed much to explanatory and predictive theory, neither have the natural sciences contributed to the reflexive analysis [a phrase we explain in due course] and discussion of values and interests. (Flyvbjerg 2001, p. 3)

Flyvbjerg (2001) sets out a range of arguments why knowledge of the human world is bound to take a fundamentally different form from knowledge of the non-human (or natural) world. As we will see, his argument can readily be applied to counselling and psychotherapy in which the approach to research epitomised by RCTs is modelled on positivist natural science and excludes from consideration the very things that distinguish the human world from that which is not human. Drawing on Flyvbjerg's analysis, supplemented by feminist critiques of positivist science, we summarise three key ways in which the world of human experience and human meaning cannot be understood on the basis of the precepts of positivism. These are concerned respectively with interpretation, location, and context.

First, in the social sciences, including counselling and psychotherapy, knowledge is always and inevitably characterised by multiple layers of interpretation. At the centre of social science research are people who have their own understandings of their worlds in which they live and the themes researchers might wish to examine. Social science researchers are typically interested in finding out about people's experiences, understandings, or opinions of some aspects of their worlds and their lives. In investigating such phenomena, researchers necessarily rely on their own interpretations of the interpretations offered by the people to whom they speak or with whom they interact. Moreover, research participants respond interpretively to what they are asked and to what researchers say about them, so layers of interpretation multiply.

Sociologist Anthony Giddens (1984) introduced the concept of the 'double hermeneutic' to describe the two-way character of interpretation in social science: on the one hand, social scientists interpret the human phenomena they study; on the other hand, the people they study make use of and respond to the knowledge generated by social science, perhaps resulting in changes to the phenomena the researchers are investigating. In the natural or non-human sciences, by contrast, objects of study – including, for example, genes, viruses, materials, and landforms – are not fundamentally interpretive in the same way as human beings. In Giddens's (1984) terms, they operate within a single or one-way hermeneutic in that natural scientists undertake interpretative work but there is no interpretive work undertaken by their objects of study. (It is of course true that natural scientists may need to take into account the impact they have on their objects of study, for example through observer effects in quantum mechanics, but only in the human world does the *same kind of* interpretive work flow in both directions.)

The ubiquity of interpretation and the double hermeneutic call into question the relevance for social science of the Comtean methodological precepts of *le réel* and *la certitude*, which together imply that it is possible to ground research firmly and unambiguously in stable, pre-interpretive empirical observations. Instead, social science research has access to rich interpretative material. So instead of offering objective, explanatory, and predictive theory, the social sciences are uniquely well placed to advance richly interpretive accounts of the human world that acknowledge the multiplicity of interpretations in play as well as the different perspectives different people bring to bear. Narrative approaches to social research in a wide range of fields, including counselling and psychotherapy, take this forward, valuing the importance of interpretation and storytelling within human culture (e.g. Clandinin and Connelly, 2000; Polkinghorne, 1988; Speedy, 2008). So too does narrative medicine (Charon, 2006).

Second and relatedly, social science researchers always work from within their own fields of study. Researchers of the human world do not have available to them a stable external vantage point, since they are human beings too: their location is internal to the world they seek to investigate. One consequence of this is that the distinction between the object of research in social science (what is studied) and the subject of the researcher is intrinsically unstable since researchers are people too. In the words of primatologist and feminist philosopher of science Donna Haraway (1988), to claim a position outside and apart from the arena of what we study (which would enable objectivity) is a 'god trick'. She and others have argued that we need to relinquish fantasies about being able to view the world from above as if we have access to something akin to a god's eye view. None of us can step outside our own immersion in the human world, and our knowledge is therefore always situated and perspectival, framed by the particular positions we occupy. We bring our experience, our learning, our passions, our beliefs, and our values into how we see the world. Consequently, however hard we might try to adhere to a principle of detached objectivity, we attempt this only because we believe it to be worthwhile. Indeed, we might say that the practice of science within a positivist mould (exemplified by the RCT) requires a passionate attachment to the necessarily human idea of dispassionate reason.

The natural sciences harness this passion in a particular way, making a sharp separation between the inspiration that leads to new insight and the rigorous, dispassionate application of the scientific method (*le précis*) to the testing of ideas about non-human objects (Bondi, 2005). But in the social sciences, including counselling and psychotherapy, that separation does not work because the supposed objects are human beings like ourselves. As well as further undercutting the Comtean precept of *la certitude*, the way in which social science researchers are positioned inside their fields of study also undermines the Comtean methodological precept of *l'utile*, because it is not possible to exclude values and beliefs in a way that can guarantee the neutrality of a science. (Whether this separation of means and ends is actually possible in the natural sciences is also debatable, but these debates are driven by different considerations.)

The 'insider' status of researchers in the social sciences may make detached objectivity and the separation of means and ends impossible, but it generates enormous potential too. Researchers have a degree of insider insight into whatever they study. While there are risks and dangers in imagining that others see, understand, and experience the world in the same way as we do, if well used, our shared humanity gives us lots of important clues about the phenomena we study. Counsellors and psychotherapists are very familiar with this as practitioners and are therefore well placed to grasp the value for developing knowledge of this insider status. Provided that we are able to hold on to an awareness of our difference from others, our insider status can be used to foster forms of curiosity that open up questions and discussions about the very things that matter most to ourselves and others. This is what is meant by reflexivity or reflexive analysis, which has strong affinities with reflective practice. The term 'reflexivity', like the double hermeneutic, refers to the two-way character of influence that pervades social research. Reflexivity acknowledges the intermingling of the subjective worlds of the researchers and those of the others in whom they are interested, and reflexive analysis seeks to understand this not from the outside but by reflecting upon what happens in our engagements with other people's subjective worlds. So, once again, instead of offering objective, explanatory, and predictive theory, the social sciences are uniquely well placed to offer something very different in the form of critically engaged, reflexive discussion of the full range of human questions and concerns about how we live.

Third, and as a corollary of the double hermeneutic and the location of researchers inside their field of study, everything in the human world is context-dependent. In other words, it is impossible to separate the entity in which we are interested – be it an aspect of a human being or of a relationship or anything else that is part of the human world – from the context in which it is situated without losing important features of the entity itself. Putting this another way, lists of the symptoms of depression, such as those contained in the guidelines issued by the National Institute for Health and Care Excellence and the Scottish Intercollegiate Guidelines Network, are abstracted from reports of various kinds made by a large number of people. The lists of symptoms (and often the reports on which they draw) take out all contextual information about the people suffering, their circumstances, and the circumstances in which their symptoms were reported. One of the consequences of this is that the list of symptoms does not actually convey what it is like to feel depressed unless we bring to it something much closer to lived experience itself, for which we draw on context-specific knowledge, whether of our own lives, or the lives of others, or perhaps what we have taken from novels and autobiographies we have read. To insist that there is a thing called depression that can be described in abstract, context-independent terms is to attempt to exclude what is utterly intrinsic to the experience, which those working therapeutically with people suffering depression seek to understand.

In the natural sciences researchers strive to develop ever more context-independent accounts of how the phenomena they seek to understand work, and as science develops, the reach of its overarching theories increases. This is well illustrated in physics where the shift from Newtonian to Einsteinian theory enabled what had previously been considered anomalies to be encompassed by the new theory and also led to the unification of understandings of phenomena previously covered by separate theories. Attempts to generate comparably universal and context-independent theory in the social sciences have been attempted by many, but their success has been limited and the progressive unification of theories has remained elusive. In Flyvbjerg's (2001, p. 40) words this failure is inevitable:

> A social science theory of the kind which imitates the natural sciences, that is a theory which makes possible explanation and prediction, requires that the concrete context of everyday human activity be excluded, but this exclusion of context makes explanation and prediction impossible.

Context-dependence renders Comte's precepts of *le précis* and *le relative* irrelevant to social science: formal, rule-based methodologies driven by technical rationality inevitably drain all that is most meaningful out of the phenomena that are most vital to living, breathing, interacting human beings, while the notion of the progressive unification of predictive theory cannot aid advancement in fields that do not seek to predict.

Context-dependence helps to explain why attempts to generate general, abstract claims in fields such as counselling and psychotherapy, in the form, for example, of explicit decision pathways to provide practitioners with rules for action, either fail to get beyond the most basic level of practice or turn out to be useless in practice. Rather than a problem to minimise if not to overcome, context-dependence – like the double hermeneutic and the situatedness of research – can become an *asset* for research in the social sciences. However, this requires the ambitions of the social sciences to be framed in very different terms from the ambitions of the natural sciences. Rather than seeking to develop abstract, explanatory, and predictive theory applicable regardless of context, social science that takes context-dependence seriously must instead be concerned with generating deep insight into particular examples. This is especially relevant in counselling and psychotherapy, where we already know that we learn through the experience of working with the particular. Research that works with the values and practices of counselling and psychotherapy therefore needs to embrace context-dependence as well as the double hermeneutic and our location inside our fields of study.

Before closing this section, we need to acknowledge that in the foregoing we have over-stated the contrast between the social and natural sciences because we have focused strongly on social science research that is concerned in some way with human *meanings*. There are branches of the social sciences, within and beyond counselling and psychotherapy, that explore phenomena in which human meanings do not play a part. One example would be demography, which is concerned with population characteristics such as age, sex, and geographical location. Demographers do successfully offer predictive models of population change, although the double hermeneutic still operates in that the findings of demographic research may influence the populations they study through impacts on migration and reproductive behaviour. In counselling and psychotherapy an example might be research about the demographic characteristics of people attending counselling sessions. Studies of this kind rely on evidence that is relatively (although never entirely) free from ambiguity and is amenable to the application of methodological principles that are very similar to those employed in the natural sciences.

We do not dispute that experience-far research grounded in the precepts of positivism may be useful for counselling and psychotherapy in a variety of ways – perhaps, for example, in guiding decisions about service provision. This is especially the case if such research does not claim to shed light on human meanings or human experience. But the precepts of positivism have been absorbed into and have come to dominate a much wider range of research in counselling and psychotherapy. We need to recognise and challenge the deeply instrumental drivers that underlie much of this research. For example, counsellors working within the British National Health Service, and in other settings too, are often expected to collect or to facilitate the collection of data from their clients using standardised questionnaires in order to evaluate the impact of their work and to generate evidence for a plethora of studies motivated by the desire to demonstrate to funders the utility or effectiveness of counselling. But to do so within methodological frameworks imported from the natural and medical sciences is a problematic strategy, because the value and meaning of what is construed as evidence is highly contestable. The limitations of such research are illustrated humorously and pointedly in a stand-up routine called 'counselling on a scale of 1 to 5', in which Jonathan Wyatt pokes fun at efforts to generate data about counselling by asking people to describe how they feel – for example how close to despair they are – on a numerical scale (see www.youtube.com/watch?v=yzkLUbglTwA), sending up studies that ignore the double hermeneutic, the situatedness of knowledge, and the context-dependence of human meanings. More conventionally, Flyvbjerg (2001, pp. 4, 168) describes attempts to emulate natural science by adopting the precepts of positivism as a 'cul-de-sac' and 'self-defeating', because social science is fundamentally different from natural science and is bound to be found wanting if evaluated according to the criteria devised for the latter.

Our interest in this book does not lie with elaborating this critique in greater depth but instead with exemplifying a very different approach to research that, we argue, is much more capable of enriching, informing, and supporting the development of practitioners in their work with clients. To do this we need to counter the chronic devaluation of experience-near ways of understanding and undertaking research in counselling and psychotherapy. In so doing we seek to close a gap between what we mean by research and by learning through practice. In order to develop our argument we turn next to what it means to know and to learn in the field of counselling and psychotherapy.

Learning through Experience

We have argued for an understanding of research that works with the interpretive, reflexive, situated, context-dependent character of the human world. We have suggested that these features of human experience are deeply familiar to practitioners in counselling and psychotherapy.

In so doing we are pointing to the idea that reflective practice might be central to ways of doing experience-near research. The fundamental purpose of research is to develop knowledge, and in order to achieve this we need to understand how practitioners become knowledgeable in the field of counselling and psychotherapy. The account of learning that we present in this section draws attention to holistic, intuitive, and embodied ways of learning and knowing that can only be acquired through practice. In the context of this understanding of learning, we distinguish between two forms of rationality: one technical and analytical; the other practical and intuitive. The former has obvious affinities with the precepts of positivism; the latter provides a basis for a radically different approach to research, which we argue is capable of cultivating and promoting the practical wisdom of counsellors and psychotherapists. It is also relevant to numerous other fields of endeavour in which practice is a fundamental source of wisdom.

A central idea in counselling and psychotherapy, developed especially in the person-centred tradition but taken up much more widely, is that people are experts in their own lives. According to this perspective, we become experts in our own lives by virtue of living them. By being alive we acquire what might be called practice-based wisdom about who we understand ourselves to be, our everyday lives, and the possibilities life offers. We embody this expertise; it shapes who we are. This way of thinking about how people become knowledgeable and expert in living their own lives translates readily into how people learn to become counsellors and psychotherapists.

A popular way of describing how learning to become a practitioner unfolds is in terms of a progression from 'unconscious incompetence' through 'conscious incompetence' to 'conscious competence' and finally to 'unconscious competence'. Because counselling and psychotherapy draw upon what appear at first glance to be universal conversational skills, learning often begins with the realisation that we have to change something with which we thought we were familiar, thereby shifting from unconscious incompetence, in which we are unaware of our lack of listening or therapeutic skill, to conscious incompetence in which that awareness has developed. Achieving conscious incompetence helps us to notice our lack of skill and therefore to begin the task of listening in a new way. After becoming consciously incompetent, the next task is to develop our conscious competence, in which we use new knowledge and guidance to think consciously about how to proceed in relation to situations with which we are presented. In the early stages of conscious competence, beginning counsellors are likely to be self-conscious, trying hard to 'get it right'. Gradually practitioners develop something a bit more like fluency, becoming more relaxed in their listening and in their capacity to respond appropriately. One sign of growing conscious competence might be how the practitioner works with and holds silence in the therapeutic relationship. However, while competence is conscious it remains quite limited, and the aim is for the developing practitioner to become unconsciously competent. Unconscious competence means that we no longer consciously and cognitively weigh up options about when to speak and what to do or say. Instead our competence is held inside us in a different way, and our proficiency relies on noncognitive and embodied ways of knowing. It is not simply that we apply rules and think through possibilities with greater speed than beginners or non-experts. Instead we work much more holistically and intuitively.

This understanding of how people learn to become practitioners is by no means unique to counselling and psychotherapy; it converges with or echoes several other accounts. In Chapter I we mentioned Donald Berwick's (2005) point that some kinds of knowledge can only be developed though practice, which he illustrated with the examples of speaking a foreign language, physical activities such as skiing and cycling, and parenting. The vital role of hours of practice in the development of high-level expertise was popularised a few years ago by Malcolm Gladwell (2008) who argued that, across a range of fields, it takes 10,000 hours to become truly expert. More than half a century ago, Jerome Bruner (1960/1977) addressed the process of education with a particular focus on improving science education in American schools. He described important and powerful components of learning as 'unconscious' (ibid., p. 8), citing the example of native language learning in which children develop a feel for grammar that gives them the capacity to communicate with a high degree of subtlety. This framing is consonant with the idea of unconscious competence. Bruner also stressed the importance of intuition, which he described as 'the intellectual technique of arriving at plausible but tentative formulations without going through the analytic steps by which such formulations would be found to be valid or invalid conclusions', arguing that it 'is a much neglected and essential feature of productive thinking' (ibid., pp. 13–14). He argued that intuitive thinking and analytical thinking are complementary, the latter characterised by explicit steps that proceed 'with relatively full awareness of the information and operations involved' (ibid., p. 57), while the former is very different, 'based seemingly on an implicit perception of the total problem' and resting on 'familiarity with the domain of knowledge involved ... which makes it possible for the thinker to leap about, skipping steps and employing short cuts' (ibid., p. 58). Although the person thinking intuitively may have 'little if any awareness' of what underlies his or her moves, afterwards it is usually possible to provide a more analytical account of the underlying rationale for the choices made (ibid., p. 58). This account will be recognisable to many counsellors and psychotherapists, who often work intuitively in the moment with their clients, reflecting later in more analytical ways on what was happening. We build into our training programmes cycles of practising and reflecting, which provide those seeking to become counsellors with repeated opportunities to connect the intuitive and analytical modes of thinking in ways that we hope will become embedded and embodied in their therapeutic practice.

In their exploration of the limits of the potential for machine-based intelligence ('artificial intelligence') Herbert and Stuart Dreyfus (1986) offer an account of human learning that, like Bruner's, differentiates between analytical and intuitive dimensions of practice and learning. They suggest that learning a new skill often begins with analytical elements, which enable the learner to recognise salient facts and characteristics of a situation and to apply generic rules for action accordingly. This involves being able to abstract key features of particular instances, which become the focus of attention. For the beginning counsellor or psychotherapist it might mean learning to recognise and respond to the emotional content of stories told by clients, effectively abstracting the feeling content from other material. For the slightly more experienced practitioner it might also mean becoming attuned to what is particular to a new situation and therefore developing the confidence to know when to ignore or bend what had initially been learned as a standardised rule, such as not asking questions. In counselling and psychotherapy, the development of analytical skill also entails the capacity to reflect on one's practice, analysing one's judgements and decisions, initially in retrospect, and then progressively integrating what Donald Schön (1983) has called reflection-in-action.

On the account advanced by Dreyfus and Dreyfus (1986), a practitioner can achieve a basic degree of competence by being able to make complex assessments of particular situations, prioritise accordingly, and assume personal responsibility for his or her actions. However, such a practitioner is not truly proficient, let alone expert. Dreyfus and Dreyfus (1986) argue that proficiency is achieved only by moving beyond the analytical to the exercise of a much more holistic and intuitive appreciation

33

of the particular, in which the need to abstract salient features and apply rules for action falls away, and the need to consciously, cognitively plan and reflect also recedes because these aspects of practice have become so deeply embodied. Instead, what comes to the fore is the capacity to grasp the particular example holistically, without the need to analyse or abstract, together with trust in one's own intuitive judgement. On this account, expert practice does not entail the logical, rational application of abstract rule-based learning but instead relies heavily on what Bruner (1960/1977, p. 8) described as unconscious 'learning structures', which are acquired and can only be acquired through experience. For counsellors and psychotherapists intuitive expertise may be manifest in greater spontaneity of a kind that can be understood in terms of inspired judgement. Practitioners operating in this way may work a great deal at 'the edge of awareness' (Gendlin, 1981) and, in psychoanalytic language, they are likely to demonstrate a deep trust in their own unconscious attunement and receptivity. The language of clinical intuition is also consistent with this understanding of expertise.

To the non-expert the proficiency of a genuine expert can seem mysterious, because intuitive ways of working are highly complex and holistic. But the rigour of intuitive rather than analytical ways of working can be understood by distinguishing between different forms of rationality. Here we draw on the work of educational philosopher Joseph Dunne (1993, 2005) who makes use of Aristotelian thought to differentiate between technical rationality (or techne) and practical rationality (or phronesis). Technical rationality has become dominant in modern societies and is often treated as if it were the only form of rationality. On Dunne's (2005, p. 373) account, technical rationality:

> puts a premium on 'objectivity' and detachment, suppressing the context-dependence of first-person experience in favour of a third-person perspective which yields generalised findings in accordance with clearly formulated, publicly agreed procedures. These procedures give an indispensible role to operations of observation and measurement, modes of testing that specify precisely what can count as counter-evidence, replicability of findings, and the adoption of a language maximally freed from possibilities of misinterpretation ... . And through these procedures knowledge is established that is both explanatory and predictive.

This echoes the approach to research that we discussed in the opening chapter, which has come to dominate the field of counselling and psychotherapy, as well as underpinning what Bruner (1960/1977) and Dreyfus and Dreyfus (1986) describe as analytical thinking and working. In contrast to this, and with close affinities to intuitive ways of thinking and working, practical rationality or *phronesis* constitutes a different kind of rationality. Dunne (2005, pp. 375–376) describes *phronesis* as 'an action-orientating form of knowledge' that is 'irreducibly experiential [in] nature' and capable of yielding 'concrete, context sensitive judgements'. As a form of rationality, it is 'the cultivated capacity to make [judgement] calls resourcefully and reliably' in a range of particular situations (ibid., p. 376). Furthermore:

> A person of judgement respects the particularity of the case, and thus does not impose on it a Procrustean application of the general rule (Procrustes was the character in Greek mythology who stretched or shortened people to make them fit the bed predesigned for their captivity) .... Judgement is more than the possession of knowledge ... because it is the ability to actuate this knowledge with relevance, appropriateness, or sensitivity to context. In each fresh actuation there is an element of creative insight through which it makes itself equal to the demands of a new situation. (Ibid., p. 376)

Dunne's account of practical rationality, inspired by his work with teachers, corresponds beautifully with the way in which we understand expertise in counselling and psychotherapy. He places emphasis on the specificity of each case such that context and example are inextricably connected, just as each client's particular way of being shapes profoundly the way an experienced practitioner works. Dunne offers a way of thinking about the rigour of intuitive ways of thinking and working that is consistent with the idea that expertise in therapeutic practice entails the achievement of unconscious competence in which embodied, intuitive, experience-near, holistic, and subjectively engaged ways of knowing are central and accorded great value.

The foregoing account of expertise is of great importance for our argument about learning, knowledge, and research in the field of counselling and psychotherapy (and it is also relevant to many other fields of endeavour). Few people would be likely to disagree that practitioners should aspire to move beyond the level of conscious competence to unconscious competence and therefore to a less technical and more intuitive, embodied, non-analytical way of working. It follows from this that if research is to contribute to this kind of development it needs to work *with* the grain of expertise and not against it. Research that does this will not require an approach or a set of skills radically different from or alien to what practitioners absorb and come to embody during and after training. Instead it will be truly consistent with and supportive of the character of knowledge and expertise in counselling and psychotherapy, speaking to practitioners in ways that enable them to deepen their understanding of what it is they do.

The approach to learning we have set out, especially the distinction between analytical and intuitive ways of thinking and practising promulgated by Bruner (1960/1977) and Dreyfus and Dreyfus (1986), together with Dunne's (2005) corresponding distinction between technical and practical rationality, provides important insight into the aversion of many practitioners to much existing research in counselling and psychotherapy. Learning to become a counsellor or psychotherapist may begin with the absorption of general, context-independent principles and practices and their application in a gradually expanding set of circumstances. However, mature or adept practitioners move beyond this cognitive, rule-based, technical, analytical approach to a much more intuitive, holistic, and contextually sensitive way of working. These practitioners become the models to which those at earlier stages in their development aspire, and they are also likely to become their mentors, teachers, and supervisors. Consequently, even beginning practitioners are likely to swiftly become aware that true proficiency cannot be achieved within a rule-based, narrowly analytical mode. They will certainly be aware that counselling and psychotherapy practice calls upon them to be personally and subjectively involved in what they do.

As we have already noted, the approach to knowledge within which most medical and psychological research operates, and which has in turn become dominant in counselling and psychotherapy, is underpinned by positivist principles and prizes technical rationality. It actively excludes non-analytical, intuitive ways of knowing. It valorises objectivity and detachment. It is, therefore, driven by and characterised by values and principles that are inherently alien to expertise in counselling and psychotherapy. We should not, therefore, be in the least surprised that many practitioners are not interested in, are actively repelled by, and/or are antagonistic towards such research: if engaging in research requires them to set aside their hard-earned, experience-near approach to practice and to take up the position of an objective, detached observer, guided only by technical rationality, their caution, dislike and distaste are entirely understandable.

The outputs of research guided by the dominant approach typically consist of more or less general, context-independent claims that can be applied only by adopting the logic of technical rationality. To take an example, Andrea Somers and colleagues (2014) ask whether psychotherapists should disclose to their clients their own psychological problems. Their study presented a sample of ordinary people (in this case undergraduate students) who might be thought of as potential clients with vignettes in the form of very brief accounts of why someone sought psychotherapy and the formulation around which the therapeutic work focused. The vignettes were presented either with or without the inclusion of a sentence noting the clinician's own history of difficulties in the same area. The research participants were then asked a battery of questions about what they thought of the psychotherapist in the vignette. The researchers found that the sample consistently rated practitioners whose own difficulties were included in the vignettes more favourably than those whose difficulties were not. For inexperienced practitioners this result might provide some reassurance about self-disclosure (intentional or otherwise), but what are more experienced practitioners meant to do with such findings? Disclosures happen in particular relationships in particular contexts, and general rules about whether or when to disclose what are inherently insensitive to these particularities. Research that can only speak to practitioners in the language of general claims is likely to be of little obvious relevance to those sufficiently competent to be working much more with clinical intuition and therefore practical rationality than with technical rationality. For these clinicians the great majority of research conducted within the dominant approach is likely to elicit a 'so what?' response at the very best.

Researching with the Grain of Learning and Practice in Counselling and Psychotherapy: The Power of Examples

In the opening section of this chapter we explained why experience-far, positivist approaches to research are not appropriate for researchers seeking to enhance their understanding and appreciation of human meanings, and we have instead argued for an approach that values the double hermeneutic, the situatedness of the researcher, and the context-dependence of knowledge. In the second section we explored the practice-based, experience-near character of expertise in counselling and psychotherapy, emphasising the central importance of embodied, holistic, and intuitive ways of knowing. So what does research that works with the grain of these values and ways of knowing look like? To a considerable extent these questions can only be answered by offering examples, such as those presented in Chapters 4 to 14 of this book. However, in this final section of this chapter we begin by offering some more general comments on such research, and then we provide an overview of how each of the chapters in parts two to four of the book contributes to knowledge in the field of counselling and psychotherapy.

Dunne (2005) concludes his exploration of the rationality of practice by reflecting briefly on the implications of his argument for research. He observes that:

> in areas such as education studies, policy studies, or nursing studies [to which we might add counselling and psychotherapy] ... the price that generalised empirical findings must pay for their very generalisability ... is a certain thinness of content. They need to be complemented, then, by thickly descriptive studies. (Ibid., p. 386)

He continues by offering a rich and vivid description of some of the characteristics of such 'thickly descriptive studies'. Echoing our point about the importance of working with the double hermeneutic, he argues that such studies 'will embrace a variety of narrative modes and be strongly hermeneutical in character. That is to say, they will tell stories' (ibid., p. 386). Moreover, rather than such stories being constructed by detached, distanced researchers, their authors will be situated within them in ways that enable them to bring to bear:

> the kind of interpretative skill that can bring out the complex interweaving of plot and characters, the dense meshing of insights and oversights, of convergent or contrary motivations and interests, of anticipated or unanticipated response from the internal environment – or irruptions from the external one – all conspiring to bring relative success or failure. (Ibid., p. 386)

Dunne's description also emphasises the importance of context and particularity, and he argues passionately for the power of examples:

> If, with their deep embeddedness in a particular milieu, these studies do indeed renounce the generalising ambitions of wider-gauge research, they are not on that account condemned to narcissism or

self-enclosure. To the contrary, when they are well done – which, among other things, will require a keenly reflective awareness of their 'point a view' – they possess what might be called epiphanic power: they disclose an exemplary significance in the setting they depict so that it proves capable of illuminating other settings – without need for re-routing through abstract generalities and, indeed, with greatest potential effect for those most deeply in the throes of the very particularity of another setting. (Ibid., p. 386)

We consider this statement inspirational, and in this book we have selected studies that we hope readers will find deeply illuminating in relation to their own experiences of therapeutic practice.

There are a number of examples of studies of the kind described by Dunne (2005) in the literature of counselling and psychotherapy, often embedded in texts that make the case for reflexive, narrative, and/or phenomenological forms of research, for example Kim Etherington's (2004) account *Becoming a Reflexive Researcher*; Linda Finlay's (2011) *Phenomenology for Psychotherapists: Researching the Lived World*; Linda Finlay and Ken Evans' (2009) *Relational-Centred Research for Psychotherapists: Exploring Meaning and Understanding*; Jane Speedy's (2008) *Narrative Inquiry and Psychotherapy*; and Jane Speedy and Jonathan Wyatt's (2014) *Creative Practitioner Inquiry in the Helping Professions*. This book, *Practitioner Research in Counselling and Psychotherapy: The Power of Examples*, seeks to expand and complement these texts through richly descriptive studies of therapeutic training and practice conducted by practitioners and, in one case, by a client. We also seek to illustrate the importance for research in counselling and psychotherapy of focusing on particular examples without what Dunne (2005, p. 386) calls 'generalising ambitions'. To do so we return to the idea of practical rationality or *phronesis* as it is deployed by Flyvbjerg (2001) in his argument for a *phronetic* approach to research in the social sciences.

Phronesis refers to the work of exercising judgement wisely in particular circumstances. Following this, the purpose of *phronetic* research is to foster and support practical wisdom and good judgement. So the approach to research that we advocate aims to work with the grain of learning to become expert, as we have laid out above. Our approach does not differentiate between knowledge that fosters practical learning and research-based knowledge; hence the close links between reflective practice and research. Because it seeks to foster good judgement, *phronetic* research requires us to pose questions about the values

39

embedded in what we do. The audiences for such research are diverse – practitioners, commissioners, policy-makers – all of whom need to be offered resources capable of encouraging wise action. The purpose is not to search for universal truths, since the domain of doing, of practical knowledge, is not of a kind that can be characterised or guided by such truths. Instead, the *phronetic* approach to research, which we showcase in this book, prioritises the particular and the context-specific, since that is how practical wisdom is exercised.

Flyvbjerg (2001) uses the term 'case study' to characterise his vision of a *phronetic* approach to social science research. There is a long tradition of case-study research in many fields within the social sciences, including but by no means limited to counselling and psychotherapy. However, the term 'case study' is a confused and confusing one. Recently, John McLeod (2010) has examined the role of case studies in the development of theory and practice in counselling and psychotherapy, placing particular emphasis on developing systematic methods for case-study research and seeking to show how clinical case studies can be enrolled in a wider project of research with generalising ambitions. This is not the particularising approach that informs Flyvbjerg's (2001) use of the term and is not consistent with the idea of a *phronetic* approach to research in counselling and psychotherapy. Our approach to case-study research is therefore radically different from that set out in Mcleod's (2010) volume.

In order to clarify our approach, it is helpful to turn briefly to debates about case-study research within the social sciences. Malcolm Tight (2010) has noted that many generic texts on social science methods make brief mention of case-study research but use the concept in a wide variety of ways. A more specialist social science literature on case study research has also developed, key proponents including Robert Stake (1995) and Robert Yin (2003). These writers seek to bring greater clarity and prestige to case-study methodology, setting out rationales for designing research that focuses on one or more cases, developing typologies of cases, and offering guidance on the tasks of the case-study researcher. Flyvbjerg (2006) has contributed to this literature by challenging criticisms and misunderstandings of the potential for in-depth study of single cases or a small number of cases to contribute to knowledge.

Although we agree with many of the arguments offered by Flyvbjerg (2001, 2006), Stake (1995), and Yin (2003) about the value of studying particular examples in context in order to develop richly descriptive accounts capable of achieving the 'epiphanic power' to which Dunne

(2005) refers, we also have some misgivings about the term 'case'. Our concerns are twofold. First, the concept of a case necessarily objectifies the entity to be explored. In other words, it tends to create distance between the researcher and that which they study. While we do not doubt the need for researchers to get sufficient distance from what they study to be able to pose searching questions, we also wish to value their passionate immersion and experiential proximity to what they study. As Dunne (2005, p. 386) argues, provided that experience-near studies are informed by 'a keenly reflective awareness of their "point of view"', they have the potential to be especially relevant for others who are themselves immersed in the particularity of another setting or milieu. Second, the concept of a case implies that it is a neatly bounded entity, and much of the guidance provided in the literature on case-study methods concerns the delimitation of the case so that it can become a well-defined object of study. However, this process militates against a genuine working with the principle that the distinction between the researcher and what he or she studies is intrinsically unstable. For these reasons, we prefer the language of 'examples', and in this book we seek to demonstrate the power of examples for research in counselling and psychotherapy.

As we noted in Chapter 1, clinical case studies and vignettes from practice have a long history in counselling and psychotherapy, occupying a central place in the development of the field and continuing to be highly valued in the education and training of practitioners. They can be understood as examples within the ambit of *phronetic* research. One of the key challenges for educators is that there can be no standard framework or methodology for such research. As we have argued above, the logic of the scientific method does not work in domains characterised by the double hermeneutic, where the researcher is located within his or her field of study and to which context is integral and not merely incidental. Instead, the approach can best be gleaned by studying examples. We can, however, point to some common features found in examples that have what Dunne (2005, p. 386) calls 'epiphanic power' as they apply to research concerned with the practice of counselling and psychotherapy. These exemplary studies engage in depth with the reality and the lived experience of therapeutic practice. In so doing they notice and attend to specific and particular details, often things that might be overlooked but that, when approached with deep curiosity, have the potential to offer new and important insights. They do not seek to abstract or generalise but to particularise in order to maximise the depth of insight. They seek to communicate and therefore offer narratives that acknowledge a range of positions and voices. Thus they contribute to conversations and dialogues and do not seek to have the last word. They are reflexive, bringing the subjectivity of the researcher (and author) into view and posing questions about the intersubjective dynamics in play. Running through all these attributes, they stay close to lived experience and are therefore experience-near.

The rigour of the kind of studies this book showcases does not come from their adherence to externally defined methods for producing, analysing, or presenting data. Instead, their rigour comes from the internal coherence of their arguments and impacts. Nor does their status as research stem from their difference from reflective practice but, rather, from their capacity to stimulate new insight and illumination. To explain what this means we consider each chapter in turn, commenting on our understanding of its particular contribution to knowledge. We do not apply commonly used labels to categorise the methodological approach of each chapter but instead use ordinary language to describe our understanding of what each author does and how each author enriches and contributes to knowledge in the field of counselling and psychotherapy.

The second part of this book focuses on experience-near accounts of coming into the field of therapeutic practice, and in each of the three chapters it includes the author interrogates an aspect of her own experience as a counsellor in training in order to offer unique insights through which they contribute to knowledge about the process of learning to becoming a practitioner. In Chapter 4, Linda Gardner focuses directly on the experience of training, which she, like many others, found deeply unsettling. She reflects on her experience, drawing especially on Wilfred Bion's theory of states of mind, to show how what she had found so unsettling was productive, formative, and necessary for her development as practitioner. Weaving together autobiographical material with reflections on what aspects of the training stirred up in her, she invites readers into her struggles and her gradually expanding appreciation of the value of not knowing in relation to herself and her clients. By drawing upon her own experience of training to become a counsellor as an example or case study of what it means to 'trust in the process' she speaks to others in the throes of their own training and to those who support them, and she contributes to the evolving body of scholarship that illuminates and brings to life the complex richness of Bion's ideas.

Next, in Chapter 5, Anna St Clair explores the question of touch in counselling practice from the perspective of a counsellor-in-training, challenging both the psychoanalytic axiom 'thou shall not touch' and the failure of other psychotherapeutic traditions to problematise touch sufficiently. Coming into counselling from a background as a dancer and dance teacher in which direct and sensitive contact between bodies is central, she offers a unique perspective on the counselling and psychotherapy literature concerned with touch. St Clair draws on ordinary moments in her counselling practice to invite her readers to think afresh about their own impulses, actions, and decisions around touch. By particularising rather than generalising, she shifts the focus of debate to how we learn about and come to embody aspects of the complex area of touch in therapeutic practice.

Completing Part II, in Chapter 6 Mags Turner explores how underlying unconscious motivations for becoming a counsellor can come into view during the course of therapeutic work. In so doing she contributes a deeply personal example that speaks to the vital interface between the personal development of practitioners and their therapeutic use of self. Presenting a feature of her experience of work with one client, Turner recognises parallels as well as differences between their lives. She draws on her counter-transference responses to trouble the pleasures and valorisation of intimacy in the therapeutic relationship. Illuminating her felt sense of an absence of intimacy in relationship to significant others in her growing-up, she recognises how this unfulfilled need can lead to re-enactment in therapeutic work. She thus provides a vivid example of how what is created within the unique dyad of a therapeutic relationship needs to be questioned and challenged in order to meet the needs of the client – and how this may also be of transformative benefit to the counsellor.

The third part of the book presents four examples in which the focus is unambiguously upon the voice of the client. Each example approaches the task of presenting the client's voice in a different way and never with objectifying certainty about the other. Through their different ways of enabling the voice of the client to be heard, each chapter makes a different kind of contribution to knowledge. Chapter 7 offers a study of the client's experience written by the client herself, who is also a practitioner. Drawing on key moments in her personal therapy, Connie Johnson illustrates how early trauma and preverbal distress may be felt within such a relationship, and she shows how, in strong therapeutic relationships, subtle ruptures can occur, be acknowledged and repaired. Her chapter also contributes to the field of counselling and disability through her acute observation of the impacts of disability within a therapeutic relationship as well as its reparative possibilities. Johnson contributes to ways of thinking with ideas from different theoretical orientations too often treated in opposition to each other: her study brings to life key tenets of the person-centred approach at the same time as making sensitive use of psychodynamic thinking.

Chapter 8 presents a rare and unusual example of therapeutic work with a long-term psychiatric in-patient, in this case a man diagnosed with schizophrenia. The practitioner, April Parkins, demonstrates the value and importance of such work, not as conventionally curative but as a way of enabling the patient's voice to be heard and his life story to be told to audiences beyond the institutional setting in which his life was enclosed. Parkins illustrates how she and her client made contact with each other, and how his active participation and self-expression led to the telling of his life story to which this chapter bears witness. Parkins draws on psychodynamic ideas to theorise the meaning of their work, offering a distinctive application of Winnicottian ideas as well as an impassioned argument for therapeutic work with people with serious psychiatric conditions.

In Chapter 9, Janette Masterton discusses bereavement counselling in prison. She shows how the impact of an in-depth, experience-near qualitative study based directly on counselling work can transform institutional practices, in this case those of the Scottish Prison Service. Masterton draws on recordings of counselling sessions to provide powerful evidence of a prisoner's experience of being bereaved behind bars. Like Parkins's client, her client wanted the story that counselling enabled him to tell to be made available to others and thereby to feel that his life and his suffering had meaning and could make a contribution to knowledge.

In Chapter 10, Linda Talbert offers a radically different way of facilitating clients' voices. Talbert develops a highly creative response to some of the ethical challenges of writing about therapeutic work. She explores tales of trauma through publicly available stories, situating herself as a reflexive practitioner in dialogue with the narratives she explores. She shows how careful readings of culturally resonant fictional or mythical narratives enable practitioners to make insights from practice available and thereby enrich practitioners' capacity for therapeutic work. Alongside this methodological contribution to knowledge, she demonstrates the centrality of stories in human life and elaborates the power and significance of narrative as a container and source of meaning-making for those who suffer and bear witness to trauma.

Part IV includes four chapters, each of which illuminates how practitioners embody and contribute to theory. Theories are ways of telling stories, which is taken up in Chapter 11, where Chris Scott explores the theme of anxiety in therapeutic work. Using the concept of narrative, he contributes to experience-near knowledge of anxiety, creatively bringing together different theories in order to offer a distinctive way of thinking about and working with clients' experiences of anxiety. As he argues, clients and counsellors arrive in counselling with their own theories – in the form of narrative accounts – of mental health symptoms including anxiety. He shows how client and counsellor co-construct a shared narrative, which holds the potential, but no guarantee, of enabling each to alter his or her own narrative in reparative ways. He offers a study of a counsellor's reflexive engagement with his own experiences within which different theories of anxiety are interwoven.

Inspired by a challenging moment of client work, in Chapter 12 Patrick Fegan makes an original contribution to the theory of counter-transferences, which he brings into dialogue with person-centred as well as psychodynamic thinking. Fegan describes how, in part through his use of clinical supervision, the concept of the counter-transference helped him to make sense of, and work with, feelings of antipathy towards a new client. But this work continued to haunt him long after it had ended. Returning once more to and deepening his engagement with the transference–counter-transference matrix enables him to offer new insight into the interplay between himself and his client. In so doing he shows how theory is lived and how that living contributes to the development of theory, in this case about the therapist's use of self.

Next, in Chapter 13, Lynne Rollo explores gender and power in the therapeutic relationship. Locating the focus of her study personally, culturally, and theoretically, she enriches ways of thinking about the embodiment of gender in the consulting room. She presents an example drawn from experiences of disconnection at the beginning of her work with a man and shows how this came to be used to inform the work. The clinical example she discusses contributes to thinking about the subtle and complex enactment of gendered power.

In the final chapter of the book, we return to the work of Wilfred Bion and to what it means to experience the 'chaos monsters' of uncertainty. In this chapter Diana Sim offers the reader an experiential way into Bion's thinking. Her work contributes to understanding the rich and complex ideas bequeathed by Bion in the way that she writes of her own experience. She thus invites the reader into a distinctive kind of relationship with her text. She offers a unique study of how theory is lived and embodied. Her account exemplifies how we can make ideas we take in from outside our own, creating something new and embodied. This embodied theory becomes a valuable resource available for therapeutic work, not as an abstraction to be applied but as a deepening capacity for being with the experience of another.

As this summary indicates, the chapters in the book express a multiplicity of voices, especially those of practitioners and their clients. Each contributor speaks in his or her own particular authorial voice and their various personal qualities offer readers diverse experiences of reading. Both writing and reading are intersubjective experiences, and different readers will experience different texts differently. Just as each therapeutic dyad is unique, so too is each reading. By cultivating and celebrating this diversity we seek to place relationality at the heart of research and scholarship, as well as practice.

Contributors to this book work in depth with their own experience as practitioners, to varying degrees writing of others as well as themselves. Remaining close to lived experience and therefore true to life in the various ways that they do poses important challenges for researchers in balancing their commitments to themselves and those others on whom their work depends with the veracity of the stories they tell. It is to these challenges that this book now turns.

References

Berwick, D. M. (2005) 'Broadening the view of evidence-based medicine', *Quality and Safety in Health Care*, 14 (5), 315–316.

Bondi, L. (2005) 'The place of emotions in research: From partitioning emotion and reason to the emotional dynamics of research relationships', in J. Davidson, L. Bondi, and M. Smith (eds) *Emotional Geographies* (Farnham: Ashgate) pp. 231–246.

Bruner, J. (1960/1977) *The Process of Education* (Cambridge, MA: Harvard University Press).

Charon, R. (2006) *Narrative Medicine: Honoring the Stories of Illness* (Oxford and New York: Oxford University Press).

Clandinin, D. J., and Connolly, F. M. (2000) *Narrative Inquiry* (San Francisco: Wiley).

Dreyfus, H., and Dreyfus, S. (1986) *Mind Over Machine: The Power of Human Intuition and Expertise in the Era of the Computer* (New York: Free Press).

Dunne, J. (1993) *Back to the Rough Ground: 'Phronesis' and 'Techne' in Modern Philosophy and in Aristotle* (London: University of Notre Dame Press).

Dunne, J. (2005) 'An intricate fabric: Understanding the rationality of practice', *Pedagogy, Culture and Society*, 13 (3), 367–389.

Etherington, K. (2004) *Becoming a Reflexive Researcher* (London: Jessica Kingsley).

Finlay, L. (2011) *Phenomenology for Psychotherapists: Researching the Lived World* (Chichester: Wiley-Blackwell).

Finlay, L. and Evans, K. (2009) *Relational-Centred Research for Psychotherapists: Exploring Meaning and Understanding* (Chichester: Wiley-Blackwell).

Flyvbjerg, B. (2001) *Making Social Science Matter* (Cambridge: Cambridge University Press).

Flyvbjerg, B. (2006) 'Five misunderstandings about case-study research', *Qualitative Inquiry*, 12 (2), 219–245.

Gendlin, E. (1981) *Focusing* (London: Bantam).

Giddens, A. (1984) *The Constitution of Society: Outline of the Theory of Structuration* (Cambridge: Polity Press).

Gladwell, M. (2008) *Outliers: The Story of Success* (New York: Little, Brown and Company).

Gregory, D. (1978) *Ideology, Science and Human Geography* (London: Hutchinson).

Habermas, J. (1972) *Knowledge and Human Interests* (London: Heinemann).

Haraway, D. (1988) 'Situated knowledges: The science question in feminism and the privilege of partial perspective', *Feminist Studies*, 14 (3), 575–599.

Keat, R., and Urry, J. (1975) *Social Theory as Science* (London: Routledge and Kegan Paul).

McLeod, J. (2010) *Case Study Research in Counselling and Psychotherapy* (London: Sage).

Polkinghorne, D. E. (1988) *Narrative Knowing and the Human Sciences* (Albany: State University of New York Press).

Schön, D. (1983) *The Reflective Practitioner: How Professionals Think in Action* (London: Temple Smith).

Somers, A., Pomerantz, A. M., Meeks, J. T., and Pawlow, L. A. (2014) 'Should psychotherapists disclose their own psychological problems?' *Counselling and Psychotherapy Research*, 14 (4), 249–255.

Speedy, J. (2008) *Narrative Inquiry and Psychotherapy* (Basingstoke and New York: Palgrave Macmillan).

Speedy, J., and Wyatt, J. (2014) *Creative Practitioner Inquiry in the Helping Professions* (Rotterdam: Sense).

Stake, R. (1995) *The Art of Case Study Research* (Thousand Oaks, CA: Sage).

Tight, M. (2010) 'The curious case of case study: A viewpoint', *International Journal of Social Research Methodology*, 13 (4), 329–339.

Yin, R. (2003) *Case Study Research: Design and Methods*, 3rd edn (Thousand Oaks, CA: Sage).

3 Rethinking Supervision and Ethics in Experience-Near Research

SIOBHAN CANAVAN AND SEAMUS PRIOR

In the preceding chapters, Liz Bondi and Judith Fewell argue for an experience-near approach to research in counselling and psychotherapy, deeply informed by practical rationality or *phronesis*. For practitioners, undertaking such research is likely to mean working closely with their own experience of therapeutic practice. This presents a range of ethical challenges, which we explore in this chapter.

In Chapter 1, Liz Bondi and Judith Fewell note the foundational importance of clinical work in the development of knowledge in counselling and psychotherapy, and they point to changing ethical and professional values as important factors in the subsequent marginalisation of clinical case studies within research. Following their argument in Chapter 2 for a return to richly descriptive studies that work closely with examples drawn from practice, this chapter discusses how this might be achieved in ways that are informed by, and consistent with, twenty-first-century ethical and professional values. A central ethical dilemma at stake is a tension between privacy and openness. On the one hand, the promise of confidentiality and privacy is foundational for the client's sense of safety and trust in the therapist, the relationship, and the process, that enables the work of therapy to take place. On the other hand, only through the exposure of practice through detailed and honest analysis and discussion can practitioners open themselves up to ethical assessment and self-assessment (Habermas, 1993). This opening up also makes accounts of practice available in a way that enables the profession to advance knowledge and articulate its position within public fora. Furthermore, therapists bear witness to and have privileged access to the stories and lives of their clients, to their problems of living and their resourceful ways of overcoming their difficulties. As Jane Speedy (2008) has argued, research constitutes an avenue for giving a voice to clients and communities who may not otherwise have one because they are marginalised or disenfranchised in public life. The management and negotiation of the underlying tension between the protection of confidentiality and the exposure entailed in research is explored in this chapter.

Chapters 4 to 14 of this book have their origins in dissertations completed by master's students with whom we and our colleagues have worked as research supervisors. The work of academic supervision has been formative for us in our development of experience-near, practice-based research, not least because it entails relationships between students and supervisors in which ethical questions are ever present. We therefore begin this chapter by reflecting on the relational complexities of research supervision that establish the context and framework within which questions of research ethics are addressed. Research supervision has an obvious relevance to educators who supervise students working on dissertations, but it also opens up complex issues of role and power that arise for all practitioners who reflect on their own clinical practice in depth and beyond the framework of clinical supervision, whether they identify as researchers or not and, if they do, whether they consider themselves novices or experts, or somewhere in between.

Our account of supervising practice-based research draws on the idea of an ethics of care, first developed by Carol Gilligan (1982) who, in the context of exploring gender differences in ethical reasoning, argued for an approach to ethics in which relationships matter. This relational approach to ethics offers an alternative to strict unwavering adherence to abstract and therefore de-contextualised ethical principles, which has a long tradition in philosophical consideration of ethics. In the second section of the chapter we explore the ethical work required when researchers (and their supervisors) undertake experience-near research that draws on their therapeutic practice. We discuss how practitioners can build on their already-established ethical sensitivity developed in therapeutic practice to address the complex ethical issues that may emerge in practice-based research. We argue that ethical mindfulness, based on relational ethics and founded on the principles of therapeutic practice, rather than a technical or procedural approach to research ethics, enables practitioners to engage in research that is closely linked to practice, experience-near, and consistent with the values of counselling and psychotherapy.

Supervising Research on Therapeutic Practice: Working in a Liminal Space

The academic literature on supervising research that derives from therapeutic practice is curiously limited. This may have as much to say about the relatively underdeveloped state of counselling and psychotherapy in the academy as it does about the interrogation of research supervision in the field. In this section some of the issues and complexities of the academic supervision of practice-related research are explored. We position both academic supervision and writing about therapeutic practice in liminal spaces. The idea of liminal space draws on the anthropologist Victor Turner's (1967) classic work on rites of passage, the relevance of which Salma Siddique (2011) has explored in relation to counselling and psychotherapy research. Siddique (ibid., p. 315, emphasis in original) writes that

> In order to move from an unknowing, not-understanding state to a position of understanding, a person needs to move through a middle, *liminal* phase. In liminality, the transitional state between two states or roles, individuals [are] 'betwixt and between'.

Siddique (ibid., p. 315) has suggested that practitioner researchers venture 'out of the comfort of the therapist's chair' into other spaces as yet unknown and therefore yet to be explored and inhabited with ease. Understood in this way the terrain of research is not one where traditional demarcations between academic supervisor and research student are secure or fixed. For an academic supervisor who is also a practitioner, and possibly a clinical supervisor, there are multiple roles to navigate and selves to gather (Etherington, 2001). For a student who is writing about his or her practice, an additional layer of complexity is created in his or her encounters in the terrain of research. Liminality can be containing, as conceptualised by Wilfred Bion (1962), and transitional as D. W. Winnicott (1971) has described. But for practitioners their experience of moving into this liminal space will vary widely. Research calls upon them to draw on their self-experience and internal worlds in new ways. For some, perhaps including those who are newly qualified, student status may be familiar, and this may make for an easier adjustment than for those coming into research with more extensive clinical experience and at greater distance from the experience of being a student or learner.

The concept of liminality has particular relevance for the supervision of academic research grounded in counselling and psychotherapy practice because of the need for student and supervisor to move 'betwixt and between' different roles, positions, and dimensions of self. It is not so much that practitioners have placed or re-placed themselves into the role of researcher, but that they are constantly re-negotiating the terrain that lies between the familiarity of their practice and its clinical supervision and the unfamiliarity of research on that practice. If professional training has fostered the capacity for tolerance of not-knowing and practicing with manifold ambiguity (Cayne and Loewenthal, 2007), practitioner research-ers may find a place to work reflexively with their academic supervisor, alongside working with their clinical supervisor and their internal world, at the same time as holding their clients in mind. For this to happen well, however, there are a number of complex intersubjective encounters in this liminal space that can have a bearing on what happens in academic supervision and that need to be navigated thoughtfully.

Sue Cornforth and Lise Bird Claiborne (2008) have helpfully noted that whereas clinical supervision takes as its focus the relationship with a third party (the client), academic supervisors support supervisees in their relationships with data from their clinical work. Both forms of supervision express a commitment to the third party of the client, but differ-ently. Supervision, in both clinical and educational settings, traditionally grounds itself firmly in an ethics of care and, as such, demands the same rigour of openness and exploration fuelled by 'what amounts to an "ethic of self-reflection"' (ibid., p. 159).

Cornforth and Claiborne (ibid., p. 160) have also argued that in both forms of supervision

> the invitation, the pleasure is in the primary relationship between supervisor and supervisee, rather than the secondary relationship between supervisee and object or other.

Reading the chapters that comprise the main body of this book, and knowing many of the students who have turned their master's disserta-tions into chapters for publication, it is possible to see 'the hand' of aca-demic supervision between the lines. However, it is also striking that only one of the chapters (by Patrick Fegan) explicitly references academic supervision, while several refer in different ways to the clinical supervi-sion of the practice they have researched. On one level this feels entirely appropriate; on another it evokes curiosity about the particular challenges of academic supervision when practitioner researchers interrogate their own practice. What follows explores some of these challenges, based on our experience of supervising master's students and informed by insights gained by a colleague who conducted a small piece of research on a closely related topic (Barbour, 2012).

Many of the practitioners who have researched their practice for this book undertook their professional training with trainers from among whom their academic supervisors were subsequently appointed. For both student and supervisor, this transition from trainee or trainer to research supervisee or supervisor is where the work begins. Quite apart from losing a training group and all its attendant supports, post-training research students are quickly exposed to a new world of epistemology, ontology, methodology, ethics and analysis that challenges their assumptions about what research is and about their place in this new, conceptually different environment. All of this can be profoundly unsettling for novice practitioner researchers. In academic supervision some supervisees may respond to this by searching for the technical knowledge or *techne* that constitutes the 'know-how' of research, even though they have been attending classes in which the argument offered in Chapter 2 is elaborated. But for novice practitioner researchers who have been so close to their practice experience, there may be an impulse to distance themselves from it, perhaps in the belief that an experience-far position is essential for what 'real researchers' do (Geertz, 1983, p. 18). Their passion for their therapeutic work may even be dulled by this process. Initially, this kind of search for the certainties presumed to be found in technical knowledge may oust the practical rationality or *phronesis* with which students will be familiar from their training and to which they have been introduced in class as an approach to knowledge and research that is consistent with the values and practices of counselling and psychotherapy. Academic supervisors confronted by this turn to *techne* are placed under pressure and may feel undermined, as if the practical wisdom of counselling and psychotherapy, which teaches us to trust the relational process of therapeutic work, is no longer enough (Dunne, 1993). But we would argue that the task for academic supervisors is to hold their nerve and perhaps also to hold the hope that in time their supervisees' trust in and passion for the practical rationality of therapeutic work will return and be augmented by the curiosity that reflecting upon one's own practice in depth both requires and enriches.

A closely related dynamic often in play in the early stages of the research process is that the locus of evaluation (Rogers, 1967) of the practitioner researcher may become externalised. For practitioners who have worked hard in training to internalise their professional locus of evaluation and to own their competence this can be deeply disturbing. In the initial stages of research supervision this kind of disturbance may be represented by over-reliance on the academic supervisor to tell the supervisee what to do and a strong 'need to know' in the approach to the research they wish to undertake. As well as holding to his or her facilitative role rather than becoming overly directive, the academic supervisor may need to acknowledge the supervisee's feelings of loss, perhaps relating to the loss of the training group and perhaps to the disorientation and lostness that is an inevitable accompaniment to entering the unfamiliar terrain of research. While this may be most acute for novice practitioner researchers, something similar recurs at some point in every researcher's experience of every project if he or she is genuinely open to the unknown.

In her developmental approach to academic supervision, Lindy Barbour (2012) cites the work of Daniel Stern (1985, p. 67) who has placed 'all learning in the domain of emergent relatedness'. Connecting psychotherapeutic practice with pedagogic theory, she describes a progression from dependency towards autonomy, with the need for academic advice and containment in early meetings between supervisor and student succeeded by a more collegial relationship later on, when the supervisee is likely to be more self-directed and more able to meet the academic supervisor as someone closer to a peer or sibling than a parent. An important element in this progression is often the realisation by supervisees of the centrality for their research of their own embodied knowledge of what they are investigating (often the therapeutic relationship) and of themselves in their encounters with others, including their clients and clinical supervisors as well as their academic supervisors. In other words, they are the experts in relation to the material they are working with. There is a parallel here between academic and clinical supervision, and, all going well practitioner researchers' self-awareness and capacity for reflexivity can be put to good use in the former as it is in the latter (Smythe, MacCulloch, and Charmley, 2009). So, just as practitioners develop an internal clinical supervisory capacity (Casement, 1985), researchers develop an internal academic supervisory capacity. Neither becomes an isolated individual, but as these internal capacities strengthen so relationships with supervisors become more equal and collegial.

Thus far we have focused on the relationship between practitioner researcher and academic supervisor. Also in the liminal terrain of practice-based research supervision in counselling and psychotherapy is the clinical supervisor, who may not be physically or actively present, but whose work with the practitioner researcher nevertheless makes its presence felt. Academic supervisor and clinical supervisor may already know one another, or they may never have met. For the academic supervisor in his or her encounters with the student, a key task is to suspend judgement of the work of the clinical supervisor. Questions the academic supervisor needs to address are: 'who am I in my (academic) supervisory self and in this (academic) supervision relationship?'; and 'what is my task and what do I need to keep in my mind?' The academic supervisor may find these questions especially helpful when the practitioner researcher is exploring aspects of his or her practice and how he or she used clinical supervision. If the academic supervisor is, or has been, a clinical supervisor, he or she may have to work hard not to 're-supervise' the practice. Embarking on lengthy discussions about details of the work enters this terrain and needs to be avoided or problematised should it happen. The task of academic supervision is to help the student to examine and pose questions about processes attendant on his or her work, not to revisit the work clinically. To take an example, in Chapter 5 Anna St Clair revisits decisions she made about whether or not to hug two clients. For the academic supervisor the task is not to reflect on these moments in relation to the therapeutic process with those clients or in other clinical work, but instead to support Anna's efforts to locate these and other vignettes from her work on a terrain in which she can explore connections among her self (including her personal history with touch and learning about touch), debates about touch in the literature, and her rich and varied experience of therapeutic relationships. For the academic supervisor the student's project needs to be held in mind, and in this context the clients with whom the student works and has worked have a presence. However, they do not become central and they are not worked with therapeutically in a direct sense, although academic supervision may, of course, generate therapeutic insights.

Practitioner researchers come to the work of research with a passion for their practice and for understanding it in new ways. A particular element of their practice, an aspect of personal learning or challenge, or a wish to know more about the dynamics of a therapeutic encounter offer trustworthy starting points. These can sustain the student when the going gets tough. The research process needs more than passion, however, and the cultivation of the capacity to think coherently and theoretically and to be curious about the work is the stuff of academic supervision. In their clinical supervision practitioner researchers are necessarily reflective but may have received or exercised little in the way of conceptual activity; in academic supervision, by contrast, conceptualising and theorising are foregrounded. Although it may take many different forms, we would suggest that conceptual work is central to the process of forming a coherent narrative about therapeutic practice and the place of the practitioner within it. Conceptualising practice and reflections on practice is not easy; it can raise awkward questions for the practitioner researcher about what really happened in the therapeutic relationship, and in the end it is likely to require returning to questions about why he or she wants to research this practice at this time in this way. This calls to mind a personal experience for one of us of working with a student who was passionate about researching aspects of suicide: the early work was theoretically complex, culturally sensitive, and historically questioning but remained experience-far until she was ready to engage, in supervision, with the softly insistent question 'why suicide?' Only then did the work of integrating personal experience, practice reflection and theoretical engagement begin. This illustrates how the academic supervisor needs to be available to meet each research student in the specificity of his or her particular study with curiosity about what the work might mean for her or him and needs to be willing to wait until he or she is ready to become curious about this.

As this discussion suggests, another boundary that requires negotiation is between the academic and the therapeutic. The idea that research may have personal therapeutic effects for researchers has been elaborated in the literature of autoethnography (for example Poulos, 2009), and we would expect researchers to be drawn to topics that are personally meaningful for them, which will sometimes engage unresolved areas in their own internal worlds. Sometimes this may be within supervisees' awareness when they embark upon their research, but for others it may emerge only after they have become immersed in their studies. Moreover, even when the awareness already exists, it is often the case that something becomes heightened or calls out to be addressed in unexpected ways – as exemplified in this book in chapters by Patrick Fegan and Mags Turner as well as by Connie Johnson's revisiting of her experience as a client. There is a risk in situations like these that students confuse the tasks of research with their own therapeutic needs and also that supervisors are tempted to cross the boundary between academic support and therapeutic engagement, a boundary that may come to feel fragile and difficult to hold with compassion and precision. In her exploration of how academics in counselling and psychotherapy work with their students, Barbour (2012) asked her informants about the differences they perceived between how they worked as academic supervisors and how they worked as clinicians. The responses they offered included the need to be proactive and directive as academic supervisors in ways they would not be as practitioners. Related to this, they also drew attention to the need to alert students to a distinction between research-for-knowledge (with personal development as a bonus) and research-for-therapy (where the students may be too close to their practice experience to be able to think about it).

Research is usually time-limited, and the great majority of our master's students need to complete their dissertations in less than twelve months from when they make the shift from professional training to research. This calls for a balance in supervision between attending to *processes* of reflection, conceptualisation, and discovery and the *task* of producing the coherent narrative of a dissertation that conforms to specific academic requirements and meets relevant academic conventions. Holding this balance is not always easy for academic supervisors. Facilitating the student's exploration and capacity to play theoretically has to be matched with the rigour of a structure oriented towards the outcome as a contribution to knowledge. One colleague conceptualises this as 'keeping the dissertation in the room', with the related task of holding the reader of the dissertation in mind. Thinking about what a well-told story might be, alongside producing a piece of work that can be creative and meaningful as well as being located academically, is always challenging. In moving between practice and research, whilst holding both positions, the most significant findings and discoveries can arise from attempts to negotiate states of being 'betwixt and between' that relate to the balance between process and task.

Practitioner researchers and their academic supervisors both have a say in how they inhabit the liminal space of academic supervision and how they negotiate their various roles and responsibilities. Both parties have a range of other experiences to guide them. Practitioner researchers have a deep embodied knowledge of their practice and their capacity to hold themselves and their clients within it; their academic supervisors have the knowledge that when students are immersed in their work to the point of feeling submerged, they can come to the surface in supervision. In the end academic supervision is about providing the right accompaniment to help the students to be curious, to see what they cannot or are not ready to see, to challenge assumptions and narrowed perspectives, and to discover new truths. It is to encourage, care, and assist practitioner researchers to work through the 'in-between-ness' of the liminal space they have entered. In practice-based research of the kind advocated and presented in this book, it is a process in which the certainties of technical rationality are relinquished in favour of the holistic, embodied, and intuitive character of practical rationality in its openness and uncertainty. For counselling and psychotherapy practitioners this may be an unnerving venture, but it is also a deeply satisfying one in which it is possible to encounter in new and rewarding ways the practice-based questions and the passions that prompted their inquiries in the first place.

From Practitioner to Practitioner-Researcher: Developing Ethical Reflexivity

Ethical questions and dilemmas are often key components of research supervision. This section considers how practitioners who select research examples drawn from their practice can develop an ethical mindfulness in relation to research that is founded on the principles of therapeutic practice, rather than seeking a technical or procedural approach to research. We argue that developing ethical reflexivity in relation to research that is grounded in the relational ethics of the therapeutic relationship is key for practitioners researching their own practice and that this is a fundamental element of a *phronetic* approach to research.

Newly qualified and more experienced practitioners will have developed an ethical mindfulness in their practice contexts, often tested by a number of ethical quandaries. They have learned how to manage the confidentiality boundary in their training and supervision. They have also learned to discuss their practice in supervision and in peer learning groups and to compose reflective case studies, demonstrating the integration of theory to practice and evidencing their competence. In each situation, they have found ways of navigating the competing ethical imperatives of their clients' rights to confidentiality and privacy and their obligation to make their practice and learning accessible and transparent for the purposes of professional development and assessment. Research, however, brings a new set of ethical considerations that many practitioner researchers find complex and challenging. Its public nature creates significant challenges to confidentiality and to the requirement to do no harm. Where the work is ongoing, practitioners' interests in researching their practice introduce a new dynamic into therapeutic relationships that needs to be understood and managed, while their clients' interests remain paramount. Even when the work is complete, issues of fidelity and trustworthiness come into play.

As discussed above, the potential anxiety aroused by the complex ethical challenges of this new situation may lead novice practitioner researchers to seek technical solutions in the form of stratagems, procedures, and checklists to minimise or even eradicate risk. As John McLeod (2010) has argued, a technical approach to the ethics of case-study research is never sufficient to eliminate the potential for harm. Instead, the task for practitioner researchers is to use their existing clinically based ethical reflexivity to think about the new ethical demands that arise when they research topics and themes inspired by their practice, perhaps focusing upon specific therapeutic relationships. This is a core dimension of *phronetic* engagement in practice-based research, which goes beyond the competent implementation of technical procedures laid down by research codes of practice and research governance frameworks. As Marilys Guillemin and Lynn Gillam (2004, p. 269) argue, 'it is within the dimension of "ethics in practice" that the researcher's ethical competence comes to the fore'.

Ethical research competence does not require new or qualitatively different skills, nor does it require the assimilation of new theories or bodies of knowledge. Rather, the research context requires practitioners to consider their practice and their relationships with clients in new ways and to articulate positions for themselves as practitioner researchers in relation to their clients. A relational rather than procedural approach to ethics takes as its starting point the relationship between practitioner and client in the context of their work together, rather than the relationship between the researcher and the academic ethical review committee with its references to abstract principles and duties applied to hypothetical, generalised persons.

In her overview of values and ethics in therapeutic practice, Gillian Proctor (2014) traces the development in ethical thinking from principlism to relationality. Following Tim Bond's (2007) elaboration of 'relational trust', she identifies a shift in professional thinking from an understanding of ethical practice as founded on the rational application of abstract principles to individualised subjects to a conceptualisation of 'ethics-in-practice' as the ongoing accomplishment of intersubjective relations of fidelity and trust between persons in context. This appreciation of relationship and context is consistent with the *phronetic* approach to research set out in this book and underpins our argument that practitioner researchers conceptualise the ethical work of research as a development of the ethical mindfulness they have cultivated in their therapeutic practice.

Accounts of the philosophical foundations of professional ethics tend to focus on three main strands: deontological, consequentialist, and virtue-based. Deontological or duty-based ethics developed from the work of Immanuel Kant and his conception of the unique inviolable personhood of the individual subject, who should not be used as a means to an end in any human action. Consequentialist thinking, developed by Jeremy Bentham and John Stuart Mill, requires the consideration of the consequences of any action by those involved in ethical decision-making. Within that strand, utilitarianism guides those making decisions to achieve the greatest good for the greatest number. In contrast to this instrumentalist thinking, virtue-based ethics, developed from Aristotelian philosophy, emphasises the moral character and motivation of the practitioner and how he or she applies his or her personal and professional values and wisdom in particular circumstances. Deontological and consequentialist ethics have served as the basis for professional codes of ethics and the identification of the ethical principles of beneficence (acting in others' best interests), non-maleficence (not doing harm to others), justice (treating others with respect, fairness, and equality), and autonomy (promoting others' right to self-determination). Virtue-based ethics has informed the development of the ethics of care and relational ethics, which underline the importance of the relationship between practitioner and client and the context in which they are located.

In counselling and psychotherapy the client usually seeks out and initiates contact with the practitioner. While power imbalances inevitably exist, the practice undertaken is first and foremost for the client, to serve his or her needs and goals. By contrast, in research, the researcher initiates the relationship with the participant and as a consequence 'bears prime responsibility' for that relationship (Clark and Sharf, 2007, p. 400): the participant is invited to enter a research project in order to help the researcher to meet his or her goals. In addition to ensuring that research participants come to no harm, any researcher working with human subjects needs to address the Kantian ethical requirement of ensuring that persons are not used as a means to an end. In practitioner research, these issues are yet more complex because it is often the case – including in several of the studies in this book – that the client has not been specifically recruited into a research contract but has entered a therapeutic contract. Only after this has the practitioner chosen to undertake research on his or her practice with the client. Consequently, in addition to practical considerations of consent-seeking, explored below, practitioner researchers are called upon to address what Speedy (2008, p. 54) terms the 'ethical discomforts' that may emerge from the sense that they are 'using' their clients for their own purposes. As Kathie Crocket and colleagues (2004) have argued, it is through the extension of relational ethics from the therapeutic setting to the research setting that this potential objectification of clients in the research process is avoided.

In contrast to ethical deliberation involving the consideration of abstract principles, such as beneficence and fidelity, and to procedural ethics, which emphasises the necessary steps to be followed for a research project to receive ethical clearance, relational ethics focuses on the actual relationships between the researcher and others involved in the research. Relational ethics is concerned with ethical conduct grounded in the intersubjective relationship between a researcher and his or her research participants in the context of their real-world interactions, where the researcher remains mindful of his or her ongoing ethical responsibilities to the other persons involved in, or implicated in, the research. As Carolyn Ellis (2007, p. 4) has argued:

> Relational ethics recognizes and values mutual respect, dignity and connectedness between researcher and researched, and between researchers and the communities in which they live and work.

In practitioner research, relational ethics requires that clients and their wellbeing are at the heart of ethical decisions within the research endeavour. Undertaking research may put practitioners into new positions in relation to the practice-related phenomenon they examine, positions that emphasise critical inquiry, observation, and questioning. However, practitioner researchers still retain their original positions as counsellors or psychotherapists, and the ethics of care remains at the forefront in their research relationships with their clients, just as in their therapeutic relationships.

One of the most demanding tasks for counsellors and psychotherapists in training is to develop their capacity to be authentically themselves and fully present as unique persons in therapeutic relationships while also occupying the role of practitioners who comport themselves within the

ambit of professional standards (Lee and Prior, 2013). When practitioners come into research, a comparable accommodation is required: they
need to find ways of being authentically engaged as persons and as practitioners in their research while expanding their identities to encompass
being researchers.

Becoming a researcher requires a positioning of the self, to use the
theory developed by Rom Harré and Luk Van Langenhove (1991), in
relation to multiple others, which will be different from positionings
within other relationships. Novice practitioner researchers are in transition from being consumers of research to becoming potential produc-
ers of research, and they are in the process of joining communities of
researchers, however conceived. Simultaneously, they begin contemplating the unknown potential readers of their research: examiners, other
students, and those who may access their research in the public domain.
The contributors to this book, for example, have reworked their dissertations with you, the reader, in mind. The principal persons in relation to whom practitioner researchers are developing their positions
are, however, the clients whose work with their practitioners is being
researched. Practitioner researchers may also need to consider their
clinical supervisors who may be directly or indirectly implicated in their
research. Sometimes, for novice practitioner researchers it is this realisation that also brings into awareness, perhaps in ways they did not
anticipate, that research exposes them in new ways too, both as persons
and as practitioners, and that this requires a new positioning in their
relationship to their own selves.

A critical step for practitioner researchers articulating their positions
is to examine their motivations and personal investments in undertaking research, both in general and in relation to the specific pieces of
work or aspects of practice on which they focus their investigation.
There may be no definitive answers to such questions, since, as Jane
Polden (1998) argues, the shadow side of personal motivation necessarily eludes even the most searching of spotlights. However, this questioning of self remains an important task in developing ethical reflexivity
as a researcher, and research supervisors will often start their work
with a new practitioner researcher with an exploration of motivation, as
illustrated in the 'why suicide?' example above. In examining their personal motivations for undertaking practice-based research, practitioner
researchers consider both the contribution they may make to others
through their work and the personal advancement they may be seeking
through their development as researchers and perhaps also through the

academic qualifications towards which they are working. Those who go on to publish from their research, such as the contributors to this book, are also called upon to address what motivates them to circulate their work in this way, including reflecting upon their aspirations to become published authors in their fields.

Seeking the consent of clients for the inclusion of their therapeutic work in research is often seen as the cornerstone of good practice, even though, as McLeod (2010) has argued, gaining fully informed and freely given consent from clients may be ethically fraught and perhaps impossible to achieve. Some of the authors in this volume, such as Janette Masterton and April Parkins, explicitly sought and gained their clients' consent for the dissertations on which their chapters are based. In both cases the clients concerned were eager for their stories to be told, and their therapists were uniquely well placed to give voice to people on the margins of society, illustrating Speedy's (2008) point about the responsibility of practitioners to help marginalised people make their stories known. Other contributors did not seek permission, judging the risks of requesting consent greater than the risks of not doing so. Instead they used other methods to protect their clients' interests, including minimising contextual information, using disguise, and writing under pseudonyms. Others again chose strategies that did not entail writing about specific clients at all, even though their work is inspired by their therapeutic practice. Even among those who did seek consent from clients for their dissertation, none re-contacted clients for permission to publish their final chapters, either because this was impossible (for example because the client had died) or because the original consent covered publication.

Underlying the decisions made by several of the contributors of this book not to seek client consent are some important complexities. Traditional approaches to the clinical case study, especially those written in the psychoanalytic tradition, assume that the study is based on the 'case' of the client, reporting his or her background, presenting issues, disclosures in therapy, and his or her process of change and growth. However, the profoundly relational nature of the counselling relationship means that any account of practice can never be a one-person study; the practitioner, his or her practice, his or her process, his or her experience, his or her history are inevitably interwoven into the account, whether he or she is explicit about this or not. The contributors to this volume are all firmly rooted in this relational understanding of therapeutic practice, and therefore they locate themselves explicitly within the processes examined in their various studies. Their work represents a variety of lenses through which therapeutic practice may be viewed. Among those who focus on single clients, some are concerned more with the client's experience, such as Janette Masterton, and others more with the dynamics of the therapeutic work and their own process, such as April Parkins, Patrick Fegan and Lynne Rollo. Connie Johnson adopts another strategy, illuminating experiences of therapeutic work by drawing on herself as client. Others, such as Chris Scott, Anna St Clair and Mags Turner, explore themes in therapeutic work that draw on specific moments or encounters with different clients but do not present detailed accounts of the clients themselves or their work in therapy. Linda Gardner, Linda Talbert and Diana Sim do not draw directly on work with any clients but instead focus on aspects of therapeutic practice in other ways, in relation to training, narrative, and engaging with theory respectively.

Whoever and however wide the readership of published research may be, practitioner researchers need to hold in mind the clients who inspire their work and to think of them as potential readers, asking themselves:

- What might my client(s) feel if they read this?
- What might my client(s) think if they read this?
- Would I be able to give this to my client(s) to read?
- What would my client(s) learn about me and our relationship if they read this?
- How faithful would they feel I have been to our relationship and the work we have done together?

Exploring these questions reaches into the heart of the ethical encounter between client and practitioner in both the therapeutic work and the research. It brings practitioner researchers back to the ontological and epistemological foundations of their practice in both areas, requiring them to address questions of knowledge, power, expertise, voice and authority. By addressing these questions, practitioners return to consider their therapeutic practice in the particular relationships examined: what was known and said by whom, what was disclosed and what was kept private, what was shared, agreed, and explicit, and in what ways might client and practitioner have differed in their understandings or their values? They ask themselves: who was I in this relationship, to my client and to my self, and who am I now in this writing, to my client and my self?

The research process, in its conduct and its publication, thus constitutes the continuation of the interpersonal dialogue between two subjects, in

Martin Buber's (2004 [1923]) sense, where the values and ethics that form the bedrock of therapeutic practice are broadened to the practice of research. This is how practitioners' ethical reflexivity can be expanded to promote their ethical competence as a practitioner researcher.

As noted above, research on therapeutic practice is always about (at least) a two-person relationship. Potential objectification of clients is obviated through the conceptualisation of practice-based research as research into the therapeutic relationship and process, into a practitioner's use of *self*, rather than being primarily focused on the client as an interesting 'case' per se. Instead of positioning the clients, their lives, their stories, as the object of research scrutiny, the rich practice examples presented in this volume investigate the therapeutic practice of the researchers, exploring the learning and development they have gained through their work. This highlights a further ethical dimension in experience-near research: that of the ethical responsibility such researchers owe to themselves as persons and as practitioners, as they expose their practice to wider scrutiny and potential critique.

While some practitioner researchers may select outstanding examples of good practice for research in order to better understand how such gains were made, others, perhaps most, find themselves turning to work that has troubled or perplexed them, that may represent unfinished business, or that proved particularly challenging. With a principal motivation to learn and develop, they select for further examination examples of work that have the most potential to contribute to their own professional development, with the hope that such research will also contribute to knowledge more broadly.

Just as in therapeutic practice, where the person of the therapist cannot be extricated from the practitioner, so in research related to practice the person of the practitioner researcher is necessarily engaged and exposed. Perhaps with the help of research supervisors, practitioner researchers need to assess the extent of self-exposure necessary for any particular project, and they need to remain mindful of their rights to privacy and their self-care. Researchers are always subject to evaluation in their research endeavours, but unlike those who enjoy the status of university positions, students may be especially vulnerable in their self-exposure because they are presenting their work for academic examination. As we have already described, research supervision needs to address this aspect of ethical reflexivity while remaining attentive to the boundary with personal therapy that may emerge in such explorations.

The relational ethics practised in researchers' relationships with their clients also applies to the research supervision relationship, where supervisors observe an ethics of care towards their practitioner researcher supervisees.

Conclusion

In this chapter we have argued for an avowedly relational approach to ethical dimensions of experience-near research, and we have turned to the values and principles of therapeutic practice to help us think about the questions at stake. Practitioner researchers' therapeutic relationships with their clients are paramount, and so too are the boundaries of confidentiality and trust within which therapeutic work takes place. Yet if concerns about these matters silence us, our work will risk becoming stultified. We are relational beings and we need to be able to explore our experiences in dialogue with others. Clinical supervision provides an important forum for such dialogue, but it still restricts knowledge of therapeutic practice to those within the profession. Finding ways to communicate the experiential realities of this work to wider audiences is surely a key task for researchers in the field of counselling and psychotherapy. The discussions we have offered in this chapter are put forth in the spirit of encouraging others to venture into this project in ways that stay as close as possible to the ordinary realities of counselling and psychotherapy.

The concept of liminality is one that we have found useful in thinking about the relational complexities of academic supervision, in which the supervisor's task is to facilitate a process of initiating novice practitioner researchers into the community of researchers. The relationship within which academic supervisors and supervisees work is one that is distinct from but can come close to boundaries with therapeutic training, clinical supervision, and personal therapy. We argue that its distinctiveness needs to be discovered in its own way by each working pair. Consequently, rather than seeking to define the limits of academic supervision, we have explored some of the themes and questions that may arise in the way supervisors and supervisees inhabit this terrain.

Over the decades since the Second World War, ethical considerations have been a factor in the marginalisation of clinical case studies from research in the field of counselling and psychotherapy. During the same period, questions of ethics in research have also been transformed, initially in medical research and more recently in social science research. This transformation is often equated with the infrastructure for research ethics review, which has grown enormously, stimulating a preoccupation with procedural requirements as well as criticisms of these procedures (Dingwall, 2008; Schrag 2011). We have argued in contrast that experience-near research needs to approach questions of ethics from a different direction, focusing not on procedures but on relationships. By drawing upon and developing the ethical reflexivity acquired through clinical practice, practitioner researchers have available to them valuable resources for thinking through the new challenges that research and publication bring. This relational approach, with its attentiveness to particularity, is rooted in and draws upon practical wisdom in a manner entirely consistent with the approach to research for which this book argues and which is exemplified in the chapters that follow.

References

Barbour, L. (2012) 'Working with postgraduate students in counselling and psychotherapy', unpublished paper, University of Edinburgh.

Bion, W. R. (1962) *Learning from Experience* (London: Karnac).

Bond, T. (2007) 'Ethics and psychotherapy: An issue of trust' in R. E. Ashcroft, A. Dawson, H. Draper, and J. R. McMillan (eds) *Principles of Healthcare Ethics* (Chichester: John Wiley) pp. 435–442.

Buber, M. (2004 [1923]) *I and Thou* (London: Continuum).

Casement, R. (1985) *Learning from the Patient* (London: Routledge).

Cayne, J., and Loewenthal, D. (2007) 'The unknown in learning to be a psychotherapist', *European Journal of Counselling and Psychotherapy*, 9 (4), 373–387.

Clark, M. C., and Sharf, B. F. (2007) 'The dark side of truths: Ethical dilemmas in researching the personal', *Qualitative Inquiry*, 13 (3), 399–416.

Cornforth, S., and Claiborne, L. B. (2008) 'When educational supervision meets clinical supervision: What can we learn from the discrepancies?' *British Journal of Guidance and Counselling*, 36 (2), 155–163.

Crocket, K., Drewery, W., McKenzie, W., Smith, L., and Winslade, J. (2004) 'Working for ethical research in practice', *International Journal of Narrative Therapy and Community Work*, 3, 61–67.

Dingwall, R. (2008) 'The ethical case against ethical regulation in humanities and social science research', *Twenty-First Century Society: Journal of the Academy of Social Sciences*, 3 (1), 1–12.

Dunne, J. (1993) *Back to the Rough Ground: 'Phronesis' and 'Techne' in Modern Philosophy and in Aristotle* (London: University of Notre Dame Press).

Ellis, C. (2007) 'Telling secrets, revealing lives: Relational ethics in research with intimate others', *Qualitative Inquiry*, 13 (1), 3–29.

Etherington, K. (2001) 'Writing qualitative research – a gathering of selves', *Counselling and Psychotherapy Research*, 1 (2), 119–125.

Geertz, C. (1983) *Local Knowledge: Further Essays in Interpretive Anthropology* (New York: Basic Books).

Gilligan, C. (1982) *In A Different Voice* (Cambridge, MA: Harvard University Press).

Guillemin, M., and Gillam, L. (2004) 'Ethics, reflexivity and "ethically important moments" in research', *Qualitative Inquiry*, 10 (2), 261–280.

Habermas, J. (1993) *Justification and Application: Remarks on Discourse Ethics* (Cambridge: Polity Press).

Harré, R., and Van Langenhove, L. (1991) 'Varieties of positioning', *Journal for the Theory of Social Behaviour*, 21 (4), 393–407.

Lee, B., and Prior, S. (2013) 'Developing therapeutic listening', *British Journal of Guidance and Counselling*, 41 (2), 91–104.

McLeod, J. (2010) *Case Study Research in Counselling and Psychotherapy* (London: Sage/BACP).

Polden, J. (1998) 'Publish and be damned', *British Journal of Psychotherapy*, 14 (3), 337–347.

Poulos, C. (2009) *Accidental Ethnography* (Walnut Creek, CA: Left Coast).

Proctor, G. (2014) *Values and Ethics in Counselling and Psychotherapy* (London: Sage).

Rogers, C. R. (1967) *On Becoming a Person: A Therapist's View of Psychotherapy* (London: Constable).

Schrag, Z. (2011) 'The case against ethics review in the social sciences', *Research Ethics*, 7 (4), 120–131.

Siddique, S. (2011) 'Being in-between: The relevance of ethnography and auto-ethnography for psychotherapy research', *Counselling and Psychotherapy Research*, 11 (4), 310–316.

Smythe, E. A., MacCulloch, T., and Charmley, R. (2009) 'Professional supervision: Trusting the wisdom that "comes"', *British Journal of Guidance and Counselling*, 37 (1), 17–25.

Speedy, J. (2008) *Narrative Inquiry and Psychotherapy* (Basingstoke: Palgrave Macmillan).

Stern, D. (1985) *The Internal World of the Infant* (New York: Basic Books).

Turner, V. (1967) *The Forest of Symbols: Aspects of Ndembu Ritual* (New York: Cornell University Press).

Winnicott, D. W. (1971) *Playing and Reality* (London: Tavistock Publications).

Part II
Coming into Therapeutic Practice

4 A Trainee Counsellor's Account of Learning to Trust in the Process

LINDA GARDNER

My Background

I stumbled across counselling around 12 years ago, having searched for some time for what it embodied without knowing its name. When I was 12 my father died, aged 40, from testicular cancer after some years of treatment. During this long period my childhood was interspersed with many visits to hospitals, periods of hope followed by despair as the cancer got treated only to spread again, until he wasted away to a painful death. Despite this I feel I had a happy childhood, and I was brought up with a strong sense of family values.

I have always had a strong creative side and was later torn between art and nursing as a career. However, the impact of my father's illness ultimately influenced me to become a nurse. On reflection this was partly to try to reduce the suffering of others and partly because hospitals, sadly, seemed part of my life. A clash of personal values occurred, however, because nursing at that time (the early 1980s) was not how I had imagined it would be. There was little time to be compassionate; the medical model was prescriptive, strict, and clinical, with patients objectified as diseases to be fixed: 'the right mastectomy in bed four', 'the colon cancer in the side room'. Pressure from senior nurses to conform was strong. Menzies Lyth (1988) offers the insight that many of these nursing practices may have been created to reduce the anxieties that might be evoked if nurses formed emotional attachments to patients.

While I tried to do what I could within the confines of the structure, it didn't feel enough. I left nursing to be a full-time mother, and when my children were at school I decided to pursue a less medical, more holistic role in nursing by embarking on mental health nurse training.

During this training I experienced the effects of staff shortages and very little in the way of holistic therapeutic care, with control and management of people being the primary focus. Extremely disillusioned, I left nursing completely to pursue a degree in behavioural science (sociology and psychology), which I hoped might offer a more holistic viewpoint and possibly lead me into a career that would feel right. It was during this degree that I took a module on counselling which I can only describe as an 'ah ha!' moment. I felt as if a light had been switched on as I was introduced to concepts that resonated with me. From the focus on feelings and emotions to the collaborative non-objectifying ethos, it just felt right. McLeod (1998, p. 354) has articulated my sense of relief in finding the kind of helping opportunity that felt as if it 'fitted' when he wrote: 'the wounded healer concept makes it possible to understand the search for wholeness and integration which characterises the lives of many counsellors and therapists and makes it possible to transform the pain of negative life experiences into a resource for helping others'.

Following my degree I did some basic counselling training and began working as a counsellor within the voluntary sector. After six years of working in this context I felt that I would benefit from in-depth counselling training and therefore embarked on an MSc in Counselling. I thought that formal academic training at university level would enable me to work with much more purpose and clarity. At that point I worked in a person-centred way and was quite resistant to psychodynamic ideas. I chose a course that was a dialogue between the person-centred and psychodynamic approaches, thinking that this would give me the academic knowledge to further confirm my view that person-centred theory was right for me.

Naïvely I had expected that, as in nursing training, there would be a set theoretical base from which we would learn to practise counselling in a specific way. Having worked as a counsellor for some years prior to doing the course, I was aware of the complexity and ambiguity of the work, but I thought that studying at university level would provide me with some answers – and it did, but not in the way I had anticipated.

The experiential and dialogical approach to teaching and learning I encountered was unfamiliar and unsettling; it deeply challenged what I had come to understand as knowledge. Through using my experience of my training as a case study, and with the help of Bion's theory of states of mind, in this chapter I try to put some of my learning into a tangible form.

Bion's work has also helped me to explore and put into words the felt sense that I had at the end of my counselling course: a feeling that I had learned something quite profound but I wasn't sure what; a sense that it had been a different type of knowledge from what I had expected. Before proceeding I have to confess that I find Bion's work quite challenging. I surprised myself when I turned to it. I have worked out my own understanding of his ideas as I have gone along, which, whilst being far from perfect as a representation of his theory, is a useful working model to support my thinking. I wish to demonstrate through these very personal struggles the value for me, and potentially for others, of Bion's concept of 'not knowing'.

My Experience of the Course

Whilst both of our tutors were firmly grounded in their own theoretical frameworks – one person-centred, the other psychodynamic – no clear indication was given as to how we students might integrate the two theories and practices, or if indeed this was the aim. We were encouraged to develop in our own way and invited to 'trust in the process', a term that both intrigued and frustrated me throughout the course.

Initially it was stressful for me to experience professional training in which there was no set base on which to learn to practise, and this stress was aggravated by the programme's dialogical nature. My nursing training (unlike counselling training) had no place for tentative exploration of different ideas about how to dress a wound or make a bed: there was a correct, exact way to do everything. There was also a great amount of fear and shame attached to doing anything wrong, which left me very anxious about making mistakes. From this I had learned that there was a 'correct' way to do everything, which I had internalised in a powerful 'rule' that was difficult to rid myself of. Prior to my counselling training I knew this at an intellectual level; however, it was only through being in relationship with the tutors and experiencing my responses of anxiety, confusion, and sheer frustration at not being told the 'right' way to be a counsellor that I truly got in touch with the emotions behind my intellectualisations.

Bion's ideas have helped me to make sense of this experience with his concept of the K link. He suggested that all emotional experiences evolve from being in relationship with someone, an idea Symington and Symington (1996, p. 26) encapsulate thus: 'an emotional experience cannot be conceived of in isolation from a relationship'. Bion (1962) argued that there are three main types of emotional connections between people, which he termed Love (L), Hate (H), and Knowledge (K). He considered the Knowledge connection, or the K link, as 'germane to learning by experience' (Bion, 1962, p. 47). The K link is different from intellectual knowledge, which is 'about' something, and refers instead to an emotional knowing 'of' the self or 'of' another that occurs in the context of a relationship. This 'process of getting to know involves pain, frustration and loneliness', which are not generally felt in finding out a factual kind of knowledge (Symington and Symington, 1996, p. 28).

The idea of emotional learning within a relationship, or K link, has clearly demarcated for me two different types of learning and knowing; knowing from cognition and knowing from experience. The idea of the K link, which I associated with my experience of learning on the course, helped me to conceptualise why I felt I was experiencing a different type of learning from what I had expected. It would seem that I was beginning to learn and to know in an emotional sense, with the learning coming from my being in relationship with another or many others, through the K link rather than through a cognitive form of knowledge. It was, as Bion suggested, at times painful, frustrating, and lonely. Never more so than in my experience of the two-hour sessions of the person-centred process group that ran for ten successive weeks and formed a specific experiential element of the programme. Prior to this experience I had an intellectual knowledge that as a person I am quiet and struggle in large groups, which often results in my avoiding such situations. It was, however, only by being in a large group and being open to the K link that I began to engage emotionally with how difficult, painful, and lonely, this was for me. My naïve hope initially was that this large group (24 students) would feel supportive and safe and that I would be able to explore my thoughts and feelings, and help others to do the same. I thought that this would lead to an increase in my self-awareness and ability to be at ease in a group. The reality, however, was very different. I learned little of how to be a facilitative person in a group, and I contributed even less by way of verbal participation. Instead I was faced with the psychic reality of myself as a quiet individual in relationship with a large group of others.

As a shy compliant child I was easily moulded into a conforming people-pleasing adult. While I embrace this at one level and get genuine pleasure from helping others, at another level it has been detrimental to me because too often I put others' needs before my own. In order to conform to what others want, it is necessary for me to 'read' them and know what the norm or expectation is. In a large nonconforming group it was impossible to do this, which rendered many of my abilities to conform useless and left me with little guide as to what was expected of me. Consequently, all I had to rely upon was my own internalised sense of how to be and what to do: only I was in control of this. This challenged me enormously, but learning to trust and accept myself in this way was one of the important lessons I learned.

While I didn't develop new confident ways of being in the group or new communication techniques, I learned something more important. I learned how to engage with my emotional felt sense and acknowledge my personal reality, including my people-pleasing defences and introverted personality traits. In doing so I developed an acceptance of a part of me that I had known intellectually but had avoided emotionally because it was too painful. Describing Bion's thinking, Symington and Symington (1996, p. 28) attributed to him the idea that

> having a piece of knowledge about oneself is not at all the same thing as getting to know oneself through experiencing those aspects of the self in the relationship with the other. To come upon one's ruthless greed in relation to another is quite a different matter from an intellectual awareness of it.

My experience is that it is only by bearing this emotionally difficult form of knowing (K) that we can get to know ourselves more fully.

Bion developed this approach further by suggesting that in getting to know oneself in this emotional sense (through the K link), there is an absolute truth of our existence, an ultimate reality, which he termed O (Bion, 1970, p. 26). It would seem that we cannot know what this is in a definitive sense, because turning it into a cognitive 'knowing about' transforms it into something else, which is therefore no longer the reality itself. O is more something that we can strive towards. Bion (1970) termed this 'becoming O' and suggested that we have an inherent resistance to becoming O because there is a perceived danger in 'being oneself one's own truth' (Grinberg, 1985 p. 177).

It is only in bearing the emotionally difficult form of knowing (K) that one can get closer to the ultimate reality of oneself (O). Our resistance to O is a resistance to our own truth and the often painful, lonely process of reaching towards that truth. The process of self-awareness and self-development in counselling training could be understood as each of us becoming closer to his or her own truth, which makes it a unique process for each student. I think this is part of what was meant by the term 'trust in the process' which so frustrated me.

Negative Capability

Bion (1970) suggested that in order to be open to finding this meaning and getting closer to the truth of ourselves (O), we need to be in a state of 'negative capability', a term he borrowed from Keats. Symington and Symington (1996, p. 169) describe negative capability as being manifest 'when a man is capable of being in uncertainties, mysteries, doubts, without any irritable reaching after fact and reason'. If we can be in this state of negative capability or 'not knowing', we are more likely to get closer to the truth of our experience; in this state we give ourselves the space to search and find our own emotional meaning rather than grabbing at an anxiety-reducing solution.

My counselling training was, for me, negative capability in action. I experienced being held in a state of negative capability or not knowing until I had managed to make my own emotional connection, both in relation to the theory and in relation to myself. Being in relationship with the tutors on the course and experiencing my emotional response of anxiety, confusion, and frustration at not being told theoretically how to be a counsellor, I learned to tolerate the pain and frustration of not knowing until I found a way that fitted for me. I could have grounded myself in either the person-centred or the psychodynamic theoretical orientation to relieve my anxiety and give me a greater sense of stability and order. However, there were ideas from both perspectives that resonated strongly with me. And so I learned to tolerate the pain and frustration of not knowing. This in turn led me to listen to my own internal knowing or, in person-centred terms, to discover my internal locus of evaluation.

The tutors on the course did not gratify my need for answers but instead empathised and supported me in the struggle that enabled the shift from old to new. If they had provided me with the answers, it would have shut down my own search for understanding. The dialogical nature of the course improved my ability to be in negative capability, with the tutors encouraging me to trust in the process until something evolved that fitted for me. As Bion suggested, this led to my getting closer to the truth of who I am and what fits for me as a counsellor.

Learning to Practise

This has, in turn, taught me how to 'be' with clients in order that the same might be facilitated in them. Bion (1970) stressed the importance of therapists trying to adhere to this state of negative capability in order to support their clients towards the possibility of developing it, and he alluded to its importance in general, such that Symington and Symington (1996, p. 169) understand him to have recommended 'that the analyst strive after negative capability not as an immediate mental discipline to be engaged in just prior to the session but rather a way of life'. This sounds a bit like a psychodynamic equivalent of the idea that to be person-centred is not an approach but 'a way of being'.

I now experience the feeling of confusion in not knowing what is happening or where we are going within a counselling session as a positive aspect of the counselling process that I try to embrace rather than escape from. As one of our tutors used to say, 'the counsellor cannot give the client the answer; it is the finding of the answer for themselves that is therapeutic'. Symington (1996, p. 145) stated that 'If the psychotherapist is not too anxious, does not feel that he has to quickly apply a plaster made up of a piece of theory or a quickly summed-up interpretation, the meaning will emerge'. I now feel relaxed enough to either just sit with my confusion or to acknowledge it, if that feels appropriate.

In relation to practice, the weekly practice and process group also had a huge impact on the way I work and make use of myself within counselling sessions. This group consisted of six or seven students plus a tutor who met together for an hour and a half each week to reflect on practice. Across the two years of the course, my group had a person-centred tutor for half of the time and a psychodynamic tutor for the other half, each one helping us to conceptualise and reflect on our practice within their respective approaches. Throughout the course I wondered why there was little skills training of the type I had experienced on previous counselling courses, in which we looked at the exact content of what was said, the responses made, and so on. Instead, the psychodynamic tutor encouraged us to respond to one another's presentations of work with clients by way of the impact the material or presenter had on us. We were encouraged to sit in silence while we listened to the case and then, one by one, without discussing anything, state what it evoked in us – our emotions, gut feelings, abstract thoughts – rather than try to make cognitive sense of the story. In hindsight I realise that we were being shown how to sense the communication from another rather than just think it. I was being taught experientially how to listen to and use other aspects of my senses, my feelings and intuition rather than just my thoughts; the whole of myself, not just my cognitive processes.

For example, towards the end of my training I began working with a client who was the mother of a long-term drug user. She presented as a very 'together' professional lady who seemed rather emotionless and very harsh in her views of her son. In our second session I noticed the anger in her tone when talking about him and could have focused on this anger. However, I also became aware in myself of a heavy knot in my stomach and found myself swallowing in the way that I do when I am trying not to cry. My reaction felt a bit strange and out of context with how she was presenting, and it was at odds with how I had felt moments before, which is an indication to me that she was having an emotional and physical impact on me. I expressed to her tentatively that while I could hear her anger, I was also getting a sense of sadness. She looked a bit confused and then tears began to well up in her eyes. From this it became evident that until that point she had not been able to allow herself to acknowledge her sadness. It was unthinkable, because in so doing she would have to acknowledge her loss of her son (in terms of what he could have been) to drugs. Prior to my training I would not have been attuned enough to the impact the client was having on me to have accessed this counter-transference response. Looking back, I think that some of this was on the edge of my awareness, as I have had a reasonable amount of practice as a counsellor, but the revelation for me was being taught in an experiential way how to attune and use this to support the counselling process.

Bion's ideas supported my understanding of this process. His term 'psychoanalytic function' (Bion, 1962), which Ogden (2004, p. 1355) has described as 'the viewing of experience simultaneously from the vantage points of the conscious and unconscious mind', is a kind of binocular thinking that I feel was being enhanced in me through the practice and process group. Bion postulated dreaming to be the main manifestation of this psychoanalytic function. He stressed in particular the importance of the work done in unconscious dreaming, which he said occurs when we are asleep but also when we are awake (Bion, 1962).

Conscious or cognitive processing of life, which we do when awake, is only a small part of the overall work done in making sense of our existence, with other processes occurring beyond our awareness. The mind is not dissimilar from the rest of our body, in which most of the functioning goes on unnoticed, but with the addition of our ability to use our conscious minds to think with simultaneously. This was an important idea for me to understand and accept at a personal level, as prior to the course I had always thought of conscious thinking as being the main working of the mind, very much along the lines of Descartes' statement 'I think therefore I am'. My medically grounded nursing training, based on scientific certainty, had probably influenced this. This has led me in the past to be less open to accepting other levels of experiencing, such as unconscious processes, which in turn had created my resistance to psychodynamic theory. Interestingly, Rogers (1995, p. 483) also alluded to something of this when he stated that 'it should be recognised that in the private world of the experience of the individual, only a small portion, and probably a very small portion, is consciously experienced'. Recent research from neuroscience also supports these ideas through evidence of right brain to right brain unconscious communication between people, much as Freud had suggested (Schore, 2003).

Bion explained that being in a state of negative capability enables us to bridge the gap between sensuous reality and psychic reality by way of intuition. In order to do this, Bion (1980, p. 11) invites us to 'Discard your memory; discard the future tense of your desire; forget them both, both what you knew and what you want, to leave space for a new idea. A thought, an idea unclaimed, may be floating around the room searching for a home.' This is similar to Freud's (1912, p. 111) encouragement to offer 'evenly suspended attention' through which the psychoanalyst can 'withhold all conscious influence from his capacity to attend and give himself over completely to his unconscious memory'.

It is not surprising, therefore, that my intuitive side also developed through my counselling training. In learning experientially in the practice and process group how to listen to my felt sense, I was enabled to tap into hitherto unacknowledged senses that were on the edge of my awareness. These days in sessions with clients I find that I often ask myself what message the client is trying to give to me. This is part of my process of zoning out from the words to the general themes and towards getting in tune with my intuition, my felt sense, and the impact the client is having on me as a whole, rather like Casement's (1985) idea of communication by impact.

I understand Bion to have suggested that at the heart of psychoanalysis is the development of our intuition, and the development of our intuition is achieved through getting closer to reality (O). This, for me, really emphasises the importance that self-awareness has in counselling; indeed I think Bion's work tells us that intuition is at the heart of our abilities as counsellors but that it can only be developed through our self-awareness and willingness to get closer to our own ultimate reality. This also endorses the importance of sticking with the client's frame of reference in counselling rather than, for example, being drawn into problem-solving, because the purpose of counselling, on Bion's account with which I agree, is to help clients access and make sense of their emotional experience.

The Ethos of Counselling

As well as being taught experientially how to use myself, I also feel that the ethos of counselling was portrayed through the teaching methods. This helped me to take in the importance of counselling as dialogical and ultimately about being in relationship. I don't recall being explicitly taught about this; instead I developed tacit knowledge of it through experiencing the relationship between the two tutors. They demonstrated in their relationship with each other a respect for the other's views, making an active effort to understand the other's perspective without necessarily agreeing with it. They demonstrated in their relationship with one another an embracing of difference, alongside a search for similarities and connections.

This mirrors the counselling relationship whereby the counsellor and client may be from different backgrounds but are trying to engage in a meaningful dialogue with one another. The counsellor needs to be able to respect and understand the client and his or her perspective, without necessarily having to be in agreement with him or her but equally without the need to be defensive about his or her own views.

While the freedom of choice afforded by the training's dialogical character made it a difficult experience for me, it also felt like a very supportive and containing experience. This seems paradoxical. Indeed even with my experience of a real sense of freedom, in no way did I feel that I was being encouraged to be a maverick counsellor doing my own thing. There were stringent professional, theoretical, and academic expectations and boundaries within which our experiences were held. However, within this was a space, not unlike the therapeutic space, where there was a freedom to find oneself, both as a counsellor and as a person. This mirrors the counselling relationship, which has boundaries that provide the safe holding of the therapeutic space in which a client can explore and 'find' the emotional truth of his or her experience.

Bion's ideas have helped me to apply thought to my experience, an experience that began with the emotional impact on me of the course, and that gradually evolved into a kind of vague felt sense of 'a thought in search of a thinker' (Bion, 1967, p. 166). At the beginning of this dialogical counselling training I was eager to know the 'right' way to be a good counsellor. I finished the course with a definitive shift towards a more relaxed attitude and less of a need for answers. I have learned experientially through the course, to live, value, even embrace the questions rather than the answers.

Conclusion: On Not Knowing

My new sense of embracing 'not knowing' feels quite different from my sense before the course of not quite knowing what I was doing. Not knowing in this new sense is not a negation of knowing but rather a knowing of a different noncognitive type, associated more with wisdom and a trust in myself to 'know' in a broad intuitive sense, which frees me up to 'not know' in the cognitive sense. Winnicott (1958, p. 260) described some of what I mean as follows: 'Acceptance of not-knowing produced tremendous relief. "Knowing" became transformed into the "the analyst knows", that is to say, "behaves reliably in active adaptation to the patients' needs".' The exact process of counselling is often unclear, and at an intuitive level I have learned to allow myself to 'not know' and 'trust in the process' until the structure and insight emerge from the relationship. In many ways I feel that I have developed my abilities as a reflective practitioner and learned to think autonomously. Both of these are important aspects of professional practice that cut across all caring professions.

Symington (1996, p. 20) suggested that:

> It is possible to have knowledge that bears no relation to our emotional state of mind.... This is the prototypical false self situation which comes about as a result of a passive reception of the academic model in whatever form it comes. We all require an inner searching activity so that our knowledge becomes assimilated to our emotional self.

The model of learning offered on my dialogical training facilitated an exploration across theoretical and experiential boundaries where I was encouraged to discover my own 'emotional shape' and my own individual way of being a counsellor.

References

Bion, W. R. (1962) *Learning from Experience* (London: Heinemann).
Bion, W. R. (1967) *Second Thoughts* (London: Heinemann).
Bion, W. R. (1970) *Attention and Interpretation* (London: Heinemann).
Bion, W. R. (1980) *Bion in New York and São Paolo* (Perthshire: Clunie Press).
Casement, P. (1985) *On Learning from the Patient* (London: Tavistock).
Freud, S. (1912) 'Recommendations to physicians practicing psychoanalysis', *The Standard Edition of the Complete Psychological Works of Sigmund Freud*, Volume XII, translated and edited by James Strachey (London: Hogarth Press) pp. 109–120.
Grinberg, L. (1985) 'Bion's contribution to the understanding of the individual and the group' in M. Pines (ed.) *Bion and Group Psychotherapy* (London: Routledge and Kegan Paul), pp. 176–191.
McLeod, J. (1998) *An Introduction to Counselling* (Buckingham: Open University Press).
Menzies Lyth, I. (1988) *Containing Anxiety in Institutions. Selected Papers* Volume I (London: Free Association).
Ogden, T. (2004) 'On holding and containing, being and dreaming', *International Journal of Psychoanalysis*, 85, 1349–1364.
Rogers, C. R. (1995) *The Carl Rogers Reader* (London: Constable).
Schore, A. (2003) *Revolutionary Connections Psychotherapy and Neuroscience* (London: Karnac).
Symington, J., and Symington, N. (1996) *The Clinical Thinking of Wilfred Bion* (London: Routledge).
Symington, N. (1996) *The Making Of A Psychotherapist* (London: Karnac).
Winnicott, D. W. (1958) *Collected Papers: Through Paediatrics to Psychoanalysis* (London: Tavistock).

5 Losing Touch: An Exploration of the Place of Touch in Therapeutic Relationships

ANNA ST CLAIR

I Can still Remember that Day ...

This was the day when the topic of touch was first introduced during my counselling training. And this was the day that marked the beginning of a significant period of confusion, uncertainty, fear, and loss. My struggle around the complexities of the subject often made me feel angry and resentful, but with time my passion and curiosity were ignited by these conflicting emotions and fuelled me into a year of research.

I discovered that touch appears in all shapes and forms. It can be 'choreographed' and it can come unexpectedly; it can be requested and refused; offered and accepted. It can also be unwanted and rejected. There are many facets and meanings of touch that need to be considered in the world of therapy. The difficulty I encountered around this subject came from my immersion in a dance culture where touch was integral, taken-for-granted, and did not seem to me at risk of being misconstrued or open to misinterpretation. Dancers use touch to portray and communicate feelings and emotion. Physical contact is also used for holding, lifting, and supporting. It is as natural as breathing.

Changing careers from dancer and dance teacher to counsellor found me struggling in many respects when it came to boundaries around touch. There were of course ethical implications to consider as a dance teacher. For example, if I wanted to correct a line or position of a student, I would always ask permission before placing my hands on his or her body. During my teacher training I was made aware of the potential sexual implications around touching a student. However, in the therapy world, touch was far more problematic and complex. This chapter brings to light the intricate and difficult aspects of touch with which I struggled as a trainee counsellor.

As a trainee I have made therapeutic mistakes and I have learned from them. When I began my practice I did not understand that clients would touch me or want to touch me. Nor did I value the possibility that I might want to touch them. There have been many occasions involving physical contact that have affected, shocked, and inspired me, and I have changed because of these experiences. In this chapter I write about these experiences with a focus on my process. When I bring to mind the clients who have helped me in my research, I do this with caution, respect and gratitude. I am without doubt indebted to them. I seek to protect the clients concerned by omitting contextual information about them.

I remember very clearly the day and moment at university when it all started. Early in my training, before I had started to see clients, we were asked to consider the implications of physical contact and in particular the impact it could have on the therapeutic relationship. My initial gut feeling was one of bewilderment, very clearly expressed (I'm sure) nonverbally by a frown! Very soon I was shocked to learn that psychodynamic practitioners refrained from physical contact, preferring to adhere to their rule of 'abstinence', meaning that they did not touch their clients at all. At that time I interpreted and internalised this as set in stone. I initially thought this approach to be ridiculous, cold, and damaging. My expression of disapproval and my dismissive attitude came from the dancer in me. I had spent all of my life being physically connected to bodies, and therefore, in my own terms, I felt very comfortable with this subject. Indeed, I felt rather conceited about the fact that I was so at ease with it. I wondered what the 'big deal' was about!

I remember driving home that evening, thinking about how absurd and ludicrous all this concern about touch was. I considered the possibility that counselling might not be for me after all. You could say that I was fired up with anger and confusion but with no knowledge about why I felt like this. Little did I realise that this was the beginning of a protracted struggle, which soon led to my overconfident feelings giving way to those of uncertainty and fear.

Over the ensuing weeks we analysed handshakes, hugs, and pats on the back, requests for physical contact and the meanings behind these requests. Did we think we were 'touchy' people and did we hug or touch others? Endless questions I never had to consider or ask before. As I began to appreciate the immensity and complexity of the topic of touch in counselling, I remember sometimes feeling slightly sick with the weight of it all and returning to my initial reaction, wondering whether it really had to be this complicated and this serious.

The Complexities of Touch

Referring to training within the psychoanalytic tradition, Orbach (2006) states that trainees can feel astonished or taken aback when they first learn about the 'taboo' on touch. She argues that it takes time for trainees to integrate the 'canonical knowledge' but that, in the end, 'ingestion of the canon' is 'endemic' in the psychoanalytical institution (Orbach, 2006, p. xiv). My own training within the framework of a dialogue between two schools of thought (person-centred and psychodynamic) required me to move between the two perspectives and consider the different views and opinions that each orientation held. Initially, this gave me the opportunity to dismiss the psychodynamic position on touch as ludicrous and to pledge my allegiance instead to the person-centred approach, which, at the time, I considered much less pedantic and hair-splitting.

But I could not escape the question: what did touch mean to me? With this weighty question hanging over me like a dark, heavy cloud, I began to exhibit some rather strange and bizarre behaviours. I seemed to form new sensory 'touch antennas' with which I tried to detect and interpret the meaning behind each moment when I touched someone, wanted to touch someone, or when someone touched me. I began to scrutinise my tutors' behaviour, watching their every move as if they held all the answers in their way of being. I was slowly driving myself mad searching for something or someone to show me how I needed to be as a trainee counsellor with regard to physical contact. Of course the answers never came. Unsure of how I felt about touch I turned to family and friends, asking them whether they thought I was a touchy person. It appeared that I did indeed touch my friends often. 'Look, you just touched my arm,' said one of my friends as I put forward my question, and I had done so, automatically, without thought.

With my presumed ease around touch shattered, coupled with fear of causing damage to my clients, I began my practice with this internal struggle, and despite my initial dismissal of the psychodynamic rule of abstinence, I decided to adhere to a 'no touch' policy. I was untouchable, and I did not touch. I had clear rules and, I thought, a rationale for practising in this way. However, I did not really understand the reasoning behind these rules. I just knew that in my confusion I needed firm and clear boundaries. However, I was soon to discover that my clients were unaware of my rules. Perhaps a 'no touching please' sign on the door of the counselling room would have made things clearer for them.

During my first year of practice, touch appeared in all shapes and forms, unobtrusive and direct. For some time my clients were the ones instigating physical contact, and it seemed that I 'gave in' each time. The first time a client put out his hand for me to shake, internally I was horrified. This was not how I had 'choreographed' my work. So I lifted my hand like a dead weight and I was taken aback by the strong and powerful grip of my client's handshake. Hiding my horror, I froze in this awkward moment as though the theory had been poured straight into my veins like cement that had already set hard, leaving me unable to move. I felt like a leper in my own skin. I was so caught up with not touching my clients that I had lost sight of the fact that they would touch me! So here it was: my first experience of physical contact with a client, with all the complexities of a handshake to consider.

The handshake at the start of the session came again at the end, as if my client needed some kind of affirmation that things were okay, that we were okay; it had a 'business as usual' kind of feel to it. I came to realise that this strong and sincere handshake might have been a poignant and powerful way to disguise a lonely and confused young boy, an aspect of the client often present in the room. The departing handshake might have been his way to ensure that there was a grown man leaving the room. I often found myself interpreting handshakes, but I had no idea where and how I learned to think about the possible meanings of a particular handshake or my feelings about it. I began to become aware of a variety of assumptions and judgements that might come to me when a hand slipped lightly through mine or when my hand was taken in a vice-like grip. I began to appreciate that a hand on an arm, a pat on the back, a hug, or a kiss on the cheek might hold many meanings and possibilities for the giver and the receiver.

Reflections on My Experience

Struggling to make sense of the question of what touch meant to me, an early memory came to me. I was five years old and in a dance class. I remember my teacher placing her hands gently on my shoulders, pressing them down to correct the line. 'Perfect,' she said. I felt a rush of pride as she smiled down at me. I was 'perfect'. Many years later, I would still get that same surge of feelings when a teacher or choreographer placed his or her hands on my shoulders. Positive memories of touch, you could say.

But what, I now wondered, if touch were to precipitate or spark off a 'rush of memories' (Hunter and Struve, 1998, p. 8) that were not so positive? What if touch were to prompt flashbacks to a negative or abusive experience? If, as an adult, I can experience a rush of positive and encouraging childhood memories when someone places their hands on my shoulders, surely detrimental and damaging memories could also be triggered. Ferenczi (1988) suggested that if a child was sexually abused, as an adult he or she would confuse sexuality for love and sexual passion for the 'tenderness' that the child had originally been seeking. Therefore, the therapist who touches such a client, for whatever reason, must surely be taking a risk of repeating what Ferenczi called a 'confusion of tongues'.

Reflecting further on my own experiences, I discovered that touch had played a significant role in my life as a dancer, onstage and offstage. It was used to praise, comfort, congratulate, greet, meet, and part. Touch was relentless: physical contact was central to the way we communicated in the artistic world. However, I now had to consider other ways by which to communicate feelings and emotions. The difficult part was trying to separate and trace the dancer thread that was woven deep in the tapestry of my memories of touch.

The teacher who placed her hands on my shoulders was my first dance teacher and I absolutely adored her. At the beginning of class she would hold out her hands and ask us to join hands to make a circle. I would rush to hold her hand, and the fact that there were at least 20 other children racing to do the same thing didn't dissuade me. I remember the elation and joy when I succeeded, coupled with feelings of smugness and relief. I felt special. At the opposite end of the spectrum, when I didn't manage to hold her hand I felt rejected and sad. I also remember feelings of anger, jealousy, and rage. Finding a partner was often a harrowing experience, especially when no one wanted to hold my hands, which left me feeling ashamed and embarrassed. It appeared that touch meant a lot to me even as a very young dancer.

Touch and Counselling

These familiar feelings and emotions made their way into the therapy room. Many months after one of my clients had shaken my hand, another client asked me for a hug. This came unexpectedly, right at the end of a session. I was taken aback and I froze in the awkwardness of the moment. My gut reaction was to make this physical connection, which I knew had taken courage to request. However, all the theory, ethical implications, and boundary issues came rushing at me, and I chose not to take up the invitation. After my refusal, my client left the room with eyes lowered, shoulders slumped, and head bowed. I cannot remember ever feeling so punishing, cold, and inhuman as I did at that moment, standing in my counsellor's robes. Shame, embarrassment, and rejection were in the room for both of us, and I wondered if our reasons for feeling like this were more similar than different. What was it that my client wanted from me in the way of physical contact that couldn't be given through words? When are words not enough?

During the next few days my stomach churned, gnawing intermittently, persistent and threatening, until I convinced myself that this client would not return the following week. I knew deep down that I had made a mistake. I knew that this particular client struggled to form relationships and that this often resulted in others turning away physically or emotionally. Further memories came as I struggled with what had happened. Several years ago I set up dance and movement classes for children who had special needs. It was difficult to 'feel' my way around in 'their' world; it was a very private world, and a place into which I was not invited. Spatial awareness was a tricky concept for many, and it was difficult for my students to work out which space belonged to whom. They struggled to separate and distinguish where their own bodies ended and where someone else's began. I recalled this when I read Farrell (2006, p. 103) who thought that certain clients wanted to hold her hands because they wanted to 'inhabit' her body or 'to find a body where they can begin to find their own'. This made sense to me in relation to my client. In the intimate and sacred space of the counselling room, a multitude of feelings were being held and contained. The moment at which I had turned away from my client happened at the end of the session, making it impossible to explore or share the feelings evoked by my response.

Citing Holroyd and Brodsky (1980), Hunter and Struve (1998, p. 137) argued that touch may be appropriate and important when working with clients who are 'socially/emotionally immature', while for Smith, Clance, and Imes (1998, p. 26) touch may be required when 'verbal interaction is insufficient'. By adhering to my 'no touch' policy I had lost my ability to be attuned. It was as if my client and I were on different wavelengths, and as with unsuccessful attempts to tune in to a radio station, we were transmitting messages that couldn't be heard because of interference.

Later I pondered whether physical contact might have been exactly what this client needed, as in the case of a soldier with whom Ferenczi worked (Thompson, 1964). This man had been shamed and humiliated following a misdemeanour and he went on to develop a mental illness. He lost interest in his personal hygiene and neglected himself. Ferenczi knew instinctively that this man needed acceptance, and despite his physically repellent state Ferenczi greeted him by embracing and hugging him. This, Ferenczi claimed, was the very moment his recovery began (Thompson, 1964; also see Rachman, 1997). Mintz (1969) echoes this, stating that when self-loathing is overwhelming, touch can move a patient towards self-acceptance.

At this early stage in my practice I seemed to have lost my confidence and natural way of being with touch. You could say that I had 'lost touch' with touch. I refused my client's request for physical contact because of my self-doubt and confusion. I was so caught up with the consequences of getting it wrong that I struggled to work out where, when, or what was the 'right' way to touch a client or whether clients actually needed physical contact of any kind. Differentiating between want and need became a very important and significant part of my thinking. A client may have wanted or requested physical contact, but as a counsellor I had to try to figure out whether this was something that he or she actually needed.

As a former dancer I came from a profession in which the only method I had for gauging what I considered to be right or wrong was the mirror. Dance studios have many mirrors. Being moulded like a piece of clay by teachers who would shape and form my body into aesthetically pleasing lines went without question. Hands were always on my body, and praise would follow with words such as 'beautiful', 'darling', 'wonderful', and 'perfect'. As a professional dancer I spent my life in pursuit of these words, in pursuit of perfection, measured initially by what was reflected back in the mirror, followed by the audience, and finally though my pupils' examination results. Out of unrelenting necessity, I searched externally for approval: I relied very much on what others told me. I *wanted* praise, attention, applause, and approval. I wanted to be the best and I wanted to be adored. Good wasn't good enough; wonderful, brilliant, and perfect were all that mattered. Hugs and applause equalled special. This was the 'food' that had nourished my soul from a very young age. Later on in my life I found that it required hard work emotionally, psychologically, and physically to sustain my 'dietary requirement', and although I *wanted* this 'food', it wasn't in fact what I *needed*.

89

When I received that strong and powerful handshake from my client, I didn't question it, nor did I bring it into the session; I just went along with it. At that time I did not have the experience, confidence, or understanding to do anything else. It was much easier for me to just assume that this was his way of being polite. However, at the same time, my gut feelings and the influence of the theory I was engaging with on my training, were telling me that there was very likely rather more going on that deserved to be thought about.

Inappropriate Touch

I was still relatively inexperienced when I was allocated another client with whom I was to make a significant mistake involving touch. It was not easy for me to maintain this therapeutic relationship. The space in which we worked was emotionally charged. It was a space where I needed to be strong and resilient, yet sensitively attuned and empathic. I knew the importance of maintaining the therapeutic frame consistently, and through almost all of our work together I achieved this. However, I was not consistent at the very end of our time together when I decided to hug him. I knew immediately that I had made a mistake. His body told me this: it felt stiff and awkward, and my embrace clearly took him by surprise. As I write this and remember that scene, my cheeks burn with embarrassment.

Reflecting on this later, I began to understand why I hugged this client. Reviewing our work together in the last session, he told me that I was an 'excellent' therapist and the 'best'. This was music to my ears, and I became very focused on these words, wanting to hear more about how marvellous I was. I would have loved for him to talk about me in this way all day! Being the best struck a chord within. I was pumped up and full of grandeur as well as being relieved that this challenging time together had come to an apparently successful end. At this moment I needed extra confirmation and validation of just how wonderful a therapist I was. Therefore I somehow imagined that I was perfectly entitled to a hug; in fact, I expected it! But he was not prepared for this demonstrative gesture and, in making this demand of him, I blundered into the space between us, this delicate space that held all the precious work we had achieved together. I knew immediately that I had made a serious mistake.

Older (1982, p. 241) suggests that 'appropriate touch becomes inappropriate when given at the wrong time, in the wrong dose, or to the wrong person', and this without question felt wrong. This hug or embrace may have come spontaneously from me, but it came from my wants and had nothing to do with him. Realising my terrible mistake, I felt as though our relationship and the work we had done was now soiled, damaged, and cheapened. I had wanted to be congratulated on a job well done, but it was the dancer who stepped forward expecting some sort of physical contact; it was the dancer who came forward for her applause, to be admired, adored, loved, touched, and congratulated, basking in the glory of her perfect performance.

I deeply regret hugging this client. I made a mistake; I knew it and he knew it. I came to understand how confusing this action might be for a client who had not been touched previously during his or her therapy (Hunter and Struve, 1998; Tune, 2001; Young, 2005). Hilton (1996) gives a compelling example parallel to the mistake I made. A colleague – a training analyst – described how he was preparing to leave the room at the end of his final day in therapy. His therapist 'put his arm on my friend's shoulder and told him how much he enjoyed working with him' (Hilton, 1996, p. 177). This had such a negative effect on the client that he felt 'as if none of the therapy had happened' and 'all of the feelings he thought he had worked through surfaced in his body as he felt the touch of the analyst' (Hilton 1996, p. 177). A mistake during the course of therapeutic work offers opportunities for repair, which is not possible at the end. Bosanquet (2006, p. 46) suggests that physical contact needs to be 'integral', happening during the session and not at the end, when it 'tends to get suspended in a kind of limbo', and that the client needs to work through feelings generated by physical connection. Empowering a client to make choices in his or her life is one of the gifts of therapy. Failing to give a client choice about how to end the therapy is disempowering and could even be viewed as abusive. I have often wondered what kind of feelings my client was left with, and I am still sad that there was no opportunity to work through any of them.

I was beginning to understand what the 'big deal' was all about on 'that' day when touch was introduced to my training. I was now in the real world of counselling with real clients who brought touch to life, in the therapy room, with all its complexities and implications. My self-awareness was growing, and I was beginning to work out where some of my feelings about touch came from, why I felt so bad when I refused a request for physical contact, why I felt awkward and stiff as I shook hands with a client, why I decided to hug a client. However, I was unprepared for the feelings that were evoked in me by another client.

When I met this client I was drawn to her like a magnet. She walked and moved gracefully, she waved her arms in sweeping gestures, drawing swirls in the air whilst using words like 'darling' and 'sweetheart'. She was a theatrical production all of her own, and she touched a very vulnerable part in me. She represented my other world, and I came alive when I was with her. Her nonverbal and verbal communication was hugely seductive for me. I was intoxicated and entranced. I felt a compulsion to hug her at the beginning and at the end of each session, but I just managed to restrain myself. One day when she arrived for her session, she stepped forward to hug me and it would have been very easy and natural for me to return this embrace, but instead I took a step back. This time it was the right decision and made it possible for us to explore her way of being.

Working through *my* need to hug this client became a significant part of supervision. It became clear that I was being pulled into a space that others also found attractive. She had a seductive aura, but this way of being wasn't working for her and although touch was something that she wanted, it was not something that she needed in her work with me. She was searching for tenderness, intimacy, and love, and I was drawn to her because she reminded me of the life I had before. She touched a part of me that was grieving for that life. I could easily have made the mistake of hugging her: it would have felt like the most natural thing to do. However, now I knew that it would have been the dancer who wanted to hug and be hugged.

The intimacy she received had always been derived through physical contact. This was all she knew. She loved being in a new relationship, which brought feelings of euphoria. She thrived on attention, admiration, and feeling special. These are without doubt intense and positive feelings. But such intensity is hard to sustain over time and can create much confusion about the nature of the relationship in question. She initiated her game in the therapy room. It was a game that she had invented for which she knew the rules and I did not. It was a bit like a game of chess, and if I had entered in unwittingly, I would have been like a pawn being moved, followed, tricked, and eventually trapped and then discarded. If I had moved in the direction she expected me to go, for example by stepping forward to hug her, I would have ended up like so many others, and when this game was over, she would set up and play the same game again with someone else. But she was tired of playing this game, and it was causing her pain and distress. She could not maintain intimate relationships, the love that she felt was short-lived, and she was alone and lonely but did not understand why. Psychologically, emotionally, and physically this pattern was taking its toll on her.

The Therapeutic Dance

The therapeutic relationship allows for a different type of connection and the possibility of a new way of being. It also offers a different form of intimacy. Learning to distinguish between physical and emotional intimacy can be an empowering experience (Hunter and Struve, 1998, p. 81). For Burch (2004, 361) closeness and intimacy 'lie on a continuum' and are 'not separate entities', but closeness lies 'in the conscious realm' whereas intimacy arises 'from the unconscious'. On this account the transference relationship would suffer if physical contact were made, perhaps preventing forms of intimacy unique to the therapeutic relationship. The therapeutic relationship is a psychological space where qualities of connection can be felt and explored. It is a touching space, but where skin does not touch skin. In this space there are moments of deeply felt relational connection between therapist and client, which moves and changes them both (Heyward, 1999).

This space can also be understood as an intimate dance. With each new therapeutic encounter the choreography changes, but the essence is always of moving in relation to one another. When all goes well the dance partners are in time, in tune, and in harmony. The rapport between them feels exclusive, and as the attachment deepens the dance changes. There are moments of close connection, and there is also space, perhaps a need for distance. As we separate, more space is created for the client to 'detach' in his or her search for autonomy. When the therapist holds the fine line between separateness and connectedness, the client is able to realise that he or she can sustain both in other relationships. Burch (2004, p. 363) suggests that even the most 'rigorously' trained analysts have 'great capacity for humanity and closeness' without the use of touch.

I grew to understand the powerful impact of withholding touch, although I also know that physical contact can be life-changing. I learned to think about the possible meanings of touch and about the significance of touch within therapeutic relationships. My initial decision to impose on my practice a 'no touch' policy soon began to feel too restrictive. It caused me to lose a very important part of myself, which affected my responsiveness, my spontaneity, and my sense of me. I had 'pulled on' the theory but it didn't fit me and I struggled to make it into something that felt like it belonged to me.

In Nancy Upper's (2004) account, professional dancer, dance teacher, and choreographer Jeff Plourde suggested that dancers feel their way into the dance they are learning, stepping inside ideas, images, and music, moving and feeling their way in the story. This in turn touches the dancer emotionally, which is then given back 'through the language of dance' (Upper, 2004, p. 115). As a counsellor I emulate this process, but instead of conveying the emotions and feelings I was experiencing through movement, I had to learn to give them back through words and through my emotional responsiveness. I learned to use the psychological space to reach out and touch my clients without necessarily touching their skin. When dances are embodied into a dancer's muscle memory they become like a second skin, natural and alive. Now if a client asks for a hug or to be held, I have more understanding and confidence to explore the request.

During my training and research I revisited aspects of my own therapy with a therapist who never touched me. I'm sure that this was influential in my initial decision to adopt a 'no touch' policy. I had many different feelings and emotions towards my therapist. I fell 'in love' with him, dreamt about him, and fantasised about our perfect life together. I wanted him to fall in love with me (or so I thought), and sometimes I hated him. I needed him to remain my therapist, which he did by holding the boundaries of our relationship without touching me physically. This was the first time in my life that I had experienced this type of closeness and love with a man. Although I didn't always know it, I did not need physical contact of any sort. My therapist helped me to distinguish between sexual and emotional intimacy, and this was indeed a 'powerful learning experience' (Hunter and Struve, 1998, p. 81). Intimacy of this kind was new for me, like an undiscovered and at times vulnerable place in which to find myself. Physical contact would have been much easier. Waddell (2002, p. 42) describes this kind of intimacy beautifully as the 'experience of being held in a primary emotional "psychic skin" equivalent to the physical skin which holds the body together'. This was the kind of 'holding' that I experienced in therapy and what I now aspire to offer my clients.

References

Bosanquet, C. (2006) 'Symbolic understanding of tactile communication in psychotherapy' in G. Galton (ed.) *Touch Papers: Dialogues on Touch in the Psychoanalytic Space* (London: Karnac) pp. 29–48.

Burch, N. (2004) 'Closeness and intimacy', *British Journal of Psychotherapy*, 20 (3), 361–372.

Farrell, E. (2006) 'The presence of the body in psychotherapy' in G. Galton (ed.) *Touch Papers: Dialogues on Touch in the Psychoanalytic Space* (London: Karnac) pp. 97–108.

Ferenczi, S. (1988) 'Confusion of tongues between adults and the child – The language of tenderness and of passion', *Contemporary Psychoanalysis*, 24, 196–206.

Heyward, C. (1999) *When Boundaries Betray Us* (Cleveland, OH: The Pilgrim Press).

Hilton, R. (1996) 'Touching in psychotherapy' in L. E. Hedges (ed.) *Therapists at Risk: Perils of the Intimacy of the Therapeutic Relationship* (Northvale: Jason Aronson) pp. 161–180.

Holroyd, J., and Brodsky, A. (1980) 'Does touching patients lead to sexual intercourse?' *Professional Psychology*, 11 (5), 807–811.

Hunter, M., and Struve, J. (1998) *The Ethical Use of Touch in Psychotherapy* (London: Sage).

Mintz, E. (1969) 'On the rationale of touch in psychotherapy', *Psychotherapy Research and Practice*, 6 (4), 232–234.

Older, J. (1982) *Touch Is Healing* (New York: Stein and Day).

Orbach, S. (2006) 'Too hot to touch' in G. Galton (ed.) *Touch Papers: Dialogues on Touch in the Psychoanalytic Space* (London: Karnac) pp. xiii–xviii.

Rachman, A. W. (1997) *Sandor Ferenczi: The Psychotherapist of Tenderness and Passion* (Northvale, NJ, and London: Aronson).

Smith, E. W. L., Clance, P. R., and Imes, S. (1998) *Touch in Psychotherapy: Theory, Research and Practice* (New York: Guildford Press).

Thompson, C. (1964) *Interpersonal Psychoanalysis: The Selected Papers of Clara M. Thompson* (New York: Basic Books).

Tune, D. (2001) 'Is touch a valid therapeutic intervention? Early returns from a qualitative study of therapist's views', *Counselling and Psychotherapy Research*, 1 (3), 167–171.

Upper, N. (2004) *Ballet Dancers in Career Transitions* (Jefferson, NC: McFarland).

Waddell, M. (2002) *Inside Lives: Psychoanalysis and the Growth of the Personality* (London: Karnac).

Young, C. (2005) 'About the ethics of professional touch', unpublished paper available at www.eabp.org/pdf/TheEthicsofTouch.pdf, accessed 22 February 2014.

Why I Became a Counsellor: Reflections on the Counter-transference

MAGS TURNER

For me and I imagine for other counsellors too, one of the pleasures of working therapeutically with others comes from what Stern (2004) has referred to as 'present moments'. In such moments there is a profound sense of shared humanity and, especially early in my counselling work, I felt deeply affirmed as a practitioner when I experienced the strong sense of connection between me and my client described by Stern. This affirmation helped me to gain confidence as a practitioner, and I soon came to feel deeply at home in my work as a counsellor, as if, in Stolorow's (2007, p. 34) terms, I had found my 'relational home'. In this chapter I reflect on 'present moments' as manifestations of the counter-transference. Using debates about the counter-transference I show how the affirmation I felt helped to illuminate my underlying unconscious motivations for working as a counsellor. In problematising moments in which I have felt a strong positive connection between myself and a client, I also make links with other, more troubling, experiences with clients, for example of dread. This prompts me to argue for understanding counter-transference experiences as likely to express simultaneously aspects of the practitioner's own unconscious concerns and aspects of the client's unconscious world.

Working with Susan

The client who initially inspired this chapter is one I shall call Susan. She was in her late twenties when she came for counselling as a result of post-natal depression following the birth of her first baby. She had had a difficult start in life and spent most of her early life in care. On her account it seems likely that her own mother was deeply depressed; she was certainly not reliably available to Susan. As a young adult, however, Susan had formed a stable, long-term relationship with her partner, who was the father of her young daughter.

Initially Susan struggled to attend sessions, missing several, sometimes arriving late and pressing for a change of time. I felt that she was testing my commitment and probably expected me to give up on her. However, I persisted and after about three months something shifted. In the session that marked the beginning of the shift I had repeated to her that I would be available at the agreed time whether or not she came. Tears came into her eyes and I welled up too. We connected in this silence, both on the edge of tears. This felt to me like a key moment of meeting, of being deeply present with one another. Her attendance continued to be somewhat erratic, and I held true to my word. Very gradually she was able to attend more consistently, and we continued to work together for about two years.

Throughout our work moments of intense connection recurred. For example in notes reflecting on session 25 I recorded that

> For me then, all sense of time seemed to stop as we both acknowledged our connection and held each other's gaze until Susan's eyes filled with tears and I duly followed. The eye contact at this point felt to me like a window into the other's soul and mind.

This has much in common with Stern's account of meeting in the 'present moment' and echoes his description of such a moment with a couple with whom he worked:

> a particularly human contact had been made – a contact that re-affirmed my belonging to other members of society, mentally, affectively and physically. I was not alone on this earth, I was part of some kind of psychological, inter-subjective human matrix. (Stern, 2004, p. 21)

My understanding at the time was that in such moments I was providing something deeply reparative in the form of maternal mirroring (Stern, 1985). In the early stages of our relationship, Susan was wary and probably fearful of allowing me to come close to her. My sense was that as she gained confidence in me as someone who was genuinely consistent and genuinely valuing of her, she began to let me come closer. I wondered if, in these moments of intense connection, she felt her true self to have been recognised and acknowledged (Bollas, 1987). Having discovered that I did not condemn or reject her, she also saw that I embraced and rejoiced in our connection. My own feelings, therefore, could be understood as expressions of a strong, positive, maternal counter-transference in which I had taken the complementary maternal role to Susan's expressions of her early childhood needs (Racker, 1957). On this understanding, Susan had projected into me aspects of herself – especially her neediness and vulnerability – that she could not fully own herself. In taking these on unconsciously, I recognised her need for a loving maternal response, hence my sense of a deeply moving, wordless connection.

However, I also want to acknowledge and pose questions about the intensity of my own feelings in these moments. I recall feeling so perfectly attuned to Susan that it seemed as if she and I merged or fused, my feelings being indistinguishable from hers, the boundaries between us dissolving. This was enormously pleasurable, as if I was completely bathed in mutual togetherness and love. In this immersion nothing else mattered; time stood still. This was rich and enriching, joyful and incredibly affirming. I felt sure that the magic of such moments was evidence of the healing power of our counselling relationship. While this healing power was designed for Susan's benefit, I felt that I was benefitting too.

Understanding the Transference–Counter-transference Relationship

I spoke of these feelings in supervision, where sometimes I felt a little anxious about the possible risks of feeling so much at one with my client. This, together with conversations with course tutors, helped me to begin a process of reflecting on what was being touched in me and took me beyond an understanding of my feelings as a complementary, maternal counter-transference response to Susan's projected neediness to consider other possibilities.

The concept of the counter-transference has been subject to extensive debate within the psychoanalytic literature. For Freud (1910) the counter-transference was a product of the analyst's own unresolved issues and signalled inadequacies in his own analysis. As such it was a problematic disturbance in the analyst's neutrality, threatening the capacity for objectivity. During Freud's lifetime questions began to be asked about whether perhaps there was a positive place for tender feelings in the analyst towards the analysand (Ferenczi, 1949 [1932]; Suttie, 1935).

But it was Heimann's (1950) seminal paper valuing the counter-transference as an important source of information about the therapeutic relationship that really opened up the discussion. Racker (1957) introduced a distinction between concordant and complementary forms of counter-transference identification: in the former, the feelings in the analyst arise from his or her identification with the analysand's predicament; in the latter, the feelings of the analyst arise from the complementary role into which they are 'pulled' by the unconscious projections of the analysand. I have suggested that some of my experiences with Susan could be understood in terms of the complementary form in which I took on the role of idealised mother. At other times, my sense was that concordant counter-transference was in operation, and I came very close to Susan's own self experience, for example when I felt empathically attuned to her and available to feel 'with' her. Notes written after session 8 provide an illustration of this:

> I recall feeling that it may have been important for her to see my reaction to her distress. I knew that I was not about to lose control of my emotions. Looking back, my tears reflected my empathic engagement with her, which I now know had some ingredient of mine in there too. My intuition at the time told me that my tearful reaction might enhance the therapeutic process.

There is debate about whether the term counter-transference should be used to include everything the practitioner feels in relation to his or her client or patient (Heimann's position) or whether it should be limited to unconscious dimensions of the practitioner's experience. There is also recognition of the potential importance of Freud's original assumption that feelings aroused in the practitioner might, at least in part, be a product of his or her own unresolved issues. While we may no longer subscribe to Freud's view that the practitioner – if fully analysed him- or herself – can or should aspire to be entirely neutral and objective, the possibility remains that unconscious responses in practitioners might interfere with their professional task, or at least generate unhelpful confusion about what is going on. Acknowledging this, Gitelson (1952) set out several different aspects of the counter-transference. First of all, he differentiated between 'the analyst's reaction to the patient as a whole and his reactions to partial aspects of the patient' (Gitelson, 1952, p. 4). He argued that the former occurs very early in the contact between practitioner and client or patient and expresses the practitioner's personality, which may facilitate the work but will also set limits on what is possible. The latter emerge more gradually and provide the valuable source of information to which Heimann (1950) referred. Gitelson (1952) differentiated among three elements of the analyst's reactions to partial aspects of the patient, pertaining to '(1) the patient's transference, (2) the material the patient brings in, and (3) the reactions of the patient to the analyst as a person'.

With the help of my supervisor, I began to think about what happened between me and Susan, trying to disentangle what was about me and what was truly about her. This was not easy, and even in retrospect I have not worked out how to apply all the differentiations Gitelson put forward. Nevertheless, his distinction between our almost instantaneous unconscious reaction to meeting new clients 'as a whole' and the much more gradual emergence of unconscious ways of relating ('reactions to partial aspects of the patient') assured me that my experience of moments of deep connection between me and Susan belonged to the gradually emerging transference relationship, which others, such as Bollas (1987), have said may remain unclear and barely understood for a very long time. Additionally, Gitelson's description of the counter-transference drew my attention to its dynamic qualities, which involve a long series of the client responding unconsciously to the practitioner, the practitioner responding to these responses, and the client responding to these responses to their own responses ... and so on!

I have suggested there is a lot of scope for confusion about what is meant by the counter-transference and whether feelings experienced by the practitioner in relation to the client are necessarily useful in relation to the work or perhaps more revealing of the practitioner's own concerns. In this context, I have found Page's (1999) notion of a continuum between a syntonic and illusory counter-transference helpful: at the syntonic end of the continuum the counter-transference is a direct response to the client, devoid of the therapist's own 'stuff'; at the illusory end of the continuum the counter-transference is dominated by the therapist's unresolved unconscious concerns. From this perspective, one aspect of our task in reflecting on the counter-transference is to 'reach a view as to the source of our emotional experience' of our clients (Page, 1999, p. 61).

Encouraged by my supervisor, I began to think of my feelings in moments of deep connection with Susan as existing somewhere on this continuum, with the potential for much movement to and fro along it. This helped me to recognise the potential influence of my early life within my work, not only with Susan but also with other clients.

Exploring my Counter-transference

I was already aware of links between my engagement with counselling and my relationship with my father. He was a great storyteller. I have a vivid early memory of a stormy winter's night when the electricity had failed. My father huddled together with me and my siblings around the open fire, and I found his storytelling utterly captivating. He did not know how to speak of his own feelings, but via the third person of the storyteller he was able to convey a great deal. It is perhaps not very surprising that, having loved to listen to him tell stories when I was a child, as an adult I should be drawn to listen to other people tell me their stories. But this did not explain the sense of fusion I experienced in moments of shared tearfulness with Susan. Nor did it explain the intensity of my feeling of pleasure and affirmation in my work as a counsellor. And so I came to consider the possibility that my formative first weeks and months might have been re-enacted in the moments of meeting in the therapy room.

I was born six weeks premature, the only girl of triplets. One of my brothers died on the day we were born. My surviving brother and I both spent several weeks in hospital. He came home two weeks before I did. Then, only one month after I came home, when we were three months old, my mother underwent major heart surgery and disappeared from our lives for the next three months. My surviving triplet brother and I, together with an older sibling and another older child, were cared for by an aunt during my mother's absence. Consequently, although the circumstances were very different, like Susan's, my mother was often absent during my early life, and even when she was present, she may well have been preoccupied, whether with the baby she had lost, or her ill-health, or her anxieties about the future, or about our care. My mother died when I was in my early twenties, a few years younger than Susan was when I first met her and before my own children were born. In my own therapy, I often experienced my mother as absent and as someone I could not really touch or reach.

According to Storr (1979), many psychotherapists have had depressed mothers. I was well aware of feeling a particular commitment to working therapeutically with women suffering post-natal depression. During my training, a tutor had drawn my attention to an underlying logic for this, linking my choice to the circumstances of my birth and early life. Discussing my work with Susan in supervision, I remembered this comment and reflected further on how my experience of 'present moments' with Susan might connect with my own background.

As a triplet in the womb and with my surviving brother after I went home from hospital, I had the experience of snuggling up very close to same-age siblings. I continue to feel a very strong bond with the brother I call my twin, which has qualities about it that no other relationships match. But I wonder if my pleasure in moments of deep connection with Susan, and especially my sense of perfect attunement, might stem from echoes of the warmth and intensity of my experience of being one of a multiple birth cohort. Perhaps my concordant counter-transference with Susan was also at least in part an illusory counter-transference experience in the sense that it was about an unconscious echo of my own perinatal experience.

The loss of an infant during a multiple pregnancy or at a multiple birth has complex impacts. It is bound to be felt by the parents, but the loss coexists with the presence and the needs of other infants. In my own family my lost triplet was always acknowledged: I grew up aware of his existence and I participated in memorialising him. But there may have been powerful and conflicting feelings around during the earliest days of my life, including grief at the loss of one baby, anxiety about the two initially very fragile survivors, and relief as both of us gained in strength and left hospital. In addition there is the question of how the two of us who survived felt. As I have already hinted, although I grew up thinking of myself as a twin, I continue to wonder if it might be more accurate to describe myself as one of triplets. Do I refer to my surviving same-age brother as my twin or as the other surviving triplet? Pionelli (1992) has used scans to observe the behaviour of twins in the womb and found strong continuities with patterns of behaviour after birth. The same is surely true of triplets, which suggests that in our interactions with each other my surviving twin/triplet brother and I may have missed our dead brother. In a similar vein, Woodward (1998) has argued that significant attachments between twins begin before birth. In this context, my attachment to my surviving same-age brother may be deeply marked by the physical disappearance from our lives of our triplet brother, by our early separation from each other while in separate incubators in hospital, and by our separate transitions from hospital to home. Now I can only wonder if some of my feelings of intimacy and oneness with Susan (and other clients), which are often triggered by recognition of losses, might somehow echo these earliest experiences in my own life.

As I have acknowledged, Susan and I had both experienced maternal absence or unavailability. I felt that I provided her with maternal mirroring and that in so doing, I provided her with a reparative experience.

But was this impulse to repair also directed towards myself? And was it driving my therapeutic work more generally?

Freud (1926, p. 136) suggested that anxiety may have its origins in the child 'missing someone who is loved and longed for' such as the mother, including a mother who is alive but not sufficiently available. Klein (1975) built on this insight to explore the unconscious life of young children in much greater depth and also took up Freud's idea of a death instinct to focus especially on destructive feelings, which she posited were felt by the baby from birth. She argued that infants fantasise about damaging their carers and that this in turn generates unconscious feelings of guilt and responsibility, which, all going well, eventually lead to an impulse to repair. Reflecting on my early life, I wonder if I felt intense, persecutory anxiety as a result of separation in hospital from my immediate siblings and from my mother. My mother's disappearance again so soon after I returned home can only have added to this. Moreover, it is likely that I – and others around me – were affected by my parents' own turbulent feelings of love and grief, fear and anxiety. From a Kleinian perspective it is possible that, unconsciously, I felt that I had caused damage to my non-surviving triplet and very likely that, again unconsciously, I felt that my destructive power had a devastating impact on my mother. According to Klein, even in the best of circumstances infants experience destructive fantasies and have no sense of the difference between thought and action. When those about whom the infant has destructive fantasies survive and constantly return to the infant without obvious signs of damage, the infant gradually comes to appreciate the difference between thought and action. However, when the infant's destructive fantasies meet a world in which the people in question really do become ill or die, unconscious guilt is likely to be greatly magnified. In my case I was exposed to death, serious illness, and inexplicable disappearances from a very early age. I can imagine that when my mother went into hospital for heart surgery my unconscious guilt was enormous, lodging in me as something for which I needed to atone in some way.

An Act of Reparation?

One way of understanding why I am drawn to work as a counsellor and have such a strong sense of feeling at home in my work is in terms of reparation: counselling provides me with the opportunity to enact my unconscious need to repair or atone, driven by the unconscious guilt that flowed from my destructive fantasies in my early life. This unconscious reparative motivation flows via my clients towards myself in the sense that in the counter-transference I give to, or enact with, clients what I long for for myself.

Thinking about this in relation to my experience of 'present moments' with Susan, perhaps for me these moments of intense connection seemed almost magically to repair all the losses of my early life and in so doing they relieved me of unconscious guilt, as well as taking me back to a previous time – perhaps even before birth. From the perspective of Page's (1999) continuum, this enacted the illusory counter-transference, since it was about my unconscious concerns rather than Susan's. There was also the illusory quality of such repair and relief. At the same time, our shared tearfulness signalled that each of us might also be acknowledging losses in our lives and therefore the ongoing need to mourn. This prompts me to think that the illusory counter-transference did not impede our work together. Rather, even if these moments were about me and my 'stuff', I was at the same time providing an appropriate and developmentally needed reparative relationship for Susan. So rather than separating out and disentangling whether my counter-transference experience was in Page's (1999) terms more syntonic or more illusory, it seems to me that it may have been both at once.

The coexistence of what Page calls syntonic and illusory forms of the counter-transference was given further emphasis for me by my reflections on a persistent feeling of dread that I experienced with another client, whom I shall call Mary. We had a lot in common, in the sense of coming from similar cultural backgrounds, being similar ages, and both having several siblings. Initially my work with Mary proceeded well, and I felt that a good therapeutic relationship was developing. But then I found myself dreading our sessions. Initially I did not understand why. I began to question my capacity to work with this client and to ask if it was ethical for me to continue. Discussing these feelings in supervision, I began to wonder whether the similarities between us, which had felt so helpful initially, were turning into impediments. Reflecting on this further, I realised that my work with Mary was probably touching on areas of unresolved grief in my life that I dreaded having to face. So, while at the beginning my similarities with Mary gave me insights that felt straightforward and valuable for the work, as the counselling developed I was being confronted by grief of my own that I did not want to face. I wept in supervision. I began to reflect more deeply on my own grief. As I did, I discovered that I could face it and I welcomed the stimulus to mourn.

At the same time, my sense of dreading the sessions with Mary began to dissipate. More than that, I was able to empathise with her in her own resistance to facing her grief. This example seems to fit with Gitelson's (1952) reference to that component of the counter-transference that pertains to material the patient or client brings: the loss and grief in Mary's story seems to have prompted my feelings of dread, which I was able to use empathically. Additionally, thinking about my sense of dread as a counter-transference experience, it seems to me that it was illusory and syntonic at the same time: it was about me and my unresolved grief, but it was also about Mary and her dread of facing her losses.

In this chapter I have explored debates about the counter-transference using examples from my work with two clients in which I was prompted to reflect carefully on the extent to which what was stirred up in me might be more about me than about my client. I found this helpful to do, and I found Page's (1999) concept of a continuum between a syntonic and an illusory counter-transference a useful guide. The idea of a continuum of this kind helped me to learn to reflect on what might be being touched within myself when strong feelings – pleasurable or difficult – are stirred up in my work with clients. It also helped me to connect my sense of feeling of finding a 'relational home' as a counsellor with my early life, which may have fuelled an unconscious reparative drive, well served by therapeutic work with others. Although the idea of a continuum ranging from syntonic to illusory served me well in developing my capacity to think about and understand the counter-transference, I came to the conclusion it is not quite right in practice. This is because, as I have illustrated, both aspects of the counter-transference can be happening at the same time, and what is called illusory may turn out to be a very helpful source of insight for the counsellor and the therapeutic work. For us as practitioners, self-awareness is vitally important, and reflecting on what we bring into our therapeutic relationships is an ongoing task.

References

Bollas, C. (1987) *The Shadow of the Object: Psychoanalysis of the Unthought Known* (London: Free Association Books).
Ferenczi, S. (1949 [1932]) 'Confusion of tongues between the adults and the child', *International Journal of Psychoanalysis*, 30, 225–230. (Paper first read at the Twelfth International Psycho-Analytical Congress, Wiesbaden, September 1932.)

Freud, S. (1910) 'The future prospects of psycho-analytic therapy', *The Standard Edition of the Complete Psychological Works of Sigmund Freud,* Volume XI, translated and edited by James Strachey (London: Hogarth Press) pp. 139–152.

Freud, S. (1926) 'Inhibitions, symptoms and anxiety', *The Standard Edition of the Complete Psychological Works of Sigmund Freud,* Volume XX, translated and edited by James Strachey (London: Hogarth Press) pp. 75–176.

Gitelson, M. (1952) 'The emotional position of the analyst in the psycho-analytic situation', *International Journal of Psychoanalysis,* 33, 1–10.

Heimann, P. (1950) 'On counter-transference', *International Journal of Psychoanalysis,* 31, 81–84.

Klein, M. (1975) *The Writings of Melanie Klein,* 4 volumes (London: Hogarth Press).

Page, S. (1999) *The Shadow and the Counsellor* (London: Routledge).

Pionelli, A. (1992) *From Fetus to Child: An Observational and Psychoanalytic Study* (London: Routledge).

Racker, H. (1957) 'The meanings and uses of countertransference', *Psychoanalytic Quarterly,* 26 (3), 303–357.

Stern, D. (1985) *The Interpersonal World of the Infant* (New York: Basic Books).

Stern, D. (2004) *The Present Moment in Psychotherapy and Everyday Life* (London and New York: Norton).

Stolorow, R. D. (2007) *Trauma and Human Existence: Autobiographical, Psychoanalytic and Philosophical Reflections* (New York: Analytic Press).

Storr, A. (1979) *The Art of Psychotherapy* (London: Secker and Warburg).

Suttie, I. D. (1935) *The Origins of Love and Hate* (London: Kegan Paul).

Woodward, J. (1998) *The Lone Twin: A Study in Bereavement and Loss* (London: Free Association Books).

Part III
Client Voices

Silent Voices

7 Working with Early Trauma in Therapy: Emerging from the Shadow of Polio

CONNIE JOHNSON

Introduction

When I first began a period of therapy, I was aware that I enjoyed the company of other people, but I also knew that a part of me felt frozen inside and lonely at times. I couldn't talk about feeling lonely but had no idea why that was. I found a therapist who reached out to welcome me, but I didn't talk about being disabled then because other things seemed more important. I had learned to bury the stories about hospital and about the daily barriers I faced, because I didn't think anyone would understand. It took time, but I learned to trust my therapist and eventually I began to talk about being a child in hospital.

During one session I found myself speaking in detail about the painful effects of one of the surgical procedures that I had endured and found highly distressing. It involved ugly pieces of metal protruding from my body, and it was very painful. Whilst I was talking about the details of this procedure, I noticed my therapist take a sharp breath and her facial expression changed abruptly. Without realising what was happening, I immediately fell silent. My therapist asked me what was happening, and I was surprised that she noticed my silence because I hadn't been aware of it myself – I was too caught up in my memories. When my therapist spoke, I began to realise that I had withdrawn because I didn't think she would want to hear about my story. I didn't want to say any more about my memory because I thought that my vivid description was too much for her to bear. It had just become too much for me to bear in that moment. My therapist very gently said she realised that her expression had frightened me, and she explained that she was imagining how painful the procedure had been – she could feel the pain of it too. She said she wanted to hear my story – she knew I had always protected other people from hearing it, but she reminded me that this was my true story and that my feelings were real. She encouraged me to talk some more.

I felt so touched by her care and warmth that I began to cry. My therapist gently took my hand and we sat together feeling the horror of that time in hospital. I told her about the doctors, nurses, and visitors staring at the ugly pieces of metal and about the questions they kept asking. But they never asked me about the pain or what it felt like to be stuck in a hospital bed when my sisters were at home or out in the sunshine playing with their friends. Even as I spoke with my therapist, I felt that I was making a fuss. I stopped talking again. I remembered that sometimes when people stared at me during that time I refused to speak to them or answer their questions. Becoming invisible was the only way to escape their intrusions. As I talked and my therapist quietly listened, we both realised how alone and distressed I had been as a child in hospital.

This was one moment in the process of finding a way to talk about my childhood illness, hospitalisation, and subsequent disability. I have always found it difficult to talk about these experiences and to understand the effects they had on my sense of self and my relationships with other people. My interest in this intensified more recently when I was living with severe physical pain and awaiting surgery. The physical pain seemed to awaken early memories of medical treatment and hospitalisation, and these memories were extremely uncomfortable because of the strong sense of shame and terror they elicited in me.

In this chapter I elaborate on what was happening for me as a child and explore why this story was so difficult to tell by investigating the layers of silencing, the feeling of abandonment and of not being understood emotionally. From there, I reflect on how I emerged from the darkness of these years so that I could retrieve the parts of myself that had previously lurked in the shadows. In so doing, I offer a case study that illustrates how early trauma and preverbal distress and disability can make their presence felt within the therapeutic relationship and how that relationship holds the possibilities of reparation.

A therapeutic process involves 'the human tendency to re-form understandings using language and other sorts of symbols in interaction with the totality of lived experience' (Warner, 2009, p. 112). Because I became ill with polio as an infant, I did not have language to describe what I was feeling at the time. I gradually came to find words by becoming aware of bodily felt sensations and associated imagery and by recalling the visual memories that I have from later childhood. My data for this case study are experiential and derive from the personal journal that I kept whilst in therapy. I have also made use of published research on infant and child-hood separation through hospitalisation and the effects of this on adult life. I have reconstructed my story autoethnographically, so that others who have either experienced medical conditions during childhood or who work therapeutically with clients who have had similar experiences may connect with it and gain insight into the traumatic effects of pro-longed childhood illness and disability.

Becoming Aware of the Shadow and Entering Psychotherapy

I was motivated to enter therapy because of my awareness of the frozen part of me that I thought of as an 'ice cube' that lay at the centre of my being. I was aware that I found it difficult to trust anyone with my deepest emotions. I was even more aware of this when, as a therapist myself, I was working with a long-term client who had been neglected by her mother and sexually abused as a child. This client talked frequently about her own frozen core, and she connected that with her childhood experiences. I realised that, if I was to remain open to this client's experi-ence and to respond to her fully with the warmth that I desired, I needed to address that inner part of myself. Alice Miller (1990, p. 116) writes:

> Only therapists who have had the opportunity to experience and work through their own traumatic past will be able to accompany patients on the path to truth about themselves and not hinder them on their way ... for they no longer have to fear the eruption in them-selves of feelings that were stifled long ago, and they know from their own experience the healing power of these feelings.

Another reason that drew me into therapy was that my daughters were in their late teens and I wanted to help them move into the next phase of their lives. I had not had an easy time in my youth, and I wondered how I would weather these years with my children. Like many mothers, I felt sad at the impending separation that would come as they moved on in their lives, and I had some sense that my responses to these events could be linked with my childhood polio experience.

I was aware of the main events in my story – that I was diagnosed with polio as a six-month-old baby and admitted to an isolation hospital where

I spent 18 days in a glass cubicle. My family could not visit me except to wave through the glass (Dowling, 1985). After that, I was placed for another two months in a general ward in the same hospital, where I was permitted brief family visits. By then it had become apparent that my illness had caused permanent paralysis in my leg, and the process of rehabilitation began.

As I talked about these experiences with my therapist, it became increasingly important that I could feel her warmth through touch and being physically held. It can be difficult to manage the area of touch with clients who have been traumatised in childhood, but touching and holding are parts of the language that infants understand (Rothschild, 2000). My therapist held me in this way freely, and regular massage became another aspect of my process of unfolding. I felt nurtured by my therapist, but I sometimes found it difficult to receive the warmth that she gave. Though I welcomed her on one level, it was easy for me to dismiss her words and to stay with the belief that I was not worthy of them. It became apparent that my keeping a distance internally was connected to my experience of aloneness and my early infant experience of separation from my mother when I was in hospital as a baby and later as a ten-year-old child.

Just before I began therapy, I had a rather dramatic experience of aloneness. I had travelled to a city that was unfamiliar to me after the funeral of an older family member. I arrived in a rather inhospitable hotel late in the evening before the day of the course I was to attend, and after unpacking I sat down and suddenly felt that everything around me was in darkness. I felt as though I was in a black hole where I was completely alone. It was as though I was lost and had no sense of the presence of any other living person. I felt very afraid. Eventually I did reach out and telephone home, but for a moment I felt abandonment more acutely than ever before. I did not understand this experience at the time, though I later learned that some therapists are familiar with it.

> The term 'black hole' conveys a catastrophic discontinuity of the self, loss of the sense of being alive; a black, psychotic depression which consumes or engulfs the personality, with a sense of losing the very floor of existence. (Spensley, 1994, p. 49)

My research on the published literature about child development and early separation sheds further light on what was happening.

Infant Distress

Though the physical symptoms of polio were highly distressing (Fisher, 1967), it was not so much the illness itself that left an emotional legacy; it was more the prolonged separation from my family that was traumatic (Rothschild, 2000), because I was separated from my parents very suddenly. Rothschild suggests that the stresses of that time would have been 'burned in' to my memory and very difficult to retrieve visually later in life. The black hole experience was a clue that something was being aroused, and the ice cube gave me an image that encapsulated something of what I was sensing.

When a baby feels anxious or unwell, she has an urge to be close to her mother, but if her mother is not present, the baby becomes more distressed. If the separation is prolonged, the baby follows a pattern of protest, withdrawal, and finally detachment (Bowlby, 1988). At around the age of six months – my age when I first became ill – a baby becomes active in exploring the world around her and she gains the confidence to do this by maintaining frequent eye contact with her mother (Holmes, 1993). In a hospital cot there was no familiar 'reference point' for me to feel such reassurance. Being in isolation because my illness was infectious was undoubtedly a terrifying experience. Even for adults, the stress of being treated in an isolation unit can quickly lead to depression and disintegration of the self (Parkinson, 2006).

Current research on neurobiology suggests that the prolonged stress of separation of an infant from her mother can affect the development of a baby's brain, with long-term effects such as a propensity to feel stressed in adult life and a distortion in the capacity to read social cues and adapt to social norms (Gerhardt, 2004). Taken to an extreme, prolonged separations can lead to psychopathology (Cozolino, 2006; Steiner, 1993). Bowlby's (1988) observations indicate that when young children return from hospital, their parents are often subjected to rejection, anger, and clinginess. My mother remembers that when I eventually left the hospital as a baby, I did not seem to want to be hugged and she felt rejected by that. That was the beginning of what Bowlby (1988) has described as a way of relating characterised by a vicious cycle in which my mother felt rejected by my detachment and her response reinforced my sense of rejection. There were shades of this when I first talked to my therapist about my childhood surgery, and it became clear that I had learned to feel that it was not safe to be with other people (Holmes, 1993).

The terror of abandonment may have been compounded by a different fear that was communicated to me from medical staff and my parents. The fear of polio was endemic at the time (Fisher, 1967; Knight, 2008), so it is not inconceivable that I could have internalised that fear through the limbic system and the activity of mirror neurons (Iacoboni and Mazziota, 2007, p. 215). The human face is of vital importance to babies, who experience unfriendly facial expressions as frightening (Ayers, 2003). I only saw the faces of strangers in hospital, and their lack of intimate connection with me could have instilled a sense of shame even at such an early age (Ayers, 2003; Cozolino, 2006; Trevarthen, 2003).

Winnicott (1960) suggests that at around the age of six months a baby begins to move from being 'merged' with her mother to seeing her as a separate person. She moves from a state of 'absolute dependency' to 'relative dependency'. Stern (1985) shares this view, suggesting that playing 'peek a boo' games is a way of experimenting with the separateness of the mother at this stage. Through play, the baby's sense of self is continually being maintained, eroded, rebuilt, and dissolved simultaneously. As this cycle continues, she learns to feel confident in knowing that when there is a rupture in relationships there can be repair, and that separation does not need to mean abandonment. But shame made repair impossible for me. Shame was one of the earliest responses to my illness and formed a blueprint that was reinforced through other experiences during my childhood and adult life.

Perhaps my saving grace was that by the time I went into hospital, I had been close to my mother for six months and may just have been able to internalise enough of her presence to 'hold her in mind' when she was absent (Stern, 1985). Brain plasticity may have been such that I could adapt to my social environment at that time, but there was clearly a residual effect, namely that of remaining 'in a state of longing for parental approval, for "social reinforcement", love and belonging, whilst having little confidence in being able to obtain these feelings' (Gerhardt 2004, p. 115). As I grew to depend on my therapist all of these longings were re-ignited, and receiving the love that she offered and trusting that sense of belonging did not prove to be straightforward.

Reaching In

I did hold my therapist in mind some of the time, but separation and reconnection were always tinged with some anxiety, and there were some particular moments when I was acutely aware of my early experience of abandonment. My therapist had to stop working for a prolonged period during my therapy, and her return date was unclear for a while, although she kept me informed about her progress. The childlike part of me found that difficult, and as time went on I lost hope that she would return. I felt quite angry about her disappearance even though as an adult I understood her circumstances. When we met again after that break, my little child felt out of connection with her, although another part of me was keen to renew the contact. I withdrew from her emotionally, but she noticed what was happening and initiated the process of connecting again. In time, I could see that this was an opportunity to experience separation and return in a more aware and understanding way – something that I could not do as a child with my mother. This experience established a new pattern of trust for me along with an experiential belief that ruptures could be repaired.

There were more subtle ruptures too. As in the story that introduced this chapter, there were times when I was talking about distressing experiences and my therapist would notice that I jumped out of connection with her by averting my eyes, changing the subject, or simply being silent. In the immediacy of the moment, she would draw my attention to what was happening and we would come back into connection again. It was as though I was falling back into the feelings of the six-month-old baby who was needing someone to understand what she was feeling – to 'come and find her' (Winnicott, 1960), because in her isolation she could not engage the attention of other people. That baby had lost her sense of agency in drawing people towards her when she needed them. My sense of shame and loss of agency may have begun in infancy, but this was also repeated during further periods of hospitalisation.

Childhood Distress

The surgery that I mentioned in the opening sequence of this chapter took place when I was ten years old. On reflection, it seems clear that I was experiencing what Rene Spitz and Katherine Wolf (1946) called 'anaclitic depression' – a severe withdrawal that has been observed in institutionalised children. I remember feeling anger and rage at being in hospital at that time, but instead of expressing how I felt, I became unhappy and distant from people around me. Steiner's (1993) idea of 'psychic retreats' explains that the powerful defences that a person builds as a response to such experiences helps to avoid the anxiety that making contact with people evokes. 'Learned helplessness' was another aspect of that state for me – a state that Herman (1994) associates with trauma. Hospital patients learn that their attempts to protest against unpleasant medical interventions do not change what is happening to them, and so they give up protesting and become compliant, losing their sense of agency (Bossert, 1994). My sense of helplessness and inability to express my emotions were also connected with the lack of empathy that was part of medical practice at the time.

Mary Westbrook's (1996, p. 2) study indicates that at the height of the polio epidemics,

> When references were made in the medical literature to children's distress, they were often in the context of warning staff of the dangers of responding too sympathetically to their patients.

When I was enduring painful procedures and my medical condition was discussed in my presence by large groups of doctors, there was very little reference to me as a whole person with emotional responses to what was happening. The physiotherapy regime was to 'work hard to recover' and for polio survivors to push themselves to the limit so that they could 'overcome' their disability. Frick (2000) reports that medical professionals grossly underestimated the distressing effect that their regimes had on children who inevitably felt disheartened when they could not meet the stringent physical demands made of them because their muscles were easily fatigued. This degree of mal-attunement was traumatic (Stolorow, 2007), but while my response of retreating into a withdrawn state provided relief from the strength of emotion, it came at the cost of feeling isolated from others (Steiner, 1993). Moustakas (1961, p. 35) writes:

> Of the many kinds of temporary abandonment, no experience is more desolating to a child than having to be in a hospital alone. The disrespect for the integrity of [her] wishes and interests, the absence of genuine human warmth, all enter into the loneliness of hospital life.

Family members tried to help me out of this state by playing board games and reading stories, but I remember being too angry to engage with these strategies. I had learned to keep these feelings to myself, but the distress I felt did not disappear, it simply went underground, and as a child and a young adult I learned to smile and to minimise the outward effects that these times in hospital had on me.

At the same time I was in therapy I received regular massage sessions that drew my attention to the tension I was holding in my body. Lying on a futon receiving a massage was a physical reminder of lying in a hospital bed, and it reconnected me with painful medical treatment. Though the massage unexpectedly evoked original sensations (Rothschild, 2000), I was now being touched with compassion and respect. Feeling safely held through massage and psychotherapy opened up a more compassionate attitude towards the young child in these memories.

During one therapy session not long before I was to have surgery, a vivid memory of the day that I was going to have the surgery as a ten-year-old began to emerge. On that day I did not know what time I would be taken to the operating theatre and I vividly remember feeling alone and afraid, anticipating being taken on a trolley along a long squeaky wooden corridor to experience something that I knew would be terrifying. That terror was beginning to resurface again. As I spoke, my therapist sat beside me and together we recalled more about that day. She asked questions that evoked my emotions while staying connected to the concrete facts of what the place looked and felt like. In the warmth of her holding, the memory became less frightening. Working in this way was building up my sense of inner strength, but there were other psycho-emotional effects of being an adult with a disability that were yet to be addressed.

Adult Effects

Mary Westbrook's (1996) research confirms that many adult survivors of polio in her study displayed signs of stress, depression, and anxiety in their adult lives and tended to judge themselves harshly, ignoring the needs of their bodies. They also found it difficult to talk about their experiences, and many did not connect events of the past with their present feelings. I was discussing all of these issues in therapy. However, I was among those whose disability was not as severe as it was for some, so it was just about possible for me to keep up with other people around me, although not without feeling a lack of belonging to either the world of the able-bodied or that of the seriously disabled (Backman, 1987). To an extent, this added to my sense of isolation, but the sense of shame I had in being disabled in this way was even more powerful and insidious for me.

As an adult with a disability that is visible, I am often subject to the 'gaze' of others – a gaze that is influenced by the negative stereotypes and prejudices about disability that are prevalent in society (Reeve, 2002). Greenberg and Paivio (1997, pp. 243–244) write:

> An early learning history of rejection, ridicule and criticism leads to deep insecurity and fear of being left alone, defenceless. These experiences can lead to the development of a core sense of self as flawed, worthless, unlovable, or bad, and therefore at risk of being abandoned. Such a core sense of self obviously is related to vulnerability, chronic anxiety, and depression.

It was deeply challenging to talk about these feelings with my therapist, because there was always a fear that in 'telling it like it is' (Zola in Westbrook, 1996, p. 5) I was laying myself open to being further ridiculed or judged. At an emotional level I was unable to fully trust that my therapist would be receptive to my stories. I did not realise that speaking out about them could protect me more effectively than isolating myself (Ayers, 2003). My experience in therapy confirmed Greenberg and Paivio's (1997, p. 235) assertion that in order to achieve the goal of self-acceptance and to overcome shame, 'people need to come out of hiding'. The conundrum is that if they do come out and they are not well received, they feel they need to retreat again, and a vicious circle ensues. For this reason it is vitally important that therapists who work with adults who have been shamed are sensitive and 'respectful of the client's need to withdraw' (Ayers, 2003, p. 237). My therapist did not push me to disclose my polio stories, but her warm, attentive, and insightful listening gradually enabled me to speak out, and this was particularly important when I was facing surgery again as an adult.

I talked with my therapist about how I might approach the surgery so that the trauma was not rekindled. I decided to write to my surgeon explaining how I felt about my childhood experiences of surgery, and I was relieved to find that he responded with kindness and understanding. I arranged a hospital visit prior to the surgery, and I was able to see where the operating theatre and recovery ward were and to speak with nursing staff about what was to happen. Friends and family knew about my fears and were a comfort to me, and I felt reassured. The evening before the surgery I had a massage session, and towards the end of the treatment I felt a sense of peace. I felt capable of accepting the necessary surgery instead of fighting my fear or trying to defend myself from it. The surgery was successful, and instead of feeling traumatised I felt confident that I had managed it without denying my feelings.

I continued with therapy and massage after the surgery and on one occasion my masseuse noticed that my shoulders were curling inwards. She said it seemed as though I was protecting my heart – the place of vulnerability. She felt that I was resisting her attempts to help me relax, and she asked me to imagine a flower opening. As soon as she said that, I stopped resisting. Both physically and emotionally this was an important moment, as I was beginning to learn to nurture my body, to let go of the tension, and to trust someone else with my vulnerability. Therapist Ton Coffeng (1996, p. 503) summarises this process thus:

> the simple act of telling what really happened, experiencing it and being believed and being supported by the therapist as a reliable parent has a healing effect. This is contrary to what happened before – the client was abused, not believed, not helped and hence mistrusted her own experience and denied the inner child.

But telling my story also meant entering into another 'black hole' and fully encountering the feelings that had been locked inside my ice cube.

Grieving

The grief spilled out spontaneously and very suddenly. It felt as though the ice cube was melting all at once like the bursting of a dam. I was overwhelmed, and all of the previous painful losses that I had experienced came flooding back until I felt that I was drowning. I grieved for that young child in hospital all alone and for the loneliness of living with a disability that I did not feel was understood by others. The grief engulfed me for a period of time so that it was difficult to function in my daily life. I was facing the emotion of the trauma that I had previously avoided or minimised, but on reflection I realise that the ability to grieve was a way of coming back into connection with myself and other people.

Although it was frightening and deeply painful, it seemed that by entering the pit of almost nonexistence, a spark of life was ignited into that frozen part for the first time. Part of the process of coming out of retreat is to recognise and acknowledge the parts that are unbearable (Steiner, 1993), so grief is a sign that trauma is beginning to be 'relegated to the past' and that healing is taking place (Rothschild, 2000). In recognising this with my therapist and in feeling her invitation to bring compassion into painful situations, I was able to come out of hiding. I allowed myself to stay in contact with my own experience in the presence of a warm relationship, but there was a moment in my grief when I became aware that I had my own inner place of warmth.

During a therapy session when I was very tearful, talking about a particularly painful bereavement, I suddenly stopped as I noticed that something else was happening. In rapt attention, my therapist quietly said 'listen'. As I listened, I began to feel very peaceful and, looking at the rug on the floor with the yellow square in the centre then seeing the trees through the glass in the sun room, I pictured a greenhouse. I felt warm and safe as I thought of that image. I felt as though I was inside the greenhouse and it had a numinous quality – a strong sense of 'beingness' – a feeling of being completely at one with myself without any judgement.

> In our safe space ... we might then become strong enough to risk reconnection with our histories, our memories and our experiences. (Etherington, 2003, p. 190)

The greenhouse image became the internal safe place that sustained me through that dark time of grieving.

As I learned to sustain myself and to seek the help of others when necessary, I felt less dependent on my therapist.

> If mourning can be worked through, the individual becomes more clearly aware of a separateness of self and object and recognises more clearly what belongs to the self and what belongs to the object. (Steiner, 1993, p. 61)

I no longer minimised the effects of having polio, and I came to adopt a kind attitude towards the disability that was part of me. My therapist had always acknowledged her own fallibility and was open to her own vulnerability, which was crucial to my trust in her and to the child in me now growing into adulthood (Ayers, 2003).

Conclusion

By unravelling the layers of shame, terror, and conditioning to remain silent that had inhibited me from talking about my experience of having polio, and through an agonising expression of grief I have developed a capacity to put words to my feelings and to bring awareness and understanding into what happened. In facing surgery again in the way that I did, my sense of agency in relation to my disability has grown stronger, and I have gained enormous relief in retrieving a lost part of myself. As a therapist, mother, daughter, friend, and partner, I am less anxious about intimate connection and separation, and I have gained an interest in further researching the emotional and relational effects of disability as experienced by other disabled people.

References

Ayers, M. (2003) *Mother-Infant Attachment and Psychoanalysis: The Eyes of Shame* (Hove: Brunner-Routledge).

Backman, M. E. (1987) 'The post-polio patient: Psychological issues', *Journal of Rehabilitation*, 53 (4), 23–26.

Bossert, E. (1994) 'Factors influencing the coping of hospitalised school-age children', *Journal of Pediatric Nursing*, 9 (5), 299–306.

Bowlby, J. (1988) *A Secure Base: Clinical Applications of Attachment Theory* (London: Routledge).

Coffeng, T. (1996) 'The delicate approach to early trauma' in R. Hutterer (ed.) *Client-Centred and Experiential Psychotherapy: A Paradigm in Motion* (Frankfurt am Main: Peter Lang) pp. 499–509.

Cozolino, L. (2006) *The Neuroscience of Human Relationships: Attachment and the Developing Social Brain* (London: Norton).

Dowling, H. F. (1985) 'Behind glass walls: The history of the Chicago Municipal Contagious Disease Hospital', *Journal of the History of Medicine and Allied Sciences*, 40, 440–461.

Etherington, K. (2003) *Trauma, the Body and Transformation: A Narrative Inquiry* (London: Jessica Kingsley).

Fisher, P. J. (1967) *The Polio Story* (London: Heinemann).

Frick, N. M. (2000) 'The contribution of childhood physical and emotional trauma to the development of the post-polio personality', Proceedings of the Ontario March of Dimes Conference on Post-Polio Sequelae (Toronto: Ontario March of Dimes, 1995, revised April 2000). Available at www.poliosurvivorsnetwork.org.uk/archive/lincolnshire/library/harvest/frick.html, accessed May 2015.

Gerhardt, S. (2004) *Why Love Matters: How Affection Shapes the Baby's Brain* (Hove: Brunner Routledge).

Greenberg, L. S., and Paivio, S. C. (1997) *Working with Emotions in Psychotherapy* (London: Guilford Press).

Herman, J. (1994) *Trauma and Recovery* (London: Pandora).

Holmes, J. (1993) *John Bowlby and Attachment Theory* (London: Routledge).

Iacoboni, M., and Mazziota, J. C. (2007) 'Mirror neuron system: Basic findings and clinical applications', *Annual Journal of Neurobiology*, 62 (3), 213–218.

Knight, C. (2008) 'The 1950s – Polio, a different war', *Journal of Orthopaedic Nursing*, 12, 106–109.

Miller, A. (1990) *Thou Shalt Not Be Aware: Society's Betrayal of the Child*, 2nd edn (London: Plato).

Moustakas, C. E. (1961) *Loneliness* (London: Prentice-Hall).

Parkinson, J. (2006) 'Experiences of selves in isolation: A psychodynamic approach to the care of patients being treated in a specialised medical hospital unit', *Psychodynamic Practice*, 12 (2), 149–163.

Reeve, D. (2002) 'Negotiating psycho-emotional dimensions of disability and their influence on identity construction', *Disability and Society*, 17 (5), 493–508.

Rothschild, B. (2000) *The Body Remembers: The Psychophysiology of Trauma and Trauma Treatment* (London: Norton).

Spensley, S. (1994) *Frances Tustin: Borderlands of Autism and Psychosis* (London: Routledge).

Spitz, R. A., and Wolf, K. M. (1946) 'Anaclitic depression: An inquiry into the genesis of psychiatric conditions in early childhood', *Psychoanalytic Study of the Child*, 2, 313–342.

Steiner, J. (1993) *Psychic Retreats: Pathological Organisations in Psychotic, Neurotic and Borderline Patients* (Hove: Brunner Routledge).

Stern, D. (1985) *The Interpersonal World of the Infant: A View from Psychoanalysis and Developmental Psychology* (New York: Basic Books).

Stolorow, R. D. (2007) *Trauma and Human Existence: Autobiographical, Psychoanalytic, and Philosophical Reflections* (London: The Analytic Press).

Trevarthen, C. (2003) 'Neuroscience and intrinsic psychodynamics: Current knowledge and potential for therapy' in J. Corrigal and H. Wilkinson (eds) *Revolutionary Connections: Psychotherapy and Neuroscience* (London: Karnac) pp. 53–78.

Warner, M. S. (2009) 'Defense or actualisation? Reconsidering the role of processing, self and agency within Rogers' theory of personality', *Person-Centred and Experiential Psychotherapies*, 8 (2), 109–126.

Westbrook, M. T. (1996) 'Early memories of having polio: Survivors' memories versus the official myths', paper presented at the First Australian International Post-Polio Conference, 'Living with the Late Effects of Polio', Sydney, November.

Winnicott, D. W. (1960) 'The theory of the parent-infant relationship', *International Journal of Psycho-Analysis*, 41: 585–595.

8 Regarding 'The Teahouse of the August Moon': Therapeutic Work with a Man with Schizophrenia within a Hospital Context

APRIL PARKINS

Introduction

David described himself as a Jekyll and Hyde character, 'a bandit with the eyes of a doe'. He arrived at his first music therapy session carrying some printed sheet music and some of his own poems as a gift to me for 'taking an interest' in him. At first he seemed pleased when I tentatively asked if he was suggesting that the poems could be used as the basis for a musical composition. A moment later he stood up abruptly and made for the door, saying that he was far too frightened to remain in the room. He said that I should do the composing; he did not want to be involved. The session had lasted for just ten minutes.

When I first met David (a pseudonym), I was a music therapist based within a psychiatric hospital, working with people who had a wide range of mental health issues. He was an in-patient with a long-standing diagnosis of schizophrenia. Our work together formed the case study on which this chapter is based. He gave his explicit permission for me to write about him and our work together, and indeed he made it clear that he was keen for me to tell his story as he understood it. He made this decision independently. Members of his family, to whom he referred occasionally and who appear in the account I offer here, would undoubtedly have perceived the events to which David made reference differently from the way he did. However, my purpose in this chapter is not to offer an objective assessment of what happened but to explore the emergence of meaning in David's communications to me as they unfolded in our work together. A case study based on my own clinical practice did not fall within the purview of the NHS ethics review process, but I nevertheless sought NHS guidance at every stage, as well as following the ethical guidance of professional bodies for music therapy and counselling.

My music therapy practice takes its theoretical stance from the psychodynamic tradition first developed by Sigmund Freud over a hundred years ago. Freud (1905, 1913) recommended that psychoanalytic treatment be confined to people whom he understood to be suffering from 'neuroses', believing that it was not possible to work with patients who had psychotic illnesses, since they would not be able to enter into a transference relationship with the analyst. However, the generation of psychoanalysts who followed in his footsteps, which included Searles, Bion, and Segal, took Freud's theories and extended them into their own psychoanalytic work with psychiatric patients who had psychotic illnesses such as schizophrenia.

The invention of chlorpromazine in 1953 and the subsequent development of other anti-psychotic medications revolutionised the treatment of people with schizophrenia (Healy, 2008). The availability of more effective pharmacological treatments has meant that medication has now become the primary form of treatment for people with severe and enduring mental illnesses. These pharmacological advances, combined with changes in the overall philosophy of care, have also brought about a shift within the organisation of mental health services, which now aim to provide 'care in the community', as opposed to in-patient psychiatric care, to the majority of people with mental health conditions. In-patient care is reserved for those who are acutely ill, and it is only those at the more severe end of the spectrum who remain in hospital for extended periods of time. As a result, it has become rare for long-term, in-depth explorative work to be offered to patients within in-patient psychiatric settings.

This case study is therefore unusual, in that it provides an example of long-term individual music therapy with a client diagnosed with paranoid schizophrenia. My work with David demonstrates the importance and value of such work in a number of ways: it is a powerful way of enabling the patient's voice to be heard; it offers a profound witnessing of a patient's life in hospital; and it demonstrates that it is possible to engage in a meaningful relationship with a severely ill patient in a way that is creative and that transcends diagnosis.

David had spent much of his adult life within institutional care because of the severity of his mental health condition. While his experience before and during his hospitalisation was deeply personal and particular, he is far from the only person to live his adult life in this kind of context. Explorative therapeutic work with an individual such as David – unpredictable, suspicious, and sometimes violent, and who experienced frequent hallucinations and delusions – would not normally have been considered appropriate. However, he was referred to me for music therapy so that he could be offered a creative outlet and a distraction from his paranoid ideas. My own aims were to give him an opportunity to express himself, initially through the medium of improvised music and later also through poetry, and to enter into a relationship with me, to whatever degree seemed possible. We worked together for a period of five years. During those years David was gradually able to find his way towards entering into a relationship with me. Within this relationship he found creative and relatively safe ways to tell and reflect on the significant stories of his life. As a result, he was able to find meaning emerging from feelings and events that he had formerly associated primarily with chaos, confusion, and distress.

David gave his consent for me to audio-record the music therapy sessions, and he made it clear that these recordings were of the utmost importance to him. Consequently, all of the quotations provided within the chapter are verbatim, coming directly from the audio-recordings. I present in italics extracts from notes I made after our sessions, which were further edited as I listened back to the audio-recordings during the preparation of the full version of the case study on which this chapter is based.

Through a series of vignettes describing the work, in chronological order, I tell something of the story of the journey that David and I made. I link these vignettes to a psychodynamic theoretical perspective, mainly using the theories of Winnicott, in order to illuminate aspects of the therapeutic relationship.

One of the principal difficulties in working at therapeutic depth with people who have schizophrenia is their difficulty in distinguishing between fantasy and reality. Winnicott's (1953) concept of potential space (also known as transitional space) provides a helpful background to thinking about the work. Ogden (1986, p. 203) describes it as an area 'between fantasy and reality', 'between the symbol and symbolised' (Ibid., 224). It includes "dream-space", analytic space' (ibid., 233–234), play space, and creativity. Thus potential space lies between subjectivity and objectivity and between the inner and outer world. Minsky (1996, p. 120) wrote that 'the strength of the transitional space compared with language is that it is creative because it is *provisional and inclusive*, like artistic experience'. Davis and Wallbridge (1981, p. 65) link the idea to relating: 'potential space is where meaningful communication takes place'.

It is within the creative and liminal space first described by Winnicott that David and I often seemed to find ourselves: between language, poetry, and music, between symbol and symbolised, between relationship and separateness, between feeling and thought.

Early Stages: Relationship and Creativity

After his abrupt departure from the first session, David subsequently agreed to return to music therapy, and he and I went on to work together on a weekly basis. In our earliest sessions, I was very wary of him and his unpredictability. My initial aim was to try to find a way of sharing music with him without frightening him away or risking his anger. We often used a piano each – I was fortunate to have two – but it was difficult to match his individual style: great sweeps of notes up and down the keyboard, musical ideas offered and retracted, shifting levels of volume, and a tempo that never remained in one place for long. Early on, despairing of ever establishing contact with him, I tried matching the disarray that I was hearing from his piano with some of my own. The piece ended after several minutes in pained laughter from us both as he spluttered in astonishment 'triumph – agony – chaos! I could not mesh with your gears!' I understood then that the issue was not primarily about a lack of awareness but rather the ability or desire to adapt and to feel comfortable with being in contact. At the same time, I noted his ambivalence towards what had been a very deliberate mis-attunement on my part.

As he became more comfortable with me, David began to articulate some of his own complex and ambivalent feelings about our relationship. One day, he arrived for his session bareheaded (he usually wore a hat, pulled low over his eyes) and smiling. Something about him seemed different, but I could not put my finger on what it was. 'I'm seeing you for the first time today,' he announced. Noting my puzzlement, he explained patiently: 'April, I'm looking at you. Usually I look past you, but today I'm **looking** at you.' With a slight shock I realised that this was true, and impulsively I asked him what it was like. He paused. Then, suddenly averting his eyes, he replied: 'Absolutely terrifying.'

Our relationship did not develop in a straightforward way. It was always necessary for me to adapt to the fluctuations in David's mental health. On one occasion he arrived at the session seeming unusually disturbed. His head and face were completely obscured by a hood, which gave him an odd, rather sinister appearance. Before sitting at the piano, he placed my chair well behind him and out of reach of any of the instruments. After playing alone, he spoke in a jumbled way about his own violence in the past – the throwing of a table against a wall, the drowning by his uncle of ten puppies. On his own face, visible now, there appeared briefly an imitation of the face of a dead puppy. This was muddled with other talk, and because of his 'mad' state I didn't know what sense to make of it, although I recall feeling disquieted by the face of the puppy.

The medium of music offered David a means towards and an experience of interrelating. Within the sessions he was able to communicate with me about what he felt able to tolerate, either explicitly (for example 'I'd like to play on my own today, with no interruptions from yourself') or in a more indirect way (for example through the inaccessibility of his face, the re-positioning of my chair, or simply through a remote, brittle silence). On days when he was able to allow my careful joining in with him, the transformation during sessions was often very moving. His response might be grudging at first, then gradually more accepting, then increasing in pleasure as we continued. Sometimes our shared playing 'worked' for him and sometimes it didn't. But at its best our musical relationship contributed to what he described as his 'lonely fumblings' becoming an experience that seemed intimate and meaningful, and that clearly felt very satisfying to him.

Fundamental to the development of our relationship in these early stages was being able to share moments of creativity. One day we spent almost the whole of the session immersed in music, as if in a long shared sequence of dreams. He later named it 'The Teahouse of the August Moon', which is the title of a book by Vern Schneider (published in 1951 and later made into a film directed by David Mann). I have chosen to use it as the title of this chapter because of its apparent meaning to David within the context of our work (that is, I am not implying any specific reference to the subject matter of the book). The music David named 'The Teahouse of the August Moon' had no predetermined direction: instead it moved through a series of atmospheres, alighting for a time within each, before moving on. To a listener I imagine that it might have sounded peculiar.

My notes record: *'what I am aware of here above all is the depth of our shared understanding within the music. We are creating it together in the moment, and it holds us in relationship. Freedom, trust, and intimacy are demonstrated by (among other things) our ability to stay together through the transitions, and the unusually long-held periods of spacious, responsive playing ...'*

If Winnicott (1953) is correct in his theory that disruption of the mother–infant relationship can contribute to the type of mental health difficulties that David developed, then it seems particularly relevant that he has been offered an experience of music therapy. 'Matching' through music implies the sharing of musical elements such as rhythm, tempo, melodic shape, level of volume, mood, and so on. This experience of attunement can replicate something of what we now believe to be similar to that which is felt by the infant during a satisfying mother–infant interaction (Winnicott, 1960). Wright (1991, p. 283) makes a comparison between maternal and paternal therapeutic perspectives within therapy, and according to his description what I endeavoured to offer to David has many similarities with Winnicott's 'maternal' therapeutic philosophy: 'holding, reflecting, being there, facilitating, enabling, and surviving; providing conditions within which growing, developing, and exploring can take place'.

According to Wright's (1991, p. 291) concept of 'two- and three-person organisation', David was primarily at the stage of 'two-person organisation'; however, his position within this organisational perspective fluctuated. Wright (1991) describes how, within the two-person organisational stage, the individual lives within a symbolic structure; in moving to the three-person stage the individual is able to use the now-familiar object-relating patterns to bring understanding and awareness to other relationships. David's fluctuation between these stages can be illustrated by the following example. One morning, on entering the music therapy room David had an aggressive altercation with a female member of staff. The session then began with him in a frightening and angry mood. He played music alone and then later, when he was less agitated, with me. At the end of the session, apparently moved by the experience, he calmly observed: 'I like music.... you're a good player.' A few moments later: 'I'm going to go and apologise to the lady'. His observation began with self-awareness ('I like music'), then it moved outward to include an awareness and acknowledgement of me ('you're a good player'), and finally to an awareness of a third person ('I'm going to go and apologise ...'), viewing himself perhaps through her eyes (an external perspective) and deciding on and carrying out the reparative act of apology. It was the playing of music that seemed to bring about this shift in his perspective, and many would perhaps argue that it was simply the 'calming' properties of music that had brought about the change. I suggest, however, that his experience of feeling contained by my presence and by the expression of our relationship within the music offered him a means of metabolising, and thus transforming, his anger (Bion, 1962).

Middle Stages (1): Identity and Symbolism

The way that David used music, and the combination of music and poetry, seemed to be as a passageway from the more ordinary, mundane outer world to the rich and sometimes strange imagery of his inner world. As I illustrate in this section, the spontaneous creation of music and poetry seemed to offer a conduit for free association, enabling him to visit some of the more remote places within himself and then providing a safe passage back to the present external world. In addition to leading him to deep images and memories, his song-poems could have been interpreted purely as artistic creations rather than as personal disclosures, and I believe that this provided him with an additional sense of safety.

Cox and Theilgaard (1987, p. xxvi) suggest that it is the therapist's capacity to pick up the 'music in the wind' that furthers the telling of the patient's story. They use the image of the Aeolian harp, once belonging to Orpheus, to suggest a manner of listening. According to the Greek legend, after Orpheus's death the harp was hung on a tree, where it continued to play as a result of the wind blowing against its strings. The creative image used by the psychotic patient may not be amenable to straightforward interpretation, but it has the power to '(touch) the depths before it stirs the surface' (ibid., p. 18).

David seems discouraged today, telling me that the piano in the large hall is very out of tune. When I ask if he'd like me to speak to someone about it he says no, that he'd be punished. He says that he wants to play a piece of his own, reciting poetry of 'whatever comes up in my mind'. He uses wind chimes, a long row of shiny gold bars hanging from a stand, to accompany his recitation. His playing is slow and steady, and his speech, when it begins, is at first clear and dramatic:

There was a soldier, on a farm

... there was mustard, there was curried oxtail,

there was steak pie on Sundays

Brussels sprouts, roast beef, Yorkshire pudding, roast potatoes

There is a longer pause here in the narrative; the wind chimes continue. The quality of his voice becomes more thoughtful.

And the river was dying, from ... (?)

It turned the river a bright pink, purple, yellow, green, blue

In the mud, the water hens along the river

The wrens further down the river ... dolphins ...

Jasper, topaz, emerald, sapphire, diamond

He continues to run his hands slowly and delicately back and forth along the chimes, steadily, like the wind, or perhaps like the flowing of the river. Combined with the measured quality of his recitation, it begins to take on an almost hypnotic quality. As his speech becomes still quieter it becomes less intelligible:

My ... photographs ... strange ...

The power of the past, in photographs

And although he has asked to play this piece on his own, for some reason it feels right to join him, and I move silently to crouch near him on the floor, reaching up to play other metal instruments: Tibetan bells, more chimes, a bell, a triangle. On the audio-recording it is hardly noticeable as being a second person but audible as an occasional slightly deeper sound during pauses in the narrative.

Days and days ... years gone by ...

Momentarily his voice becomes harsh and louder:

Men ...

Then his voice subsides again, his speech still deliberate, but slower. At the time I understood very few of the words but in my playing was responding simply to the sombre, now sparse quality of his speech:

My dog, dead in the road ...

Bells ringing

From the first (church?)

My mother –

My own fault ...

Drowning

Puppies

I don't know why *(this phrase is half-sung, on a rising pitch)*

130

Then he murmured:

> ... I didn't protest ...
>
> ... house ...
>
> ... up steps ...

The piece closes here, and the sound of the chimes ceases.

We revert back to the present. He speaks about himself and me, making a comparison:

> I see you that sensitive there, April, making a contribution. I can't understand.... I can't feel the same way. I feel as though I'm a brute. I have been made that way. I used to have the sensitivity ...

He shares evocative memories of his younger days, the Beatles, the Rolling Stones, the beauty, the love.

> But I lost it. I had it. Things in my own mind turned bad, April. Always on hospital medication, a long list, another drug to take ...

I say to him that he seems very sad about what he has lost, but he doesn't answer, beginning instead to play. It takes some time before we can settle into playing together, but it comes eventually, first with excitement and then resolution, then sitting together in silence.

David's poems came about in an entirely spontaneous manner, and although I rarely felt confident of 'understanding' them in a conventional sense, his choice of words and manner of speaking invariably conveyed depth, intention, and vivid imagery. The material he offered had some similarity to the mysterious qualities of a dream, which Ogden (1997, p. 153) writes: 'cannot be translated into a linear, verbally-symbolised narrative without losing touch with *the effect* created by the dream experience itself, the experience of dreaming as opposed to the meaning of the dream'. This seems to suggest that, at the same time that we gain understanding through being able to symbolise an experience verbally we also lose touch with some aspect of that experience.

Music and the musical instruments became significant metaphors for David's identity, feelings, and relationships with others. Love, his love of playing, the need to care for, to tune, to make out-of-tune, 'to be knackered', 'bashed to pieces', a recipient of 'umpteen people venting their frustrations' and a fascination with their destruction have all been features of the sessions.

The sight of an unwanted piano dumped in the hospital grounds has made an impression on David. He speaks about it in connection with his fascination with 'ripped-out' music today after his 'wild cacophony' of playing. The disintegrating piano, left to the mercy of the elements, has brought to his mind his love of Jimi Hendrix: the 'chemically-induced violent distortion of sound', and the supreme act of destruction in setting fire to his guitar when on stage. David identifies with Hendrix: 'Music meant a lot to him, had an awful lot of … sadness not the word … ' *I suggest, 'anguish?'* 'Yes – similar. Tormented.' *And later, near the end of the session, he speaks of some quite different qualities 'freshness, sweetness, virginal …' and asks if I can harmonise some of the written music that he has left with me. In previous weeks he has described me as someone who tries to* 'add harmony to disharmony'.

The instruments and aspects of the music offered David an opportunity, through projection, to describe his feelings about himself. He would identify with the piano, one day complaining about it being 'wrecked', on another day that it was inhabited by 'a ghost, a spirit, a presence, an emanation', and on yet another day he would express his love for it. He had ambivalent feelings about improving the condition of the various pianos that we used, wondering at one moment if one of them could perhaps be tuned but in the next moment rejecting the offer.

His frustration with the piano has become centred on a single note. He hammers at it, angry and disparaging: 'a bum note – listen to that! That's not a **note**!' *Sitting at the other piano, and scarcely conscious of what I am doing, I echo the note on my own piano. I try to play it the way he plays it, loudly, harshly, trying to hear what he is hearing. But the tone of the two pianos is slightly different, and although I am trying to match him, my touch on the piano is different too. We play the note, back and forth, while he continues to complain vociferously. I add in a chord, further down in the bass, with the offending note still audible at the top. He stops hammering to listen. I play the note again, with another chord. I am not using conventional harmony and the chords are not particularly related, but the note remains poised at the top, an integral part of each chord. He remains completely still, as if transfixed, while I play ten or so chords, resolving it carefully at the end. Something has shifted in the room and outwardly he is completely calm, but I also sense, somehow, his inner excitement.* 'Lovely …' *He wants to do it too and tries, making small splodges of sound on his piano. He asks me to show him how, but two of us sitting at one piano is not comfortable for him and he gives up quickly, gently handing the task back to me:* '**You** put it right.'

Judging from David's response, I believe that this experience was for him one of the most meaningful moments within our work together. The stark 'bum note' (which, at that moment, I believe represented *him*) was altered through its inclusion within a harmonic context. It was as if this ugly, unwelcome note had been accepted and given a place within which to 'be'. When played alone, the note had felt harsh, isolated, and static, but the underpinning harmony that I offered seemed to transform it into something that he found both beautiful and meaningful.

This episode seems to have something in common with Winnicott's (1971) description of the way that fantasy can be transformed into imagination by the creativity of the potential space. 'Fantasying' suggests a dissociative state: 'an isolated phenomenon, absorbing energy but not contributing-in either to dreaming or to living' (Winnicott, 1971, p. 26). It is static and does not progress. Imagination, on the other hand, is what becomes of fantasy when it is transformed by the creativity of the potential space (Ogden, 1986). It has life, energy, and meaning.

Middle Stages (2): Symbolism

Both Klein and Winnicott made extensive contributions to the understanding of symbolism and its role in psychological development and well-being. Klein, in identifying the paranoid-schizoid and depressive positions, said that the inability to symbolise was one of the defining features of the developmentally more primitive paranoid-schizoid position. Within this position, 'One's symbols do not reflect a layering of personal meaning to be interpreted and understood; *one's symbols are what they stand for*' (Ogden, 1986, p. 65, my italics). Events are experienced without being interpreted, and the qualities of 'as' and 'as if' remain undifferentiated. It is unsurprising that there seems to be a link between the loss of the ability to symbolise and psychosis (Taylor, 1997, p. 61).

In our work together David used a developing form of symbolism, which I suggest assisted him in managing separations. In the earliest period of our work, when his mental health was at its most unstable, there were a number of occasions when he was not allowed to leave the ward to attend his music therapy session. When I went there to see him, he would often give me something to take back – some tattered pages of printed music or sheets of his own distinctive musical writing. It is as if it was important for him to be represented through a tangible object that, within this context, made reference to an aspect of him as well as to an aspect of our relationship.

My understanding was that David was using the sheets of music as a symbol, in Segal's words, 'not to deny but to overcome loss' (Segal, 1986, p. 57). That he was not doing this consciously suggests that the object is at an earlier, partially symbolised stage, perhaps closer to Winnicott's concept of the transitional object.

An internal world such as David's, with its extremely persecutory nature, was in many ways like Klein's paranoid-schizoid position. Inhabiting this frightening place, within which he often believed that others were harming or intending to harm him, required the aid of defences, and those with which David was familiar – splitting and projection – are consistent with Klein's description of this position.

I have already offered several examples of David's projection of parts of himself into musical instruments and musical sounds. The theme of the split within him between good and evil was never far away, and he expressed it in different ways, sometimes through musical metaphor:

Harmony, with the sound of a single tone ... surrounded by strife and terror almost.... Music tends to destroy itself ... chords ... a viability towards ... harmonised, prayer-like music ... *anything* can be fermented ...

Sometimes it was the contrast between us that described the two extremes. I was often identified as representing the side of good: 'April with her kind, deep heart; David with a heart of stone. It's not that he can't feel things, but ...'

Later Stages: Witness and Meaning

David sits at the far end of the room, using the guitar. At his request, I am sitting some distance away. He was diagnosed with cancer just over a week ago, and he told me about this during the session last week. He said that it was not a surprise. His singing is powerful today and he accompanies his own songs, returning again and again to the theme of recent months, the blackbird: 'fall down dead'. The songs and poems sometimes seem continuous, blending into one another. He holds the guitar upright, like a cello, strumming it to accompany his poems.

... The finest burgundy.
My sister's birth.
My father ... my sister's head.
The minister he said 'bless the child'
Place ... laid them ... on your own heads ...
Fraternal, maternal
My brother's disgust
Hear a tale saying such.
Corner shop ...
Change for a coin
I sell my cup in place.

He stops playing the guitar here; his voice becomes quieter, intent, as if going to a deeper place.

My mother and father, dead departed
Stones, flowers, the grave which was there.
They lay in their boxes of black teak and brass handles
Open box (lights?)
Nothing inside
Earth and dust and grave, bones,
A book,
silver
hand-painted
scribed
altered
church
burnt
edges frayed
Fires of Sodom, Eden, Paradise of Dante Alighieri

He resumes the guitar here, as if resurfacing, back to the present:

Venezia, Siena, Roma
Bluebirds come back
To southern parts.

135

Within months, David's health began to deteriorate visibly, and he understood that he was dying. Themes in the sessions were of guilt, sorrow, and anger in relation to his history with his family and to his own decisions in the earlier stages of his life.

Material that came up in earlier sessions re-emerged, and sometimes I was able to place the pieces together, as one might with a jigsaw puzzle. He told me a more complete version of a story that had emerged at least twice before, and when I put it alongside the other, odd and disconnected references to 'cold water' and 'kitchen', it suddenly all made sense.

He has been playing the guitar, using the harmonica as a slide on the fretboard. As he stops, his words appear suddenly as if from nowhere: 'Ten dead puppies, though … ten dead puppies'. Dimly I connect these words to a story, half-told, from long ago. He wants to tell me more now, and he also doesn't want to tell me, as if he fears that it might contaminate me somehow. His phrases are at first halting, and then they become more fluent.

> My mother … big dog … bitch dog … not old … big collie – I can't remember. But anyway, these puppies we had, ten of. My uncle – I could … tell you the story but it might haunt you …

He hesitates, then gathers himself:

> But, tell the story. Ten puppies, half-blind. My mother, for some reason, wanted them destroyed. I don't know … but … put (?) powder into the sink – kitchen – prepared to …

His voice is hushed, almost breaking:

> You can guess the rest … my uncle used the sink, cold water … you can guess the rest.

Almost whispering now, he struggles to articulate the unspeakable final sentence:

> He drowned them…

It had often seemed to me that symbolic meaning within David's material was not unattainable. He and I were fortunate to have had the luxury of time, which allowed material to be re-told and to be presented in different ways. The story about the drowned puppies was given a series of 'tellings' in different modalities, each of which represented a different form of symbolism: first in a briefly re-enacted representation, later in a musical/poetic form, and finally in a hesitant but clearly spoken and linear form. Although I do not believe that it was intentional on his part, he communicated the multi-layers and meanings of the story through the different manners of his expression.

My understanding increased with each of these re-visits. The first time, witnessing his rendition of the face of the dead puppy, I felt unease and distaste, as if being confronted with something unpleasant that I didn't understand. The second time, within the musical poem, I could not distinguish many of the words of the story, but I was acutely aware of the overall tone, the spacing, and the almost hypnotic atmosphere. Its compelling quality affected me to such an extent that I was moved to join in with him, at the very point when he began to refer explicitly to his past. The third time he told the story directly and intentionally, with reference to me as the listener and with concern for the impact that it might have. And although the story was in itself horrible, I also felt some relief at gaining an understanding of what he had experienced.

'Music itself is a witnessing presence' (Rose, 2004, p. 129). This refers to the commonly described feeling that many of us seem to experience when we feel that certain music 'speaks' deeply to us, that it resonates with us, and that there is a sense of it having been created 'in our own image [supporting] the illusion that reality is self-centred' (Rose, 2004, pp. 92–93). This feeling is perhaps even more pronounced when, as in this situation, David directly created the music that we were hearing. Music was not the only witness within our sessions: there was also my presence, and that of the audio-recorder. The latter was an essential component of our work. He explained its importance by saying that it is 'part of your soul on record' or 'part of you that will remain alive forever'.

I suggest that the act of witnessing also relates to the concept of metaphorical 'holding'. Winnicott (1945) describes 'the patient's need to be known in all his bits and pieces by one person, the analyst. To be known means to feel integrated at least in the person of the analyst.' To this end, it is the audio-recordings that have become invaluable for me as I struggle to make sense of, remember, understand, and integrate all of the disparate and confusing fragments of material. It is difficult to know what David's sense of this might be, but I suggest that his deep valuing of the work may have some relationship to his awareness, on some level, that I am making this attempt to 'gather in the bits' with which he has presented me.

Conclusion

In the writing of this chapter it has been very liberating to have had the freedom not to conform to the language of 'evidence', 'outcomes', and 'validity' that has become so prevalent in the world of the health service today. The standard measurement tools used in mental health settings would not, in my opinion, have been of any real assistance in assessing David's response to music therapy. It is possible that some positive change in David's emotional well-being during the period of therapeutic contact might have been registered, but against the backdrop of his severe, fluctuating mental health problem, the frequent changes in his medication, and the volatility of day-to-day life, it would not have been possible to attribute this to any one particular cause. At most the standardised tools, with their focus on outcome rather than process, might have given an incomplete and ambiguous answer to the question of 'what' happened but without offering any insight into the much more interesting and relevant questions about 'how' or 'why'.

Within this chapter I have presented a way of thinking, rather than a conclusive argument. My intention has been to convey complexity and uncertainty, while at the same time providing a coherent means of understanding and interpreting. The broad, creative, and sometimes elusive nature of potential space has the capacity to encompass the depth and unpredictability of David's and my work. Returning to the descriptions offered at the beginning of this chapter, we are reminded that potential space offers a place in which 'meaningful communication' can take place. Within our working relationship there was space for fantasy and reality, for play and creativity, and for developing symbols to emerge and be tentatively understood. The relationship of this work to the underlying theory of potential space is one of mutuality, in that Winnicott's concept offers us a way to think about and make sense of the material, and at the same time the details of the work illuminate and bring to life aspects of his theory.

As for the debate about whether psychologically based treatments can be useful for people with severe mental illnesses, it is likely that this will continue for many years to come. What I have presented here is a single case study, and as such it makes no claim towards generalisation. However, I hope that it will be a reminder that within the current climate of 'one size fits all' we should not forget the needs of the individual.

I believe that it was very significant that David gave me his permission to write more publicly about our work together at around the same time that he was diagnosed with cancer. As such, this description of our work can also be understood to be part of his legacy, ensuring that his memory, and part of his soul, can remain alive after his death.

I continued to work with David until his last days. During one of our final meetings, after asking me whether we had any time left in the session, he spoke about our work together, focusing on what had been difficult about it and what had been good.

> Just to say, even after all this time, April, I still can't handle it. I'll always be unable to find myself at ease, particularly (with) ladies … sometimes … pedestal…. I can't do that. What I can do – I could use … work – just work done. Work to do, work done. Work achieved. Which is something.

References

Bion, W. R. (1962) *Learning from Experience* (London: Heinemann).

Cox, M., and Theilgaard, A. (1987) *Mutative Metaphors in Psychotherapy: The Aeolian Mode* (London: Tavistock).

Davis, M., and Wallbridge, D. (1981) *Boundary and Space: An Introduction to the Work of D. W. Winnicott* (London: Karnac).

Freud, S. (1905) 'On psychotherapy', *The Standard Edition of the Complete Psychological Works of Sigmund Freud*, Volume VII, translated and edited by James Strachey (London: Hogarth Press) pp. 255–268.

Freud, S. (1913) 'On beginning the treatment', *The Standard Edition of the Complete Psychological Works of Sigmund Freud*, Volume XII, translated and edited by James Strachey (London: Hogarth Press) pp. 121–144.

Healy, D. (2008) 'The intersection of psychopharmacology and psychiatry in the second half of the twentieth century' in E. R. Wallace and J. Gach (eds) *History of Psychiatry and Medical Psychology* (Boston, MA: Springer) pp. 419–437.

Minsky, R. (1996) *Psychoanalysis and Gender* (London and New York: Routledge).

Ogden, T. H. (1986) *The Matrix of the Mind: Object Relations and the Psychoanalytic Dialogue* (Northvale, NJ, and London: Jason Aronson).

Ogden, T. H. (1997) *Reverie and Interpretation: Sensing Something Human* (London: Karnac).

Rose, G. J. (2004) *Between Couch and Piano: Psychoanalysis, Music, Art and Neuroscience* (Hove and New York: Brunner-Routledge).

Segal, H. (1986) *The Work of Hanna Segal: A Kleinian Approach to Clinical Practice* (London: Free Association Books).

Taylor, D. (1997) 'The psychoanalytic approach to psychotic aspects of the personality: Its relevance to the National Health Service' in C. Mace and F. Margison (eds) *Psychotherapy of Psychosis* (London: Gaskell) pp. 49–62.

Winnicott, D. W. (1945) 'Primitive emotional development', *International Journal of Psycho-Analysis*, 26, 137–143. Reproduced in *Collected Papers: Through Paediatrics to Psycho-analysis* (London: Tavistock, 1958).

Winnicott, D. W. (1953) 'Transitional objects and transitional phenomena – a study of the first not-me possession', *International Journal of Psycho-Analysis*, 34, 89–97. Reproduced in *Collected Papers: Through Paediatrics to Psycho-analysis* (London: Tavistock, 1958) and in *Playing and Reality* (London: Tavistock, 1971).

Winnicott, D. W. (1960) 'The theory of the parent-infant relationship', *International Journal of Psycho-Analysis*, 41, 585–595. Reproduced in *The Maturational Processes and the Facilitating Environment* (London: Hogarth, 1965).

Winnicott, D.W. (1971) 'Dreaming, fantasying and living: A case history describing a primary dissociation' in *Playing and Reality* (London: Tavistock) pp. 26–37.

Wright, K. (1991) *Vision and Separation: Between Mother and Baby* (London: Free Association Books).

9 A Secret Sorrow: Making a Difference to Bereavement in Prison

All Alone
Nobody kens I'm grieving
Nobody sees me greet
I break my heart at night
When the jail is fast asleep

Billy

Introduction

The above poem tells a powerful story about the lived experience of bereavement in prison. It and other client narratives were given voice in my research, which has informed and changed the practices of the Scottish Prison Service in relation to bereavement care for prisoners.

For many years, I have offered counselling, on a voluntary basis, to male inmates of a Scottish prison. Early in this period (beginning in 1999) I set up and developed a bereavement counselling service within this setting under the auspices of what is now known as Cruse Bereavement Care Scotland. The ethos of counselling, with its emphasis on openness and trust, and that of a closed, disempowering prison regime, which necessarily prioritises security above all else, are worlds apart, and yet each can serve the other in the interests of prisoner care.

Although much has been researched and written about bereavement over the past recent decades, very little reference is ever made in the literature to the experience of grief within prison. As I have journeyed the paths of grief alongside my prisoner clients, I have been witness to an aspect of human experience that is largely hidden from everyday life and lived in silence. McLeod (2001, p. 7) points out that an important role for counselling research is to document such 'critical dilemmas in living' and make them available to others, which became a key purpose in my own study.

As I embarked on my research I felt a strong need, from a personal, professional, moral, social, and political perspective, to enable the marginalised voices of bereaved prisoners to be heard and shared amongst other parties, especially the Scottish Prison Service, in order that these voices might become a force for change in bereavement care for prisoners through better-informed practices. This need arose from my prolonged, passionate interest and involvement in my counselling work with clients who dare to set out on the road towards personal truthfulness whilst doing time. It was embedded in the deepest of respect for those who struggle, on the edge of our society, towards 'becoming themselves' (Rogers, 1961).

Bearing witness to my clients' grief within the prison walls and analysing my encounters with them within a qualitative research paradigm not only deeply informed my practice but also profoundly influenced the understandings and practices of dealing with grieving prisoners within the prison service. My research aimed to formally record and explore the lived experience of bereavement in prison with a view to sharing this with others in the hope of improving bereavement care within the prisoner population. It did this through telling the stories of former imprisoned clients whose experience of bereavement was shared with me within our counselling work together. As such, this was a qualitative practitioner research study rooted in counselling practice. It might be assumed that a quantitative research study, with its emphasis on numbers and statistics, reliability and validity, might have been more in keeping with the world of locks, bars, and disciplined routine that is prison. However, this chapter demonstrates how the power of storied lives, as lived, spoke to the Scottish Prison Service in a meaningful and enabling way.

Existing literature demonstrates that prisoners suffer dramatic loss as a direct result of incarceration (Stevenson and McCutchen, 2006). Additionally, many inmates have also suffered severe loss prior to imprisonment (Hammersley and Ayling, 2006). The Scottish prisoner population, for example, is characterised by social deprivation and exclusion with high levels of mental ill health, substance use, and childhood abuse (Houchin, 2005). It is against the backdrop of such legacies of loss that a prisoner's experience of bereavement, in response to the death of someone significant, is lived.

According to Rosenblatt (2008, p. 208), 'culture creates, influences, shapes, limits, and defines grieving, sometimes profoundly'. Significantly, grief can be influenced by the imposition of the immediate sociocultural environment and its prescriptive norms to the extent it is 'disenfranchised' (Doka, 1989). It is the experience of disenfranchised grief on which I focus in this chapter (also see Masterton, 2014a).

Disenfranchised Grief

Disenfranchised grief is defined as 'the grief that persons experience when they incur a loss that is not or cannot be openly acknowledged, publicly mourned, or socially supported' (Doka 1989, p. 4). Grief can be disenfranchised with regard to unrecognised relationships (e.g. extramarital affair); unrecognised losses (e.g. abortion); and unrecognised grievers (e.g. young children and very old persons) (Doka, 1989). Circumstances surrounding the death (e.g. AIDS-related death) and the ways in which individuals grieve (e.g. wailing where stoicism is expected) can also disenfranchise grief (Doka, 2002). Disenfranchised grief is recognised as a risk factor in bereavement (Parkes, 2002). Whilst it tends to exacerbate grief, it leaves people to grieve alone (Doka, 1989). Where bereaved persons perceive themselves to be without support, a complicated bereavement can be expected (Rando, 1993).

Many years' experience of working as a counsellor practitioner with bereaved male inmates of a Scottish prison has given me extensive and intimate inside knowledge about an aspect of human experience that is typically suffered in silence and laden with the risk of a complicated bereavement. This chapter aims to demonstrate how I built on existing knowledge about disenfranchised grief in prison by drawing on my counselling work with bereaved prisoners and focusing on the bereavement experience as lived and described by one of my clients in his own words. It also demonstrates how new insights brought about a force for change in bereavement care for the Scottish prisoner population through more informed practices.

I chose a qualitative case-based approach to explore the experience of bereavement in prison, since this research strategy has the ability to shed maximum light on human experience, as lived, within its real-life context (Edwards, 1998; Schneider, 1999). My evidence consisted of records from a set of individual case studies relating to a small group of eight bereaved imprisoned clients who had completed their counselling work with me. Any one of these clients would have demonstrated the trauma and anguish experienced by bereaved prisoners; for reasons of space, in this chapter I have selected just one.

Disenfranchised Grief and Craig's Story

My 22-year-old client, Craig, was 10 when his mum died on the operating table whilst receiving surgery for cancer. Shortly afterwards, Craig's dad, Archie, turned to drink and subjected Craig and his 8-year-old brother, Robbie, to severe emotional and physical abuse and neglect for 18 months until the boys were taken into care, never to see their father again. Archie was killed at work two years later, after falling off a high roof under the influence of alcohol.

During their three-year stay in care, Craig and Robbie suffered horrific emotional and physical abuse at the hands of two care workers. Robbie was also frequently sexually abused by these men, the witnessing of which Craig was forced to endure. In an attempt to escape the horrendous pain of their lived realities, the brothers began to smoke cigarettes and sniff lighter-gas and glue before going on to drink alcohol and then smoke cannabis.

When Craig was 15, he and Robbie were placed in foster care. Craig stopped using substances but started stealing and then drug dealing in order to fund his brother's continuing drug use, which escalated into a heroin addiction after their foster mum was diagnosed with advanced bowel cancer.

It was Craig's drug dealing that eventually led to his three-year prison sentence, which began on a Tuesday. On the following Sunday, 19-year-old Robbie hanged himself in the flat the two brothers had shared for nearly three years.

Ten months after Robbie's suicide, Craig referred himself to Cruse Bereavement Care Scotland for bereavement counselling, on the advice of one of the prison's addiction workers. Craig and I worked together for 36 sessions. What follows is part of his story, which highlights recurrent themes relating to the experience of becoming bereaved in prison. All verbatim data presented were transcribed from audio-taped counselling sessions.

Craig was shocked beyond belief to learn of Robbie's suicide from the prison officer in charge of the admission hall, a response commonly experienced by prisoners (Ferszt, 2002) whose bereavements are often due to sudden, unexpected, and traumatic deaths (Finlay and Jones, 2000; Vaswani, 2008).

> I just couldn't believe what the screw [prison officer] was telling me.... My baby brother dead ... hanged himself.... I thought, no, this can't be right ... this can't be happening to me. (session 10)

Craig was desperate to find out exactly what had happened, to make sure that Robbie was indeed dead, and to be with his much-loved maternal grandmother who was his only known living relative.

> My head was all mixed up with questions.... I was bursting to see my granny ... and I needed to see Robbie with my own eyes. (session 10)

Clearly, Craig was in need of family support, which could help considerably towards reducing the impact of sudden loss (Reed, 1998). He also needed to view Robbie's dead body, a practice that can help to make real the fact of death (Worden, 2010), particularly with sudden, unexpected loss (Hodgkinson, 1995). A brief private phone call to the grandmother was all that was allowed.

Craig felt enormously guilty about Robbie's death.

> I started thinking right away that I was to blame for Robbie dying ... that if I hadn't got the jail it would never have happened.... The guilt just got bigger and bigger.... I felt absolutely totally ashamed of myself. (session 12)

Guilt, which is a common manifestation of grief (Worden, 2010), can be exacerbated where there has been a suicide (Wertheimer, 2001). It is referred to consistently as a component of prisoners' grief (e.g. Finlay and Jones, 2000) and can be intense when the death is perceived as a consequence of imprisonment (Potter, 1999). Further, it can be intensified by disenfranchising circumstances such as a stigmatised death like suicide (Doka, 2002).

Arguably, Craig's loss of his brother had the potential to render him acutely vulnerable at a time when, as a newcomer to prison, he had more than enough to cope with in terms of loss and change. Notably, of the 81 completed suicides in Scottish penal establishments between 1995 and 2000, the majority (68 per cent) occurred within the first month of custody, with risk being greatest during the first week (Power et al., 2003).

On admission to prison, which is a 'total' institution, that is a powerful 24-hours-a-day, day-in–day-out socialising machine, Craig experienced a 'mortification of the self' (Goffman, 1961):

> I had enough on my plate without my baby brother dying.... It's hard in the beginning ... when you're not jail-wise.... You pretend you're okay ... but you're wary ... and scared.... It's a different world.... You've lost just about everything....You're grieving for the life you had outside.... It cuts the soul out of you....You're not Craig any more.... You're a prison number....You wear jail clothes....You don't have your own bits and pieces.... I was only five days into my sentence when I got told Robbie had taken his life.... It cut the soul right out of me.... It was like I was dying inside ... like I was the dead one. (session 10)

Stripped of much that defined his former identity, and separated from roles in which he had previously felt affirmed, Craig lost his soul. Robbie's death intensified this loss and left Craig feeling mortally wounded. From that first dreadful Sunday in prison to the next, Craig's shock and disbelief continued. 'Nothing felt like real any more'. He felt 'so lost... absolutely totally lonely...and empty' (session 10).

It was intensely alienating for Craig to be so isolated from his grandmother at this time and cut off from funeral rituals, which provide an opportunity to confirm the reality of loss within a context of support (Rando, 1984). He had to wait until the Friday before receiving confirmation that he had permission to be present at Robbie's burial for half an hour. This was to take place on the following Monday after a funeral service in the church that Craig was not permitted to attend, much to his chagrin. 'I was gutted at not getting to the church.... I wanted to be there for Robbie...sing for him and everything' (session 12).

Craig felt tortured during the time before the funeral. His daily phone calls to his grandmother were 'like medicine, a wee dose of life juice' during this period of his mourning (session 10). However, he felt extremely guilty about not being at home to lend her support, a point referred to in the literature (Potter, 1999), and so deeply ashamed to be imprisoned. He convinced himself that his imprisonment was the reason for Robbie's suicide. He even refused to let his grandmother visit him, when the suggestion of a private visit was raised by prison staff.

I didn't want my granny anywhere near this poxy place.... I was ashamed enough ... without her seeing me here ... in amongst all the other cons [inmates]. (session 10)

As if the days of that 'absolute purest black week' weren't bad enough for Craig, the nights were 'a million times worse' (session 10). Tired and worn out as he was, he could not sleep. There was simply no escape from the darkest darkness that had become his waking life. Lying on his bunk, staring into the night's void, Craig hungered for death.

It was very, very black thoughts that were in my head ... going round and round ... absolutely all night long....All I wanted was to be away ... to be dead ... and be beside my baby brother ... and my mum. (session 10)

Craig was escorted to Robbie's burial by three male prison officers who were not known to him, handcuffed from the time he left prison until he was returned. The burial was heart-wrenchingly painful for Craig. 'I felt gutted ... absolutely totally broken hearted'. His guilt and shame about Robbie's death, coupled with the embarrassment and shame he felt through being there in handcuffs ('there's no dignity with that.... You feel a disgrace ... a total embarrassment'), caused him to feel undeserving of the supportive presence of those around him. 'I didn't deserve any sympathy.... Everything was all my fault' (session 12).

After returning to prison, Craig felt increasingly distressed. 'I was getting totally mangled with it all.... The hurting was squeezing the life out of me' (session 12). Lying awake in the dark that night, his heart and soul wrung with pain, Craig's distress reached fever pitch.

It got desperate....I was bursting to greet [cry] ... really bawl my eyes out and let it all out ... but you can't do nothing like that in a place like this....You'd be labelled a weakling ... a pathetic wimp ... or a psycho....And once that happens, you're done for ....The cons prey on any weaknesses like that....And if the staff think you're losing it and going mad ... they take over and put you on special watch....You can end up in a suicide cell for 23 hours a day ... with a mattress and blanket for company ... nothing else ... and you wear a goonie [hospital gown].... You're not the boss of yourself in a situation like that....You're helpless ... and if the mental teams say you need medicated ... you can end up feeling totally powerless.... Being on watch is torture.... Everybody says it's enough to push you right over the edge. (session 12)

Craig had a huge need to give expression to his emotional distress. The prison culture, which is not conducive towards such behaviour (De Viggiani, 2006; Ferszt, 2002; Harner, Hentz, and Evangelista, 2011; Schetky, 1998), prevented him from doing so. Craig feared being seen as a 'weakling' and exploited by fellow inmates on account of his vulnerability. He also feared being perceived as 'mad' and placed in an anti-ligature cell on a system of observation and care that he regarded as punitive and controlling rather than supportive; a response highlighted in the study of Harner, Hentz, and Evangelista (2011).

Fearful of what might happen should he cry, Craig reached for his pen and, with the sharp edge of its broken-off clip, tore lines into his left arm, causing tears of blood to flow.

> I'd never done anything like that before.... It was my way of dealing with the really bad feelings inside me.... I couldn't handle them any more....The pain of cutting myself was better than the absolute total purest agony inside me.... It took the lid off everything for a while ... got me through that night in one piece.... Nobody found out.... I used my socks as bandages. (session 16)

Craig's need to harm himself physically was not unusual. In their research, Roth and Presse (2003) have shown that when confronted with intense emotional pain prisoners may self-harm in order to relieve the unbearable intensity of their suffering. It is as if the physical pain becomes a bearable substitute for that which cannot be borne emotionally.

Within a few weeks of Robbie's funeral, Craig turned to illicit drugs given to him by his heroin-addicted cellmate in order to escape from his relentless and merciless crushing grief.

> I never wanted to be a smackhead [heroin addict] ... but I was desperate for something ... that would blank out some of the shit that kept on coming at me ... all the time....There was no mercy to it.... It felt like I was being squashed to death ... by a ton of grief. (session 4)

Craig's grief was given particular weight by mounting feelings of anger. Anger is commonly experienced in response to loss (Worden, 2010) and is cited as a major component of prisoners' grief (Finlay and Jones, 2000). As Doka (2002) notes, anger can be intensified by disenfranchising circumstances, of which imprisonment is an example. Craig lived in constant fear of giving expression to this experience due to the threat of disciplinary action. The thought of being sent to the segregation unit – 'that place scrambles your brain with loneliness' – acted as a strong motivator for Craig to hide his rage. Whenever his 'purest raging anger about 12 long shit years of nothing but death and total fucking misery' threatened to overwhelm, Craig cut his arms 'at night ... in secret' in order to 'deal with the absolute total nightmare agony inside' (session 19).

What made Craig's grief even heavier to bear was that he felt completely alone with it. Although he sorely needed to have a 'right big heart-to-heart with somebody sound' (session 10), he found this impossible to do within the prison milieu for fear of breaking down and crying. He became overwhelmed by a grief he felt forced to confine behind the bars of his own inner prison. As the first anniversary of Robbie's death loomed on the horizon, he decided to seek bereavement counselling in order to liberate this secret sorrow.

> I want to grieve for Robbie ... talk about him and remember everything about him ... feel what I need to feel ... without having to blank out the bad stuff with drugs. (session 3)

For Craig, the experience of counselling was 'like coming in from the cold' (session 10) and 'like getting a hug with big strong arms you can absolutely totally trust' (session 12). In session 22 he explained to me: 'If it wasn't for you and the absolute strong and purest caring way you do your counselling job with us boys in here, I'd probably be dead by now'. During session 22, Craig pondered out loud:

> The way I see things ... counselling puts the soul back into you ... and it gives you a dose of self-respect....And it's getting my soul back that's helped me stay away from the drugs ... and it's helping me get my head round all the sadness and everybody dying on me and all the shit ... all the bad stuff that was piled up inside me.

The story of Craig depicts the lived experience of bereavement in prison as a deeply distressing and despairing one. It portrays how the powerful sociocultural prescriptions of the prison environment can limit the grief of prisoners from being openly acknowledged, publicly mourned, or socially supported to the extent it is profoundly 'disenfranchised' (Doka, 1989).

Separated from kith and kin and excluded from important healing rituals, prisoners can experience themselves as being completely alone with their grief. Isolated behind bars, there is simply no real context of community and support within which their experience of mourning can be. Notably, sadness cannot be, due to the fear of being perceived as weak; anger cannot be, due to the fear of disciplinary action; distress, in general, cannot be, due to the fear of being seen as mentally ill and at risk of suicide. Unable to be the truth of their experience, prisoners are unable to confront the reality of their loss and to process and integrate their grief. It remains a confined encounter; a secret sorrow. Significantly, this secret sorrow is experienced against the backdrop of lives that have often been swamped by loss and trauma from an early age. It is also experienced in the light of the relentless and enduring living loss that is incarceration. As with Craig, prisoners can make a bid to escape their prison of grief through the use of illegal drugs and by way of self-harming. All said, disenfranchised grief has the power to impact hugely negatively on the coping ability of prisoners doing time. It also has the potential to complicate their process of transition back into the community following liberation from prison.

Making a Difference

On the basis of my research, it was clear to me that a contextually informed, sensitive understanding of the experience of loss, as it is lived by prisoners, could enable prison staff to develop support systems capable of ensuring a level of care more attuned to the immediate needs of bereaved inmates. I therefore began to share the findings of my study with members of staff from my local prison – from the governor, who makes provision for care, to various staff groups, who are involved in the delivery of care – with a view to raising awareness of this secret sorrow and the harm it can cause to prisoners. My continuing dialogue with the prison staff about the harm unacknowledged grief can do has enabled them to appreciate that bereaved prisoners can conceal their distress for fear that staff will see them as mentally ill, at risk of suicide, and in need of being isolated within an anti-ligature cell or disciplinary segregation. When these insights are communicated by prison staff to grieving inmates, bereaved prisoners can immediately feel more recognised in their experience. Understanding how despairing prisoners can feel in the early days after learning of a death, especially on returning to prison post-funeral, has encouraged residential, chaplaincy, and other staff to be more available to inmates at such critical points. This type of contact can help to make prisoners aware of the full range of support services available, including that of Cruse Bereavement Care Scotland. Being admitted to prison shortly after becoming bereaved was highlighted in one of my case studies as a particularly distressing and threatening experience (also see Masterton, 2014b). This insight prompted healthcare staff to consider enquiring about any recent losses when interviewing prisoners as part of the reception process.

Simple, practical initiatives such as these can immediately make a difference. They are examples of how doing a little can help a lot to validate and support prisoners at crucial points in their bereavement process. They also demonstrate how a small qualitative case study undertaken by a practitioner researcher brought about a significant change in bereavement care for imprisoned persons through more informed practices.

The power of Craig's storied life, along with the stories of the others in my research, spoke to the heart of the Scottish Prison Service, which recognised that if practices were improved across all prisons in Scotland, many of the difficulties the staff encountered with bereaved prisoners could be reduced. Since I completed my study, the Scottish Prison Service has worked with the evidence and recommendations I made available in a variety of ways. For example, at the time of writing, the Service is working in partnership with Cruse Bereavement Care Scotland to replicate in other Scottish prisons the counselling service I set up in my local prison. These developments provide powerful evidence of the potential influence of qualitative case-study research that remains close to lived experience.

References

De Viggiani, N. (2006) 'Surviving prison: Exploring prison social life as a determinant of health', *International Journal of Prisoner Health*, 2 (2). 71–89.

Doka, K. (ed.) (1989) *Disenfranchised Grief: Recognizing Hidden Sorrow* (Lexington, MA: Lexington Books).

Doka, K. (ed.) (2002) *Disenfranchised Grief: New Directions, Challenges and Strategies for Practice* (Champaign, IL: Research Press).

Edwards, D. (1998) 'Types of case study work: A conceptual framework for case-based research', *Journal of Humanistic Psychology*, 38 (3), 36–70.

Ferszt, G. (2002) 'Grief experiences of women in prison following the death of a loved one', *Illness, Crisis and Loss*, 10 (3), 242–254.

Finlay, I., and Jones, N. (2000) 'Unresolved grief in young offenders in prison', *British Journal of General Practice*, 50 (456), 569–570.

Goffman, E. (1961) *Asylums: Essays on the Social Situation of Mental Patients and Other Inmates* (Garden City, NY: Anchor Books).

Hammersley, P., and Ayling, D. (2006) 'Loss intervention project for adult male prisoners – a project in progress', *Prison Service Journal*, 166, 22–25.

Harner, H., Hentz, P., and Evangelista, M. (2011) 'Grief interrupted: The experience of loss among incarcerated women', *Qualitative Health Research*, 21 (4): 454–464.

Hodgkinson, P. (1995) 'Viewing the bodies after disaster: Does it help?' *Bereavement Care*, 14 (1), 2–4.

Houchin, R. (2005) *Social Exclusion and Imprisonment in Scotland: A Report* (Glasgow: Glasgow Caledonian University).

Masterton, J. (2014a) 'A confined encounter: The lived experience of bereavement in prison', *Bereavement Care*, 33 (2), 52–62.

Masterton, J. (2014b) 'Bereavement counselling in Edinburgh Prison', *Counselling in Scotland*, Winter/Spring, 4–6.

McLeod, J. (2001) 'Developing a research tradition consistent with the practices and values of counselling and psychotherapy: Why counselling and psychotherapy research is necessary', *Counselling and Psychotherapy Research*, 1 (1), 3–11.

Parkes, C. (2002) 'Grief: Lessons from the past, visions for the future', *Death Studies*, 26, 367–385.

Potter, M. (1999) '"Inside" grief: Bereavement in a prison environment', *Bereavement Care*, 18 (2), 22–25.

Power, K., Swanson, V., Luke, R., Jackson, C., and Biggam, F. (2003) 'Act and care: Evaluation of the revised SPS suicide risk management strategy', Scottish Prison Service Occasional Paper Series 01/2003.

Rando, T. (1984) *Grief, Dying and Death: Clinical Interventions for Caregivers* (Champaign, IL: Research Press).

Rando, T. (1993) *Treatment of Complicated Mourning* (Champaign, IL: Research Press).

Reed, M. (1998) 'Predicting grief symptomatology among the suddenly bereaved', *Suicide and Life-Threatening Behavior*, 28 (3), 285–300.

Rogers, C. (1961) *On Becoming a Person: A Therapist's View of Psychotherapy* (London: Constable).

Rosenblatt, P. (2008) 'Grief across cultures: A review and research agenda' in M. Stroebe, R. Hansson, H. Schut, and W. Stroebe (eds) *Handbook of Bereavement Research and Practice: Advances in Theory and Intervention* (Washington, DC: American Psychological Association) pp. 207–222.

Roth, B., and Presse, L. (2003) 'Nursing interventions for parasuicidal behaviors in female offenders', *Journal of Psychosocial Nursing and Mental Health Services*, 41 (9), 20–29.

Schetky, D. (1998) 'Mourning in prison: Mission impossible?' *Journal of the American Academy of Psychiatry and the Law*, 26 (3), 383–391.

Schneider, K. (1999) 'Multiple-case depth research: Bringing experience-near closer', *Journal of Clinical Psychology*, 55 (12), 1531–1540.

Stevenson, R., and McCutchen, R. (2006) 'When meaning has lost its way: Life and loss "behind bars"', *Illness, Crisis and Loss*, 14 (2), 103–119.

Vaswani, N. (2008) 'Persistent offender profile: "Focus on bereavement"', Briefing Paper 13, Criminal Justice Social Work Development Service for Scotland.

Wertheimer, A. (2001) *A Special Scar: The Experiences of People Bereaved by Suicide*, (Bristol: Taylor and Francis).

Worden, W. (2010) *Grief Counselling and Grief Therapy: A Handbook for the Mental Health Practitioner*, 4th edn (Hove: Routledge).

10 'Reading the Wound': Using Stories to Open Up the Nature of Trauma

LINDA TALBERT

Introduction

That trauma tales should span the vast stretches of time that distance the ancient world from the modern comes as no surprise. Trauma takes little notice of time zones or historical eras and has long been the subject of song and story. 'Human beings are storytellers by nature ... the story appears in every known culture' (McAdams, 1993, 26). To paraphrase one of the more renowned of these storytellers, it is a truth universally acknowledged that a person in possession of a good story must be in search of an audience. Whether it is a rather plain governess addressing her 'dear reader', a child returning from a trip to the circus, an astro-physicist propounding his newest theory, or the Brothers Grimm setting off on 'once upon a time', all storytellers are seeking to be heard by someone. They are looking, Frank (1995, 335) says, 'to find others who will answer their story's call for relationship'. This is especially true of the two 'wounded storytellers', ancient and modern, whose voices are heard here and with whom I collaborate in this research story.

In a matter of a few sentences you may have noticed how effortlessly we have already entered into a storytelling relationship, and we are not alone. Besides myself as researcher and my two research subjects, I have also summoned a whole host of other characters whom you may know, love, or heartily dislike: Elizabeth Bennet, Jane Eyre, your favour-ite nephew, Stephen Hawking, giants and dragons, and who knows what else. That chorus of voices and the dialogues they spark in our heads are also part of the nature of storytelling. The creation of story takes place in an inter-subjective space where many things may happen, almost anyone or anything can enter, and where the tale takes on a co-constructive, collaborative mind of its own (Bruner, 1990; Frank, 1995; Polkinghorne, 2004; White, 2004; Etherington, 2009; Crossley, 2000; Speedy, 2008; Hermans, 1999). As you can see from the preceding bracketed list of names, we have also already begun to draw upon the many other research voices who join this dialogue and contribute to the story that I am proposing we now begin.

The impetus for this research story is rooted in my clinical experience as a counsellor. Listening to the stories of my clients is the milieu in which I have formed understandings of the impact of trauma on them and on me. I have been a witness to these stories, a hearer of them in a private, confidential space, where I was trusted to help put the tellers' terrors and triumphs into words. Because I have been trusted in this way, I consider the content of these stories privileged, sacred, and securely held behind a closed door. My clients and their stories *will not* enter this research space, but my experience of them, at least that part of the experience that is strictly and ethically speaking my own, *will.*

To give voice and voices to this lived experience of hearing trauma tales in the counselling setting, I have invited two literary characters to join me in a conversation, an embodied dialogical exchange between persons. My two research collaborators are the proverbial, persevering Job from the pages of the Bible (TM, 2002; TNIV, 2005) and Mack, a modern 'Everyman' from a novel called *The Shack* (Young, 2007). Though they are divided from each other across a gulf of time and culture, there are striking similarities in their stories. They are two middle-aged, successful businessmen, devoted to their large families, worshippers of a Judeo-Christian God, deep thinkers, and solid citizens, who are, 'one day', struck, knocked over, and crushed by the entry of trauma.

The *DSM IV* labels trauma as arising from 'direct personal experience ... witnessing ... or learning about unexpected or violent death, serious harm or threat of death ... to a family member or close associate' (Frances, Pincus, and First, 1994, p. 424). Stolorow (2007, p. 10) offers a more poignant metaphor for the experience of trauma as a state 'in which severe emotional pain cannot find a relational home in which it can be held'. In 'one day' Job is the victim of two natural disasters, lightning strike and violent wind, which claim the lives of all ten of his children. His modern counterpart, Mack, endures the abduction and murder of his beloved six-year-old daughter by a serial killer and paedophile. Both men's stories fit the *DSM IV* definition of trauma events, and the men themselves more than qualify for the unwanted and unsought designation of 'trauma victim'. Both stories also bear witness to the kinds of severe emotional pain that cry out for containment in a relational home.

A counsellor hearing such stories is several degrees removed and shielded by the professional boundaries of the counselling setting, its supportive resources, and her distance from the actual trauma event. She cannot be classified as a victim of her client's trauma. However, in the appropriate therapeutic mutual intimacy of the counselling relationship she does witness, learn about, and directly experience her client's responses and, sometimes, re-enactments of the original traumatic event. This can lead to the kind of parallel phenomenon that Pearlman and Saakvitne (1995) have described as 'vicarious traumatisation'. In a different way and quite apart from her client's story, the counsellor, too, needs to find a reflective space and a 'relational home' in which the powerful impacts of traumatic material can be held, understood, and stored appropriately.

'To derive personal meaning from a bad event', McAdams (1993) argues, it is necessary to construct a story. Human beings yearn 'to make sense of subjective experience through narrative rather than empirical fact' (McAdams, 1993, p. 49). By using these two men, their trauma tales, and the dialogue between us, this chapter focuses on the ways in which narrative functions as a container and meaning maker for trauma survivors and their counsellors, who together try to find their way through the dark labyrinths of disorientation and devastation that often characterise trauma.

Reading and engaging with fictional literature offers a 'painted' but still transparent window into the way real human beings deal with appalling and tragic circumstances in their lives (Frank, 2007). Hartman (1995, p. 537), a literary theorist, argues that a disciplined exploration of literature or indeed other forms of artistic expression can help us to 'read the wound' that trauma embodies.

'Reading the wound' in this way has the potential to provide an alternative form of reflective practice by offering rich sources of trauma material and narrative without the ethical issues of client confidentiality or the impact of the charged nature of these stories on the therapist herself. Literature offers a detached distance from which to view some of the realities that must be faced in doing this kind of work. 'Reading the wound' makes available a safe, replenishing, reflective space for counsellors to think about, symbolise, and construct meaning for their work. Such texts provide a particular kind of containment and support for practitioners, particularly those working with trauma.

Taking my lead from a fundamental tenet of the humanistic approach, I situate myself, reflexively, in this research conversation in an authentically empathic 'as if' position (Rogers, 1967). I enter these literary creations and engage with their main characters, Job and Mack, 'as if' I were hearing their accounts first hand and face to face, allowing their stories to impact me as a listening reader, collaborating and constructing with them a research narrative about trauma that includes all our voices. Both of the texts I am using here, *Job* (TNIV; TM) and *The Shack* (Young, 2007), contain narratives that are dialogical in format. Within their literary frameworks, both Job and Mack voice frequent, first-person, descriptive observations about their experience of trauma. In order to evoke some of the authenticity of their voices and the creative dynamism of the juxtaposition of ancient and modern, I quote directly and frequently from what they say about their experience and weave these excerpted fragments of speech into the conversations I construct with them. These conversations range across four main topics relevant to trauma work: the impact of visceral content, the importance of empathic witness, the intensity of affect, and the resultant challenges to existential understandings of self in the world. Each dialogue (printed in italics) is followed by a commentary reflecting on insights for praxis.

Embodied Experience

Linda: *One of my real interests in your stories is how containment works. As a counsellor, I have felt what it's like to be in on the construction of these stories. Creating the narrative, the flow of finding words and making sense is so often interrupted by fragmented trauma material – highly charged shards of feelings, thoughts, and sensations that, while fiercely attached to and essential to the narrative, resist containment in it.*

There can even be a kind of pseudo-corporeality to these intrusions. Both your stories contain examples of these sudden, alarming interruptions. I wonder if you could say a bit about what that was like for you.

Mack: *I guess the first thing that strikes me in what you've said is how little I was aware of the impact of my stuff, my trauma 'material' as you call it, on myself and others. I didn't think I needed any other container than my own head. For the longest time I thought I was keeping it inside my own head, and that's what I thought I was supposed to do, you know, the 'dumb manly thing' and all that (Young, 2007, p. 22).*

When I finally made that journey to the shack where my daughter was killed, it was as if I couldn't keep the stuff under wraps any more (74). 'Flashes of visual memory' and a kind of 'stabbing blistering fury' seemed to assault me 'in waves' and I actually did taste 'bile and blood in my mouth' (74). They were as much in my body as in my mind's eye, if that makes any sense. When I finally got in sight of the shack, 'I retched so strongly it brought me to my knees' (75). I guess I came to a point where I literally couldn't 'digest' that stuff anymore, and it had to come out.

Job: *Yes, that is something of what it was like for me too. Dread and fear are so hard to stomach. 'Sighing' was the 'only food' I could eat, and my groans seemed to gush out like 'vomit' (TNIV, 3.24; TM, 3.24). The terrors do seem to invade your body as well as your head. It's so easy to get caught up, swept away by the memories of what has happened, they can dominate and fill the horizon so completely, it's difficult to see or think about anything else.*

Sometimes 'my terrors' seemed to 'overtake me like a flood'. I can hear the terrifying roar of the 'tempest', and it literally 'snatches me away in the night'. That moan of the cruel 'east wind' and the image of it striking my son's house, all that dust and chaos and collapse, the sight and sound 'sweeps me out of my place' (TM, 27.20–22). There is only 'turmoil' (TNIV, 3.26), 'frightening dreams by night' and 'terrifying visions' by day (TNIV, 7.14).

Mack: *Yes, I know those moments when the waking dreams are just as terrible as the sleeping ones. I kept having the same nightmare where I'm 'stuck in cloying mud' and I can just glimpse my little Missy 'running down the wooded path ahead' of me and she has no idea of the danger she's in. 'I frantically try to scream warnings to her' but 'no sound' emerges, and I'm 'always too late and too impotent to save her'. I wake 'bolt upright in bed', 'sweat dripping' everywhere. Then 'waves of nausea and regret and guilt roll over me like some surreal tidal flood' (25).*

Linda: *It seems for both of you, the emergence of these images, sensations, thoughts, and feelings, whether in flashbacks or nightmares or other embodied experiences, threaten your capacity to contain, 'digest', make sense of, and move through what has happened to you. They cloud your field of view as they storm into your bodies. Listening to you, I'm also aware of how powerful these charged bits of the story are for me and the ways in which I am impacted by them, swept out of my place by them, and feel some of the relentless assault and impotent helplessness that they can trail in their wake.*

Trauma is an embodied experience. The indistinguishable intermingling of body, sensation, and mind in trauma experience is well attested. Even across an immense cultural, social, and temporal divide, Job's and Mack's stories share similar evidences and manifestations of the visceral impact of trauma. Some are evident in the dialogues above. Elsewhere in his story Job speaks of the 'weight' (TNIV, 6.2) of his anguish, and he frequently uses metaphors of the body to describe the ways in which his suffering has penetrated his being (TNIV, 16.8,13).

Both protagonists' accounts (in the excerpted fragments above and in their trauma tales) reflect the immediacy, intrusiveness, and toxicity of these disconnected lightning flashes of pain and memory. Herman (1992, p. 177) suggests 'A narrative that does not include the traumatic imagery and bodily sensations is barren and incomplete. The ultimate goal ... is to put the story, including its imagery, into words'. Pearlman and Saakvitne (1995) point to the equally powerful impact of dissociated material and sensorimotor experience on the counsellor working with trauma stories.

There is a particular kind of contagion attached to these bits of re-enacted trauma experience, which requires vigilance and a careful weighing up of the therapist's responses. Otherwise the therapist can be 'pulled across boundaries' she doesn't want to cross into the 'liminal spaces' that Frank (2008, p. 122) says constitute the danger zone in listening to the tales of 'wounded storytellers'. In these spaces of heightened tension, powerful affect, and penetrating embodiment, it is easy to be both overwhelmed and outwitted (Pearlman and Saakvitne, 1995).

In the introduction to *The Shack*, the narrator's account of Mack's early family history includes a description of the brutal beating he once received from his drunken father. Even though this episode is a literary creation in a populist work of 'fiction', its plausibility still evoked traces of an embodied response in me, as a reader, coming across it for the first time. It also took me, immediately, to painfully real parallels with one of my clients.

As I read this literary depiction of an incident of torture, I was *struck* on several levels. First, bodily, which I experienced as an inward recoil, as if evading a blow, then the sound of a camera shutter flashing and the flickering cinematic image of a shivering and vulnerable 13-year-old boy tied to a tree. This was followed by, or perhaps simultaneously shot through with, a potent mix of feelings: disgust, horror, sorrow, anger at the perpetrator, and shame over the possible voyeurism implicated in contemplating (even for a brief moment) such a scene.

Eventually these responses were transformed into thought, and this graphic scene from Mack's past became a significant biographical detail, important in understanding his attachment history. For me as an engaged reader of his story, the sequence was first embodied, then imaginal and sensory, then affective, and finally cognitive. I am not suggesting that this is a normative sequencing of response, for me or any other counsellor, when hearing this kind of account. However, it does illustrate the role of literary texts in simulating and surfacing these kinds of responses. An engaged literary reading can provide opportunities for gaining awareness of what is evoked and how it is experienced. It can sharpen skills for acknowledging, monitoring, and using this information for the benefit of clients, thus offering a contained reflective space.

Part of becoming an adequate container is learning to 'digest' and therapeutically empathise with highly visceral material; unwittingly entertaining responses that mirror the client's state too closely, or worse, can be punitive or dismissing of his or her lived experience. Ignoring or underestimating the potency of this form of denial risks a damaging re-enactment of the original trauma in the therapy space. Embodying, sensing, imagining, feeling, and reflecting, while at the same time maintaining the capacity to observe and think about what is happening, are qualities of presence essential to trauma work. For a practitioner to embody such qualities calls for continuous development and practice (Garland, 2004). Engaging with literary accounts of trauma can surface and supplement this development of awareness and highlight the important synergies between the effective management of embodied sensation and the offering of empathic presence.

Empathic Engagement

Linda: *What seems more clear now is that containment takes place when the fractures caused by trauma are storied more coherently but that this can't happen without an empathic witness who can be trusted to hear your story without reacting in ways that replicate the original trauma.*

I know from my own experience with trauma clients that often the first story that needs to be told and processed is a story of these painful additional woundings, a form of 'friendly fire' I suppose you could call it, that takes place when the person you choose to tell your story to isn't trustworthy or just can't hear it in the way you need to tell it.

Job: *Indeed, that is a truly deep form of anguish. For me there was a moment when my Comforters would no longer even 'look me in the eye' (TNIV, 6.28).*

Like 'intermittent streams' they might gush at the spring thaw, but in the 'dry season' they 'cease to flow' (TNIV, 6.17). They kept trying to 'correct what I said', in fact I counted 'ten times' they 'reproached me' and 'shamelessly attacked' even the most intimate things I said about myself (TNIV, 19.3). Finally I had to speak out in the 'anguish of my spirit' to let them know (TNIV, 12.3) that their 'maxims were proverbs of ashes' and their 'defenses were defenses of clay' (TNIV, 13.12).

Mack: I wanted to cheer when I read that part of your story. Especially when you said, 'You are miserable comforters all of you' (TNIV, 16.2). Those guys deserved to be sent packing. Some people 'only want to hear what they are used to hearing' (Young, 2007, p. 9).

Job: Yes… it was a more painful reality than they were able to digest. I remember saying at the time, 'My spirit is broken … my plans are shattered … who can see any hope for me?' (TNIV, 17.1, 11, 15). Eventually, I gave up expecting any understanding or help from my 'Comforters'. I knew I needed to address my pain to a different audience.

Mack: I guess until I heard your story I didn't realise how fortunate I was in the friend I chose to help me write my story down. It wasn't easy though. It took me two years before I could even start talking to him about it. Even then it was 'difficult for me to look him in the eye' (Young, 2007, p. 12).

Job's and Mack's need for a trustworthy, empathic listener is undeniable. Both stories have much to say about how trauma victims approach or find access to an empathic witness. For the trauma sufferer, 'Recovery can take place only within the context of relationships; it cannot occur in isolation' (Herman, 1992, p. 133). In order to construct narratives of the self after trauma, 'we need not only the words with which to tell our stories but also an audience able and willing to hear us and to understand our words as we intend them' (Brison, 1997, p. 21). Both Mack's and Job's stories reflect this critical symbiosis between the need to find words to construct a narrative and the cry for a witness, to connect empathically with a real person. What is 'inside' the psyche of the trauma sufferer needs words and language to symbolise and shape it but also a flesh and blood 'other', a 'Thou' in Buber's (1937) terms, to witness and welcome it.

Rejected by the 'Comforters' and bitterly alienated from his wife and community, Job struggles with the seeming incoherence of his 'impetuous words' and longs for the 'weight' of his anguish to 'be placed on the scales' (TNIV, 6.2). His plaintive, deeply relational cry to the Comforters,

'Have pity on me, my friends, have pity' (TNIV, 19.21), is followed almost immediately by his equally agonised call for a containing narrative, 'Oh, that my words were recorded, that they were written on a scroll, that they were inscribed with an iron tool on lead or engraved in rock forever!' (TNIV, 19.23, 24). As the story progresses, his voice becomes more and more insistent that his pain be heard by someone who can actually contain the enormity of his suffering. Levy (2004, p. 53) assesses this kind of 'validation of a survivor's experience [as] probably the most containing therapeutic gesture a therapist can make' to a client. My reading of Job's and Mack's stories and the conversation above highlighted for me again just how essential the establishment of a trustworthy relational container is – and that trauma sufferers come with very different and often very damaged capacities for this.

Emotional Expression

Linda: *As I read your stories and interact with you more, I'm impressed by the sheer range of emotions, and intensity of affects that surface, activate, and accompany your journeys. I wonder if you could say a little bit about these and maybe how they affected your significant relationships.*

Mack: *Phew, that's a tall order. I'm not even sure where to start. I guess it's no accident my narrative sort of begins in the midst of an ice storm. I didn't realize it at the time, but I was living in a 'frozen world', numb, detached, and constantly on guard, fearful that any contact or 'conversation [with anyone] might tear the scab off my wounded heart' (Young, 2007, p. 12).*

Job: *I experienced deep alienation from my wife, who experienced her grief and pain very differently. Like Mack, I was struck dumb and could not even speak or relate for a long time. My first emotion after awakening from that terrible silence was an overwhelming longing for self-annihilation, just not to exist anymore (TNIV, 3.3, 11, 16). How 'I longed for death that did not come' (TNIV, 3.21).*

Mack: *Being a victim of that level of attack and chaos ... well ... it's just isolating, isn't it? You feel cut off from the world of 'normal', whatever that is. Handling my own emotions was bad enough, but the impact on my other daughter, Kate ... seeing her shut down like that was agony.*

Linda: *You both not only had to deal with the trauma yourselves and your own emotions, but you also had to come to terms with how those around you, especially those you love and care about, were responding. There is something* *about the experience of trauma that seems to heighten sensitivity and increase anxiety about the appropriateness of our emotions, not just for clients but for counsellors too. I have often observed how intently aware trauma clients are of how their trauma stories are impacting me emotionally. Maybe it's my imagination, but sometimes I have an uncanny sense that certain of my clients have keener antennae for my emotional reactions to their story than I do.*

Naming, expressing, and integrating the powerful emotions that accompany trauma can often be one of the most intractable aspects and difficult tasks for survivors, their families, and their helpers to negotiate. There is some evidence to suggest that emotional responses laid down in trauma are encoded differently from other affective memories (Ogden, Minton, and Pain, 2006; Williams and Banyard, 1999). The immediate impact of trauma is often a 'period of shock and denial – the event is too large and too horrible to be taken in all at once, and the mind protects itself by trying to shut down' (Garland, 2004, p. 37).

This 'functional alexithymia' is evident in both men's stories and serves an early adaptive role in helping them both catch up with the magnitude of the events that have befallen them (Ogden, Minton, and Pain, 2006, p. 13). Both characters display at different points in their stories the desire for an ultimate form of numbness, when it seems 'the only way to regain control over one's life [is] to end it' (Brison, 1997, p. 32). They also both refer to the 'deep chasm' of isolation that separates their traumatised worlds from the 'horizons of normal everydayness', which seem no longer available to them (Stolorow, 2007, p. 16; Miller and Tougaw, 2002). According to Levy (2004, p. 51), 'managing and containing [the client's] powerful feelings of hatred and death' pose one of the most difficult emotional challenges of trauma work.

Some clients develop highly effective radar for how the therapist is feeling and responding to the details of the story, and they can use this monitoring to help navigate the murky, trauma-generated fogs that often blur the boundaries between what is 'real' and what is illusion. Seeing the counsellor's 'real' human responses to details and events that have become locked in the eerie world of nightmare and flashback can reground and reconnect the client to more authentic ownership of her or his own emotions and responses (Levy and Lemma, 2004). Clients are 'particularly sensitive to any pretense, withholding or falseness on the part of the therapist' (Pearlman and Saakvitne, 1995, p. 299). Counsellors can veer between extremes of 'insensitivity and over-identification as a way of dealing with [their] own emotional reactions to horror stories'

(Boehnlein, 2007, p. 272). Engaging with examples of these dynamics at work in literary texts provides a uniquely useful reflective space and a less charged atmosphere for the counsellor to consider her own responses to these powerful affects.

Existential Explorations

Linda: *In a very helpful way your stories have acted as a kind of safe holding environment for my own observations and feelings as I attempt to make sense of and reflect on what has happened to me in the process of listening to trauma voices and containing what they project into me.*

Trauma does so much more than just shake your body and psyche. It can disrupt the whole foundation you've based your life on and leave gaping fissures in what used to be the solid ground of how you saw the world and who you are in it (Pearlman and Saakvitne, 1995).

Mack: *It was a bit like that ... the ground did seem to open up and threaten to swallow me whole a few times. There's this disbelief, almost like a rip in the fabric of the universe, and you just can't take in what is happening. I remember just asking the air, 'How could this happen?' (Young, 2007, p. 53).*

It took me a long time to come to terms with the existence of that level of evil in the world and, even worse than that, that God hadn't done anything to stop it. I mean ... that monster paedophile was out there, lurking in the woods, stalking my little girl, for God's sake! ... I blamed God for it with every fibre of my being. In that frozen time before I went back to the shack, I didn't know who I was or what I believed anymore.

Job: *Yes, I too have seen the terrors of 'Leviathan', that chaos crouches in the deep places of the world, and no man can tame this beast or bend it to his will (TNIV, 41.1–34). 'Iron it treats like straw and bronze like rotten wood' (TNIV, 41.27). I had been a whole person. I became a 'shadow' (TNIV, 17.7). It was a monumental struggle with the nature of evil in the world and how the Almighty orders the universe. I screamed for justice, because God seemed so silent and indifferent to the infamy ... I say infamy ... that had been perpetrated upon me.*

Mack: *Infamy ... yes, that's the right word. There was a time when I couldn't speak of it without reliving it, as if it were happening now. I know I can never erase what happened and it will always cause pain, but I've found my way to some kind of 'meaning' for it that makes sense to me, at least, even if to no one else.*

Job: *Yes, what I experienced in the whirlwind, like what you experienced in the shack, changed everything, but it's very difficult to explain to people exactly 'how' that happened.*

Linda: *I hear in both your narratives a re-evaluation of the values and assumptions you held or thought you held before the trauma. There is a powerful subtext for you both in the overturning of your conventional and socially constructed views of God's character and nature and how you thought the world worked.*

Job: *Everything seemed so clear before tragedy swept into my life and changed all the rules. I thought it was simple, God took care of the good, protected the innocent, and punished the wicked. After the children died, and the way they died, well … I just couldn't make sense of it anymore. Like you, Mack, I thought this Creator that I had worshipped all my life sat and watched the 'calamity and sudden death' that hit my family and he just 'folded his arms' and 'stood aloof from the despair of the innocent' (TM, 9.23).*

Trauma lives up to its etymological meaning of 'wound', and often the deepest wound to deal with is the impact on the victim's personal world view, spirituality, and sense of identity. Maslow (1968, p. 206) stresses the importance of these aspects when he says, 'the human being needs a framework of values, a philosophy of life, a religion or religion-surrogate to live by and understand by, in about the same sense he needs sunlight, calcium or love'. Pearlman and Saakvitne (1995, p. 308) relate this to the counsellor's task by stating, 'Therapists who have no room in their formulations … for the nonmaterial, intangible aspects of human experience may be at a loss in the face of the deep spiritual wound experienced by survivors of traumatic life events'.

Howard (1991) argues that an engaged interface with literature or 'culture tales' opens windows on the spiritual and existential explorations of others. Whether the tales are fictional or not, the interface with them can be a valid and useful form of empathy development and engagement with clients' idiosyncratic existential quests, especially when those world views may differ markedly from the therapist's own frames of reference. Whether a client's spirituality includes belief in God or some other non-material, transcendent reality, trauma almost always requires a painful reassessment of these core beliefs.

Rousseau and Measham (2007) point to the importance of acknowledging with trauma victims the seeming random absurdity of what has happened to them. That chaos and evil exist in a seemingly ordered world, that

165

paedophiles stalk little girls, and that tornados strike and crush houses and families are hard truths to take in. That the destruction of the innocent *doesn't* make sense is part of the *process* of making sense of what has happened. 'Meaninglessness is an integral part of the experience of trauma for many people' (Rousseau and Measham, 2007, p. 280). Both Mack and Job engage powerfully with this process in their stories, and while they don't completely abandon their original beliefs, they challenge and discard many of their previous assumptions and embrace new, more personalised, relational understandings. Their belief systems cease to be rigid rationales on which they try to build an airtight case for their own rights to safety, control, and an unclouded sky. Instead, they embrace ambiguity, ambivalence, and a more realistic perception of uncertainty. Their existential angst does not become more rationally explained but more safely contained within an intimate, empathic relationship with a God who has become more present, more real, more alive to them. This new relationship and transformed view of the very centre of their belief system holds them while they learn to hold themselves.

How each of their culminating epiphanies actually transpires remains shrouded in varying degrees of ambiguity and mystery in both stories. However, there is no doubt about the ways in which their relational and profoundly personal epiphanies have restored new meanings to their worlds, coherence to their understandings of themselves, and a life-giving reconnection with their families and communities.

Of all the ways these two texts have revealed and illuminated the dark labyrinths of tragic suffering, it is this ambiguity and mystery that I find the most meaningful aspect of both men's experience and the one that accords the most with the journeys I have made with trauma clients as well as the personal faith reassessments their stories have engendered in me. Trauma almost never ends in easy answers, but it often finds its way to profound transformations.

Conclusion

Both men's stories, my imaginal dialogues with them, and the narrative our voices have created together have led to the emergence of new collaborative meanings and a differently generated knowledge base from which to view the experience of trauma for clients and counsellors. This juxtaposition of two trauma voices, one from the ancient world of the Near East and the other from a contemporary citizen of the West, opened up a reflective space of interest and vitality for 'reading the wound'. The use of these literary characters and my empathic engagement with them fostered an environment in which the realities of my own trauma practice work, its impacts on me, and its meanings could be freely and ethically brought into an inter-subjective space. As a result a new narrative has been co-constructed that embodies the two original aims of this chapter: to illuminate the role of literary narratives and imagined dialogues in surfacing insights about trauma's impact on client and counsellor; and the creation of a containing story, a meaningful reflective space and 'relational home' for my own counsellor experiences of trauma work. The real life trauma tales of my own clients, although unvoiced here, have still in some sense been mute witnesses, present in the background throughout this story. They stand in solemn, silent solidarity with Job and Mack, and in that strange, deeply wise community of shared suffering, I like to think they have also been heard, and honoured.

References

Boehnlein, J. (2007) 'Religion and spirituality after trauma' in L. Kirmayer, R. Lemelson, and M. Barad (eds) *Understanding Trauma: Integrating Biological, Clinical and Cultural Perspectives* (Cambridge and New York: Cambridge University Press) pp. 259–274.

Brison, S. (1997) 'Outliving oneself' in D. Meyers (ed.) *Feminists Rethink the Self* (Boulder, CO: Westview Press) pp. 12–39.

Bruner, J. (1990) *Acts of Meaning* (Cambridge and London: Harvard University Press).

Buber, M. (1937) *I and Thou* (Edinburgh: T. and T. Clark).

Crossley, M. (2000) *Introducing Narrative Psychology: Self, Trauma and the Construction of Meaning* (Buckingham and Philadelphia: Open University Press).

Etherington, K. (2009) 'Life story research: A relevant methodology for counsellors and psychotherapists', *Counselling and Psychotherapy Research*, 9 (4), 225–233.

Frances, S., Pincus, H., First, M., et al. (eds) (1994) *Diagnostic and Statistical Manual of Mental Disorders IV* (Washington, DC: American Psychiatric Association).

Frank, A. (1995) *The Wounded Storyteller: Body, Illness and Ethics* (Chicago and London: University of Chicago Press).

Frank, A. (2007) 'Interview through a painted window: On narrative, medicine, and method', *International Journal of Qualitative Methods*, 6 (3), 121–139.

Frank, A. (2008) 'Caring for the Dead' in L. Hyden and J. Brockmeier (eds) *Health, Illness and Culture: Broken Narratives* (New York: Routledge) pp. 122–130.

Garland, C. (2004) 'Traumatic events and their impact on symbolic functioning' in S. Levy and A. Lemma (eds) *The Perversion of Loss* (London and Philadelphia: Whurr Publishers) pp. 37–49.

Hartman, G. (1995) 'On traumatic knowledge and literary studies', *New Literary History*, 26 (3), 537–562.

Herman, J. (1992) *Trauma and Recovery* (New York: Basic Books).

Hermans, H. (1999) 'Self-narrative as meaning construction: The dynamics of self-investigation', *Journal of Clinical Psychology*, 55 (10), 1193–1211.

Howard, G. (1991) 'Culture tales: A narrative approach to thinking, cross-cultural psychology, and psychotherapy', *American Psychologist*, 46 (3), 187–197.

Levy, S. (2004) 'Containment and validation: Working with survivors of trauma' in S. Levy and A. Lemma (eds) *The Perversion of Loss* (London and Philadelphia: Whurr Publishers) pp. 50–70.

Levy, S., and Lemma, A. (eds) (2004) *The Perversion of Loss* (London and Philadelphia: Whurr Publishers).

Maslow, A. (1968) *Toward a Psychology of Being* (New York: Van Nostrand).

McAdams, D. (1993) *The Stories We Live By: Personal Myths and the Making of the Self* (New York: Guilford Press).

Miller, N., and Tougaw, J. (2002) *Extremities: Trauma, Testimony and Community* (Urbana and Chicago: University of Illinois Press).

Ogden, P., Minton, K., and Pain, C. (2006) *Trauma and the Body* (New York: Norton).

Pearlman, L. A., and Saakvitne, K. W. (1995) *Trauma and the Therapist* (New York and London: Norton).

Polkinghorne, D. (2004) 'Narrative therapy and postmodernism' in L. Angus and J. McLeod (eds) *The Handbook of Narrative and Psychotherapy* (London: Sage) pp. 53–67.

Rogers, C. (1967) *On Becoming a Person: A Therapist's View of Psychotherapy* (London: Constable).

Rousseau, C., and Measham, T. (2007) 'Posttraumatic suffering as a source of trans-formation: A clinical perspective' in L. Kirmayer, R. Lemelson, and M. Barad (eds) *Understanding Trauma: Integrating Biological, Clinical and Cultural Perspectives* (Cambridge and New York: Cambridge University Press) pp. 275–294.

Speedy, J. (2008) *Narrative Inquiry and Psychotherapy* (Basingstoke and New York: Palgrave MacMillan).

Stolorow, R. (2007) *Trauma and Human Existence: Autobiographical, Psychoanalytic, and Philosophical Reflections* (New York and East Sussex: The Analytic Press).

TM (*The Message: The Bible in Contemporary Language*) (2002) (Colorado Springs: NavPress).

TNIV (*Today's New International Version*) (2005) (Grand Rapids: International Bible Society).

White, M. (2004) 'Folk psychology and narrative practices' in L Angus and J. McLeod (eds), *The Handbook of Narrative and Psychotherapy* (London: Sage) pp. 59–84.

Williams, L., and Banyard, V. (eds) (1999) *Trauma and Memory* (Thousand Oaks and London: Sage).

Young, W. P. (2007) *The Shack* (London: Hodder and Stoughton).

Part IV
Embodying Theory

11 An Investigation of Narratives of Anxiety

CHRIS SCOTT

Introduction

Conducting research into problematic adulthood anxiety would appear to be a timely undertaking. In recent years, national newspapers have reported results of studies that indicate an upward trend in the numbers of adults experiencing disruptive levels of general anxiety (Martin, 2009). Studies have also highlighted that despite the considerable impact of anxiety upon the general population's wellbeing and on healthcare costs, it remains under-researched when compared with depression (Kroenke et al., 2007). These findings indicate that my own perception that problematic anxiety is one of the issues most commonly presented by clients referred to counsellors in general practice does indeed reflect wider trends.

In light of the above, counselling practitioners need to be equipped with effective ways of improving the experience of people living with anxiety. However, the effectiveness of psychological therapies to significantly and consistently alter the impact of anxiety upon people's lives is in doubt. A Cochrane review of the clinical efficacy of psychological therapies in the treatment of generalised anxiety disorder (Hunot et al., 2007) commented that even when clinical trials assessed a particular type of intervention as 'successful', this status was based only upon its being more successful than an alternative intervention, including no intervention at all. According to the same review 'successful' trials typically report clinically significant change in fewer than 50 per cent of the research participants. In addition, the review could find no basis for concluding that any of the psychotherapeutic modalities were more or less successful than others, suggesting that any form of psychological therapy could expect roughly equivalent outcomes. As a counsellor, these findings are potent for me. They resonate with my sense of some of my own clinical encounters when I have been left feeling relatively ineffective, or only partially effective, in attempting to facilitate a significant change in other peoples' difficulties with anxiety.

Any of these points would seem sufficient motivation to conduct further research on treatment for anxiety. However, more than any of these considerations, it is my own relationship with anxiety that provides the greatest impetus behind my desire to study problematic anxiety. I approach this subject with a lifetime of experiencing frequently uncomfortable, limiting, and at times distressing levels of anxiety. Anxiety exerts an enduring influence upon my quality of life with a pervasiveness that I regard as unrivalled by any other experiences. Unfortunately, my past experiences of being in consulting rooms as the client were as disappointing and unproductive as some of my current experiences of being there as the counsellor.

Following from these points is my conviction that existing counselling traditions and their associated conceptualisations of adulthood anxiety are insufficient to fully address the complex phenomenon of problematic adult anxiety. I suggest that this is reflected both in my own experiences and in existing research on the efficacy of psychotherapeutic interventions in the treatment of adult anxiety disorders, where often only minor improvements are reported (e.g. Bower, Rowland, and Gracely, 2003).

In my own experience of living with anxiety, the most significant changes seem to occur for me through alterations in the way I understand, attach meaning to, and describe the experience. As a counselling practitioner, I sense that the encounters in which I have witnessed significant shifts in clients' relationships with their anxiety have occurred when I have responded to the aspect of their anxiety that is most relevant for them. Central to this has been working with their stories of their anxiety. The principal idea explored in this chapter, therefore, is that of narrative processes in the lived experience of anxiety. I argue for the potential significance of narrative as a major factor in addressing and working with problematic anxiety.

The development of my awareness of my own anxiety has followed a predictable and repetitive course. Again and again I have turned to the considerable literature on the topic in the hope of finding a way to resolve my difficulties. As I now reflect, I can recognise that this searching followed a consistent pattern. I would strive to find a description of anxiety that fitted my own, anticipating that with this recognition, potential mastery and resolution would follow. In contemplating this internal drive, I become aware of its childlike and naïve quality. At times I believed that I had found my anxiety contained in the writings of others.

These moments led to an almost euphoric sense of hope, which I can only compare to my adolescent love affairs, where the first moments of a romantic relationship would encourage the fantasy of a merged and lifelong bond, only for the novelty to wear thin and the cold disappointment of reality to dawn all too soon.

Acceptance of the inevitable futility of this process, perhaps also combined with increased age and a degree of emotional maturity, eventually led me to attempt a radically different approach, which I set out in this chapter. Here the starting point is to describe my own experience of anxiety phenomenologically and to explore my narratives of and about this experience. By turning my attention inward rather than directing it towards the expert literature, I offer an experience-near source of lived material from which to develop my analysis.

Drawing upon the work of psychologist Bruner (1990), McLeod (1997) has conceptualised narrative as a process of making sense of our experiences, as well as a process of communicating this story to others. In addition, McLeod (1997) has highlighted how narrative can act as an important counterbalance to more positivist approaches to knowledge, which certainly dominate existing research about anxiety. My aim in this chapter is to begin with stories of anxiety as they are communicated by ourselves and others, and only then to connect these accounts with more conventionally scientific research.

In approaching my theme from a personal vantage point, I draw on both my own direct experience of anxiety and what I have learned as a counselling practitioner from others whose struggles and attempts to alter their experiences of anxiety I have witnessed. Indeed my own narrative has become entwined with those of my clients: while I impact upon the stories of anxiety that clients bring, their stories also impact on mine. Writing this story leads to the potential for my narrative once again to evolve and change. In recognition of this fact, building my own narrative into the chapter is both necessary and appropriate.

What Is Anxiety?

How do I know when I am anxious; how do I perceive and become conscious of anxiety? My answer to these questions begins with physical experiences, including a churning sensation in my stomach, breathlessness, raised heartbeat, sweating, and muscle pain in specific areas such as my neck, chest, and shoulders. Next, linking to these physical sensations, I can at times also identify changes in my mental state. These are harder to specify, as they are more elusive, vague, and more challenging to describe, but they would typically include a sense of my mind speeding up and racing but in an incoherent and confused fashion. I might characterise my mental state as one in which I am disorientated and slightly bewildered. Finally, there is an emotional aspect to my anxiety. I tend to use words such as fear and terror to describe the emotion of anxiety. While the word 'anxiety' is itself regarded as an emotion, I prefer to conceptualise anxiety as an interplay among these physical, mental, and emotional experiences.

For me, these experiences constitute the core of my anxiety and the story I tell of what it is to suffer anxiety. The core features are consistent, and I can relatively easily become aware of them. As a practitioner, I am frequently introduced to the personal experiences of anxiety of others, which may be similar to or different from my own. Quite often people talk of worries that are more specific than mine, for example about death or chronic illness. While the specific content may vary widely, there is much in common in the way these worries are experienced in the sense of being repetitive, constant, and seemingly uncontrollable. Often the content of worries is described as unwanted thoughts, such as a father imagining setting fire to his child's school, a commuter fantasising about jumping in front of the morning train, or a wife drawn towards smothering her husband. A client may offer examples such as obsessing over trivial details or over the thought of causing an accident. While these experiences of anxiety are less familiar to me personally, they still exist for me and I can sympathise with the emotional impact such mental occurrences entail.

With clients who describe themselves as suffering from anxiety I have adopted the habit of asking, 'How did you know you were anxious?' This invites them to narrate their stories of anxiety. As with my own process, many clients relay the physical aspects of their experience first. The list of physical changes is quite extensive, but some features recur with particular frequency. In addition to my own physical symptoms, feeling a tingling or pins and needles, the need to pass urine or defecate, cold and hot flushes, shaking and trembling, twitching and weakness are all commonly highlighted. When clients can verbalise the mental aspect of their anxiety, they often talk of feeling weird, unreal, disconnected, unable to focus or concentrate, or dizziness, and occasionally a sense of being unable to control themselves, such as forgetting how to walk, or a feeling that they are out of proportion relative to other people or the room they are in (whether abnormally small or large).

An international panel of experts recently distilled the phenomenon of depression into aspects that could be regarded as sufficiently distinctive and consistent as to constitute the core aspects of depression (Seta, 2008). A definitive and concise equivalent does not appear to exist for anxiety. However, combining my personal and clinical experience with a model provided by Sanders and Wills (2003, p. 17) and information from the National Institute for Health and Clinical Excellence (now National Institute for Health and Care Excellence) guidelines (NICE, 2011) and the American Psychiatric Association (2000), I offer an initial attempt at this task in Figure 11.1.

Physical	Cognitive/ emotional	Functional/ behavioural
Palpitations	Feeling unreal, derealisation, depersonalisation	Sleep disturbance
Shortness of breath		Increased bowel frequency
Gasping		
Numbness or tingling in hands and feet	Feeling faint, dizzy	Need to urinate
Sweating	Startled response	Jumpiness
Hot and cold	Feeling 'weird'	Exhaustion
Muscular twitches	Nervousness	Loss of appetite
Twitchiness, tics	Fear	Inability to concentrate
Vomiting, nausea	Apprehension	
Irregular heart beat and pulse	Disorientation	Tiredness
Lump in throat	Confusion	Increased appetite
Chest pains	Fugue	
Numb legs and arms	Restlessness	
Aches and pains	Feeling speeded up	
Weakness		
Breathlessness, increased breathing rate	Distraction	
Choking	Sense of floating or falling	
Stomach pains, cramps	Sense of loss of control	
Churning stomach		
Dry mouth	Insecurity	
Shaking		
Headaches		

Figure 11.1 Examples of core features of anxiety

175

Different people may experience only some aspects of this model or report entirely unique, idiosyncratic manifestations of their anxiety. Figure 11.1 could be expanded to include reference to those genetic, hormonal, and neurotransmitter processes that research indicates are also core aspects of anxiety (Martin et al., 1988; Hettema et al., 2005; Pine and Leibenluft, 2008), although these are process of which sufferers are not directly aware.

Reactions to Anxiety

'[Anxiety] causes people to pursue many maladaptive coping avenues' (Kabat-Zinn, 1990, p. 334). When the core features of anxiety are triggered, our seemingly natural reaction is to do something. In taking action we may try to control, overcome, or get rid of our arousal as swiftly as is possible. For some, our response will have become so automatic that it operates as if it were a natural reflex.

My own response to anxiety has altered considerably over the years. When I first became disturbed by anxiety as a teenager, my reactions were often extreme. Perhaps the sense of bewilderment around the physical, functional, and emotional changes I experienced drove me to take drastic action. Or perhaps these experiences triggered anxiety (perhaps unconscious) from a much earlier, immature time in my life. Whatever the reason, I would alter my actions or lifestyle to control the anxiety that arose in me. Turning to alcohol seemed effective for a while. My mind could follow a logic that noticed going to school, being in social situations, and being alone all included the dreaded sensations of nervousness, nausea, tension, and confusion. Under the influence of alcohol my experience of these situations seemed to be transformed. From a state of apprehension and a desire to be invisible, alcohol brought confidence, conversation, humour, and a carefree attitude that was such a welcome escape from my anxious state. Similarly smoking seemed to take the edge off my symptoms – never as successfully as alcohol but sufficiently well to enable me to get through the school day and most notably to cope with the periods of time when I was alone.

Over time these coping mechanisms would gradually become less successful. Anxiety seemed to be winning, and I would therefore redouble my efforts to cope. Avoiding school, avoiding other people, and withdrawing would bring short-term relief. However, when these strategies failed I would simply return to an earlier pattern and get caught in a never-ending cycle of anxiety and destructive behaviours. These attempts were typically characterised by extremes: using alcohol or avoiding alcohol, being alone or avoiding being alone. Unfortunately, by their very nature, these extremes would result in my replacing the problem of anxiety with a new problem. Even as a youth, I was aware that these measures were impacting negatively upon my health, education, and relationships.

In addition to altering my behaviour in the hope of gaining some control over my anxiety, the way I used my mind also seemed to change. I would slip into my imagination to fantasise my way out of anxiety, escaping into childhood memories or images of future success. Linked to this use of my mind were elaborate mental rituals that I would follow in the belief they could offer protection. I place prayer in this category, because I would spend enormous amounts of time in conversation with a God I hoped existed as well as with deceased relatives. In particular I tried to cope with anxiety through imaginary dialogue with my grandmother, whose death shortly before my thirteenth birthday had seemed to pre-cipitate the rise of my anxiety. The content or outcome of these prayers seemed to be less important than the sense of reassurance the process provided.

Just as I have stories to tell of my reactions to anxiety, so counselling clients often describe their responses to the core features of their anxiety, which typically involve attempting to control, express, com-municate, or mask their symptoms. In so doing, they alter patterns of behaviour. At times it can seem that attending counselling may itself be a behaviour designed to do something to relieve or cure anxiety. The range of actions described by clients seeking to relieve their anxiety suggests that many people make numerous attempts to find a resolu-tion before they consider counselling as a possibility. Perhaps counselling becomes a relevant option for people only when their other attempts to control their experiences have become unsuccessful, dissatisfying, or problematic in some way.

Prior to accessing counselling, my experience of attempting to control my anxiety seemed to compound the distorted way in which I perceived myself, others, and life in general. My repeated unsuccessful attempts had led to a sense of futility and hopelessness that I brought into my counselling encounters. I found that this triggered a feeling of depend-ence on the counsellor, who represented the last chance to find a cure for the primary source of distress in my life. The harmful or destructive lifestyle changes I had already made had significantly altered my perception of myself. Witnessing this process in others, I have found that this altered perception of self is often powerfully charged emotionally. For example, clients' stories of anxiety may come to include references to themselves as pathetic, stupid, dependent, needy, hostile, or defective, with inevitable consequences for their self-esteem. This aspect of the narrative may draw on a wide array of different emotions, thoughts, and behaviours that are far removed from the original focus upon anxiety but have become integral and fundamental to the client's personal story of anxiety. I would argue that the way our self-concept and our perceptions of others alter is a critical aspect of the anxiety storyline. The very processes of escape, avoidance, and reassurance-seeking will almost certainly cause an impairment and erosion of the quality of life, and we may reflect upon missed opportunities, damaged relationships, loss, and limited or unsatisfying experiences. When my own attempts to control my anxiety negatively impacted upon my life, it is perhaps not surprising that I attributed these losses to my anxiety. This would stir in me a set of difficult emotions connected to loss, including regret, guilt, despair, anger, and self-loathing. Narratives of reactions to anxiety therefore include important stories of and about the self of the sufferer.

Understanding Anxiety

It appears to be a human trait to attach meaning to our experiences (Hayes, Strossahl, and Wilson, 2003). However, 'virtually all people live within a life narrative that leaves some aspects of their experience poorly explicated' (Warner, 1997, p. 137). We strive to make sense of the way we feel and who we are, perhaps in the hope that by gaining understanding we will increase our sense of control and lessen our sense of hopelessness. Narrative is the process of making meaning out of our experience and, when we experience anxiety, it appears that for many of us the need to understand the process can become particularly important.

The moment I first became aware of being troubled by anxiety was not the first time I had experienced anxiety. Intermittently during my childhood, and perhaps my infancy, I experienced moments of anxiety and fearfulness. I had no language for these experiences and no way to conceptualise them in my mind. At the time I lacked any concept of these states having meaning or significance. By the time I reached my early teenage years this had changed. The first time I became consciously distressed by anxiety was the first time it occurred to me that the way I felt was unusual or different from other people's experiences of life. I became intimidated by the seeming inevitability of feeling out of control. The problem with the way my narrative formed was that I lacked an adequate language and could draw only from a limited range of ideas. For a teenager from an emotionally uncommunicative family, living in a conservative, Scottish working-class rural community, the range of information available to help construct a narrative was limited and skewed. People in my community rarely discussed anxiety; they didn't seem to experience it and were even hostile to the concept. To acknowledge fear in such an environment was unthinkable, and this inevitably impacted upon the way I formed an under-standing of my experiences and my perception of myself.

In trying to understand what was occurring, I tended to assume that the symptoms of my anxiety were social in origin. The social explanation I formed to help comprehend my state of being made other people the source of my fears. My fears of collapsing, vomiting, public ridicule, and acting inappropriately were only difficulties if other people were there to witness my shame. Allied to this was a newly forming awareness that contact with other people triggered the anxiety state. I began to design a socially orientated storyline in which other people were dangerous, harmful and threatening. Contact with others was therefore the trigger for anxiety as well as for anger towards others. It was to take me a long time to begin to use a psychological framework to comprehend my experiences.

When I am working with clients, comparable themes emerge in their stories of anxiety. Perhaps I ignore or miss other pieces of informa-tion that are present and tune into the aspects of their narratives that resonate with my own. However, I consistently encounter clients who, without necessarily verbalising their concerns in these terms, appear to have questions of four kinds: What is occurring within me when I'm anxious? Why am I experiencing anxiety? What do I need to do to stop this experience? What do these experiences say about me, other people, or life in general? While clients may come looking for answers from me, I have learned that taking the time to hear their own responses to these questions offers access to their personal narratives and can be a very valuable and productive part of the therapeutic process.

Like me, clients make sense of their experiences of anxiety based upon what is culturally available to them, and this process begins long before they access counselling. Their narratives are as varied as the literature on the subject and are often strongly held. Ideas about genetics, neurology, environment, society, personality, spirituality, nature, nutrition, and cognition are all presented as sources of distress. Sometimes more than one explanation can be present for a client, and each person's narrative evolves during counselling. Usually it will expand to include a psychological definition, which often then operates alongside understandings formed prior to counselling and which still maintains some significance or truth for the person. Clients' evolving narratives constitute their own personal, idiosyncratic model of anxiety.

Professionally sanctioned narratives of anxiety are offered within the various theoretical frameworks for therapeutic work. These narratives tend to emphasise, minimise, or disregard different elements of the wide range of processes that can be regarded as constituting the phenomenon of anxiety. As counsellors, we may be working from a frame of reference in which anxiety does not exist as a distinctive entity, and we may pursue other parts of our client's experience to confirm this. For example, some practitioners hold the belief that anxiety is a manifestation of an evolutionary survival response, while others insist that anxiety is an expression of insecurity or a defence, prompting investigation of formative relationships and experiences.

In observing myself in practice, I recognise that it is easy to become animated, interested, quizzical, or encouraging when a client begins to unwrap the layers of meaning that resonate with my preferred formulations. It is also easy for me to unwittingly communicate confusion, lack of interest, frustration, or mild annoyance when clients deviate from a storyline that I find more recognisable and comfortable. I have learned that the key task in working with narrative is not determining whether a storyline is objectively true, false or distorted. Rather the story as it currently stands needs to be accepted and heard if it is to be given the opportunity to change.

A Tripartite Model of Anxiety

Bringing together the themes discussed in this chapter, I offer a tripartite model of anxiety, based on a dynamic interplay between arousal, reaction, and narrative (Figure 11.2).

Narrative permeates the experience of anxiety in numerous ways and acts as the glue that binds the whole process together. If I believe that anxious arousal is intolerable, my reaction to it is triggered. Similarly, if

Figure 11.2 A tripartite model of anxiety

I believe that my reactions have significantly impacted upon the quality of my life, I may become despondent and hopeless. These constitute narratives, which operate at different levels within the phenomenon of anxiety. Narratives may take the form of stories about self, often communicated in comments such as 'this proves I'm pathetic' or 'I hate my body'. Narratives may also relate to others, displayed through comments such as 'I don't know anyone else who feels like this' or 'this is all my mother's fault'. For some people, narratives may focus on their anxious arousal, with statements such as 'I hate this feeling' and 'my biggest enemy is my anxiety'. Sometimes narratives focus on the consequences of living with anxiety, for example 'it was because of anxiety that I dropped out of university' or 'I lost my wife because I was so anxious – we couldn't go anywhere and she'd had enough'. Or they may focus on the consequences for others of living with anxiety: 'my father spent twenty years in and out of psychiatric hospitals because of anxiety'; 'my grandmother died from a panic attack'. Narratives may relate to the future, often pessimistically, as in 'what's the point: if this is how life feels I think I've had enough' or 'who would want to be with me – even I don't want to be with me'. Narratives may address the therapeutic encounter, for example 'you're my last chance' or 'I've tried everything and nothing works'. This broad range of examples highlights the way narratives operate across many aspects of the complex experience of anxiety. They also serve to emphasise that those experiencing anxiety will form their own idiosyncratic relationship to and explanation of the phenomenon. In addition, these examples illustrate how the nature, content, and focus of the narratives all carry emotional impacts, which may be as great as, and potentially more acute than, the anxiety itself.

Narratives of anxiety have implications for our internal relationships with ourselves and with our external relational world of objects and others, as illustrated in Figure 11.3.

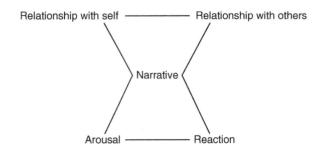

Figure 11.3 The systemic process of anxiety narratives

Conclusion

The central conclusion of this chapter is that our relationship with anxiety, which is principally carried in our personal narratives, can be a highly significant part of the experience. Bringing attention to our relationship with anxiety often leads to changes in our narratives, which, at least for some people, can prove to be a fundamental part of the therapeutic process. To conceptualise and respond adequately to individual experiences of anxiety, practitioners need to hold an awareness of the myriad ways in which it may be understood and narrated, which, I have suggested, requires an openness beyond characterisations associated with any single therapeutic tradition.

Perhaps the only real difference between my anxiety as a 12-year-old compared to my anxiety as a 42-year-old is how I relate to it. The core symptoms are still present, and at times I still continue to avoid, escape, and look for reassurance. The difference now is that my story of anxiety has changed. I no longer look for meaning behind these feelings or behaviours. I have stopped resenting, regretting, worrying about, and fearing the experience or the impact it has had, and instead I practise accepting and being in contact with the actual experience. This feels more grounded and healthy than a simple resignation and is a process of being present with myself rather than the alternatives of self-loathing, accusation, and limitation.

Reflecting upon the experience of having explored and written about narratives of anxiety, I am aware that what I have presented here is a meta-narrative. This chapter tells a story of the story of anxiety. I am also aware that the process of writing has impacted upon my own story of anxiety, and once again the narrative changes slightly for me.

My original thinking and writing were more politically focused and the language was at times more confrontational than in the final result. As this chapter emerged, I recognised that as my anxiety about finding an identity as a writer subsided, the sense of frustration and apprehension gave way to a quieter, more contained and considered narrative voice.

References

American Psychiatric Association (2000) *Diagnostic and Statistical Manual of Mental Disorders,* 4th edn (Washington: American Psychiatric Association).

Bower, P., Rowland, N., and Gracely, E. J. (2003) 'The clinical effectiveness of counselling in primary care: A systematic review and meta-analysis', *Journal of Psychological Medicine,* 33 (2), 203–215.

Bruner, J. (1990) *Acts of Meaning* (Cambridge, MA: Harvard University Press).

Hayes, S., Strossahl, K., and Wilson, K. (2003) *Acceptance and Commitment Therapy: An Experiential Approach to Behaviour Change* (London and New York: Guilford Press).

Hettema, J. M., Prescott, C. A., Myers, J. M., Neale, M. C., and Kendler, K. S. (2005) 'The structure of genetic and environmental risk factors for anxiety disorders in men and women', *The Archive of General Psychiatry,* 62, 182–189.

Hunot, V., Churchill, R., Teixeira, V., and Silva de Lima, M. (2007) 'Psychological therapies for generalized anxiety disorder' (Review), *The Cochrane Library,* Issue 1. DOI: 10.1002/14651858.CD001848.pub4.

Kabat-Zinn, J. (1990) *Full Catastrophe Living* (New York: Delta).

Kroenke, K., Spitzer, R. L., Williams, J. B., Monahan, P. O., and Löwe, B. (2007) 'Anxiety disorders in primary care: Prevalence, impairment, comorbidity, and detection, *Annals of Internal Medicine,* 146 (5), 317–325.

Martin, N. G., Jardine, R., Andrews, G., and Heath, A. C. (1988), 'Anxiety disorders and neuroticism: Are there genetic factors specific to panic?' *Acta Psychiatrica Scandinavica,* 77, 698–706.

Martin, D. (2009) 'Sharp rise in depression and anxiety as QUARTER of middle-aged women suffer "common mental disorder"'. www.dailymail.co.uk/health/article-1129802/Sharp-rise-depression-anxiety-QUARTER-middle-aged-women-suffer-common-mental-disorder.html#ixzz1TsL2fBKw. Accessed: 3 August 2011.

McLeod, J. (1997) *Narrative and Psychotherapy* (London, Sage).

NICE (2011) *Quick Reference Guide: Generalised anxiety disorder and panic disorder (with or without agoraphobia) in adults; Clinical Guideline 113.* (London, National Institute for Health and Clinical Excellence).

Pine, D. S., and Leibenluft, E. (2008) State-of-Science Review: SR-E12. 'Neurocognition and neuroimaging in anxiety disorders: Implications for treatment and functional outcome'. *Foresight Report: Mental Capital and Wellbeing* (London: The Government Office for Science).

Sanders, D., and Wills, F. (2003) *Counselling for Anxiety Problems* (London, Sage).

Seta, J. P. (editor-in-chief) (2008) 'The core of depression', *Medicographia*, 30 (1), Issue 94.

Warner, M. S. (1997) 'Does empathy cure? A theoretical consideration of empathy, processing and personal narrative' in A. C. Bohart and L. S. Greenberg (eds) *Empathy Reconsidered: New Directions in Psychotherapy* (Washington, DC: American Psychological Association) pp. 125–140.

12 Hauntings: On Discovering the Lived Experience of Counter-transference

PATRICK FEGAN

Introduction

When I was invited to contribute to this book I was initially thrilled and honoured to be asked, as one would be in response to such an invitation. However, this was followed by a strong sense of trepidation as I realised that I would have to return to a very difficult time and place in my learning as a counsellor and reflect on a study I had undertaken six years earlier. Then I remembered what Freud had said about ghosts:

> A thing which has not been understood inevitably reappears; like an unlaid ghost, it cannot rest until the mystery has been resolved and the spell broken. (Freud, 1909, p. 122)

As I finalised this chapter I was reminded of the time a few months earlier when I was in discussion with my tutor about the first draft of my contribution to this book. As I sat with her I was inwardly struck by a wave of emotion that conveyed to me a depth of compassion for a small abandoned child lying in his cot in a children's home, waiting for someone to attend to his cries, waiting for that someone who didn't come. In my compassion for that little boy there is no trepidation, no fear, no rejection, and no sense of recoiling away from him; there is only acceptance and an embracing.

This is the story of how my work with one particular client (whom I shall call Andrew) contributed to my finding this place of compassion and self-acceptance, where I could offer comfort and a sense of safety to my very early self without the fear of annihilation. It is also a story of my journey of understanding as a person and how it has influenced and continues to influence my professional development as a counsellor.

My hope for this chapter is that it will reveal the ever-deepening layers of understanding that arose out of my work with Andrew and how this growing understanding enabled me to gain a greater capacity to be in empathic attunement with him. This in turn enabled me to:

> respond to the client's perception of reality at that moment, as opposed to one's own or some 'objective' or external view of what is real.... At the same time, he or she retains a sense of self, as opposed to being swamped by or 'fusing' with the client's experience. (Greenberg, Rice, and Elliot, 1993, p. 104)

The route by which I achieved this entailed moving between, and seeking to develop, concepts drawn from the person-centred and psychodynamic approaches on which my counselling training drew.

The First Session with Andrew

I still hold a vivid memory of the first time Andrew and I met and the wave of feelings that engulfed me in our first session. He told me that he was in a relationship that he was finding increasingly difficult to maintain and manage, because his partner had ceased contact with him and had requested that he not initiate any contact, at least for the time being. The reason his partner gave for this stance was that he needed to assess their relationship in response to other life events that he was going through. Meanwhile, Andrew was experiencing acute anxiety that was making it difficult for him to cope with his daily life, and this had prompted him to seek my help.

Andrew found himself in a place of utter panic and in the grip of a desperate determination to reconnect to his partner, no matter how briefly, to alleviate the stress he was feeling. He persisted despite knowing the potential cost of going against his partner's express wishes. His attempts at reconnection took the form of an on-going series of texts to his partner expressing his undying love for him.

As Andrew read out loud some of his texts I found myself inwardly recoiling from him. Outwardly I expressed, as best I could, a supportive empathic stance toward him. But I felt at the time as if I was suffocating and being trapped in a snare from which there was no escape. I had never before come across such a strong negative reaction towards a client. What was also reverberating through me was the thought that I shouldn't be feeling like this: I recognised how my capacity to be empathically attuned to him was being negatively affected and how my ability to be congruent was compromised. My thoughts and feelings made it very difficult for me to stay with his frame of reference.

The quality of Andrew's reading of his texts that jumped out at me most and that I can still recall vividly many years later was the emotional pleading and begging for the smallest acknowledgement that his partner was still there for him. Emotionally his situation was clearly devastating. He was in pain. He was bereft. But my panic was only heightened when Andrew told me that he would find it very useful to have someone to talk to because he was 'wearing out' the few friends he had. At this point, some 25 minutes into the session, I too was feeling repelled and worn down by him. It was as if the more he endeavoured to pull me towards him, the more I wanted to pull away.

What also concerned me was my awareness of the dichotomy between how I was presenting and how I was feeling. In meeting Andrew I seemed to be able to establish a rapport and be in psychological contact with him but this was increasingly at odds with my internal stance towards him. Added to this was my fear that should I disengage from him, he would fall apart. I was feeling trapped. This recounting of the first session may seem rather dramatic, but it reflects the intensity of feelings I was experiencing in my counter-transference towards Andrew.

Explorations in Supervision

In light of the intensity and nature of my initial experience of Andrew, I felt it was imperative that I take my work with him to supervision in order to understand my responses and to ascertain if it was possible for me to continue to work therapeutically with him. Exploring my feelings towards Andrew in supervision, I became aware that I associated him with my adopted mother. I recalled memories of sitting with my adopted mother night after night until the wee small hours of the morning from when I was about eight years old until my late teens. Each night she would wring her heart out to me and tell me how important it was that I was there for her, listening and understanding. I can recall her saying to me 'You are the only one who understands me, who is there for me. Do you realise how important this is to me?' This reminded me very much of the quality of Andrew's pleas to his partner and his declaration to me about:

> how useful it was to have someone to talk to as, living on my own, I don't have a great deal of support around me and I can't speak to my family about my sexuality; and I am wearing out the few friends I have.

In his book *Healing the Shame that Binds You*, John Bradshaw (1988) describes the kind of relationship I had with my adopted mother as a process whereby the child takes on the role of supplying his or her parent's narcissistic gratification and only in so doing secures love and a sense of being needed and not abandoned. Bradshaw describes the consequence of such a relationship as one in which there is no one to mirror the child's feelings and drives or to nurture the child's needs. Any child, he says, growing up in such an environment has been mortally wounded by this narcissistic deprivation. A consequence of this experience of my adopted mother was a growing resentment that I held towards her, which stemmed from my slow realisation that no matter how much I invested in her, my needs would not be met. There was no one there for me. I felt that my mother suppressed my identity and growing independence as a person and that in my battles with her, when I was struggling to hold on to myself, she wore me out. I realised that I was scared of the same dynamic in relation to Andrew.

In supervision I came to the realisation that Andrew's presentation was akin to that of my adopted mother's in terms of their similar expression of acute unmet need. Both my adopted mother and Andrew shared an underlying melancholy in their communication of pain and hurt. I began to connect this quality with Bradshaw's (1988) concept of narcissistic gratification. Could it be that the melancholy they both expressed arose from their own early experiences of not being mirrored or nurtured by their own primary caregivers? A crucial aspect of this quality of expressed melancholy emerged later in relation to myself as a result of my deepening understanding of the forces at play between Andrew and me, a point to which I return.

At the time, I used the insights I had to think about Andrew's transference relationship with me. Internally, he was a child in search of a parent, an ideal parent, who in this case was going to be me. In my fantasy, the price I would have to pay in meeting him in this was an on-going repression of myself, which I was not prepared to do. This refusal was expressed in my maintaining a distance from Andrew, at the same time as hoping that I could still be empathic. This distance was not neutral, in that it possessed a flavour of rebellion and resistance against him. This led me to wonder about how, despite my resentment towards my mother, I had met her in her neediness, whereas with Andrew I was struggling to imagine how, within professional constraints, I could do the same. What was different this time? The answer to this was that I was no longer the little child with an aching need to experience being met.

Exploring My Counter-transference

During this time of working with Andrew I was also, through my experience and growing understanding of my counter-transference, dealing with delayed grief resulting from the loss of my mother and from the realisation that, in my adopted parents, I did not have anyone who validated me when I was growing up. This is painful to write about even now. I was only able to approach these feelings and express them because, on my counselling course, I had for the first time gained an experience of being genuinely met and 'contained' in the sense of Bion's (1962a, 1962b) model of maternal 'containment'. This sense of being genuinely met and contained occurred time after time. Even when I was in the midst of one of my many smogs of ambivalence, I was still met. For the first time in my life I began to trust that I belonged, that I was not alone. It was a profoundly moving experience. At the time of beginning my work with Andrew, in my counselling training we had recently watched together the film *Secrets and Lies* by Mike Leigh. This concerns the developing relationship between a mother and the daughter she had given up for adoption. The film touched me deeply. As a result of my felt experience of the film and the experience for the first time of feeling safe, listened to, heard and indeed seen, I was able to release the feelings of loss and isolation that I had held onto for so long.

The impact of my experience of affirmation and the sense of belonging I gained in my training modelled for me a far healthier way of enabling one to get one's needs met. I didn't have to go to the 'other' first to get some scraps of nourishment from the table. It was OK to be me. I did not have to deny myself in my meeting with the other.

With Andrew I felt as if I was being pulled into a way of relating that I had experienced with my adopted mother. The difference now was that

I also held an experience of being genuinely met and, having found the courage to embrace this new way of relating and being, I was not about to go back into a situation in which I felt I would be obliterated and lost. My wariness of close empathic contact with Andrew arose from the dread I felt at the thought of being trapped by him in the very same way that my mother had entrapped me. I am reminded here of Bion's (1961, p. 149) description of the unique quality of counter-transference:

> The analyst feels he is being manipulated so as to play a part, no matter how difficult to recognize, in somebody else's phantasy – or he would if it were not for what in recollection I can only call a temporary loss of insight, a sense of experiencing strong feelings.

This is echoed by Money-Kyrle (1956, pp. 361–362), who states that

> The analyst ... unfortunately is not omniscient. In particular, his understanding fails whenever the patient corresponds too closely with some aspect of himself which he has not yet learnt to understand.... when the interplay between introjection and projection, which characterises the analytic process, breaks down, the analyst may tend to get stuck.

I was at risk of losing my insight and was indeed stuck. This situation was creating tension and conflict in my work with Andrew between my needs as a person and my requirements as a counsellor to work ethically, which meant being fully present and genuine. How could I be genuine when internally I felt repelled?

I came to understand that the experience of being met on the course heightened my counter-transferential reaction to Andrew by unconsciously strengthening my desire to 'act out' against him and thus to treat him as I would have liked to have treated my adopted mother, namely by not meeting her needs at the expense of mine. Hence my impulse to hold back from Andrew. But I also knew that this would be disastrous for both of us. Heimann (1950) emphasises the threat of this kind of counter-transferential enactment, drawing attention to the danger that the analyst will act out strong feelings and insisting that the first task in such circumstances is to prevent this from happening. For me supervision was crucial in enabling me to achieve this.

As my supervision sessions progressed I became less agitated in relation to my work with Andrew. The exploration of my counter-transference enabled me to settle within myself and to relax in myself enough to allow myself to connect with his frame of reference. As a result I was able to become more robust in my ability to experience empathy towards Andrew. These outcomes of my supervision enabled me to continue to work with him. On reflection, a key aspect of my 'settling' was the result of untangling, in dialogue with my supervisor, what was 'my stuff' and what was the client's. The process by which this was achieved involved my supervisor helping me to explore both the feelings I held towards Andrew and how these may have been echoed aspects of other significant relationships in my life. What was occurring was what Pick (1985, p. 164) describes as the second task of therapy:

> Having recognised counter-transference and having avoided acting it out in a destructive manner, the analyst must attempt to undo the inevitable tangle in his mind between what is more directly patient produced, and what is more a function of his own personal response to that production. If he can do this, the analyst can then try to understand what the patient is projecting, along with the motive behind it.

Over time, in our work together, although Andrew still presented as anxious, the number of texts declined and he spent less time talking about his partner and more time talking about himself. An outcome of on-going supervision was that I was better able to engage empathically with Andrew without feeling threatened by doing so. This was expressed in the changing quality of the stance I spoke of earlier, which became less rebellious and more accepting as I worked through the counter-transference and began to break the association between Andrew and my adopted mother. I was becoming better placed to separate my issues from his, as a result of working through the complexities of my counter-transference. This enabled me to become more tolerant internally of being empathically engaged with Andrew.

An illustration of this is that on one occasion I became quite angry and irritated by Andrew's partner's apparent lack of understanding of the pain and hurt Andrew was experiencing as a result of their separation. This could be understood as a projection into me of Andrew's anger. However, I think that empathy feels different from this kind of projective process because it involves an active imagining of how the other feels or of entering into an 'as if' stance, which were qualities of how I remember feeling at that time. An outcome of this for me was that I felt safer and reassured by my increasing capacity to be containing of myself in relation to Andrew. I found myself better able to reciprocate the trust he placed in me, and this continued until our work together concluded.

Making Sense

About a year after my work with Andrew ended, I decided to advance my studies by proceeding from my postgraduate diploma in counselling to complete a master's degree. Because I had had such a powerful experience in my work with Andrew, I decided to draw on it as the basis for my master's dissertation. Another feature that played an important part in my decision to undertake this study was the fact that I still felt strongly connected to Andrew. This connection felt more than psychological; almost physiological or cellular. It was as if there was unfinished business between us that I couldn't understand but that I felt instinctively was of huge consequence in relation to my ability to be 'present' in my work as a counsellor.

My understanding of this situation began to develop through an exploration of the dynamic of my working relationship with my dissertation supervisor. As with Andrew my relationship with him involved a struggle to hold on to myself. But whereas with Andrew this struggle was characterised by an initial pulling away and maintaining a 'safe' distance, with my supervisor it was a pulling towards. I found my supervisor to be an inspirational figure; he was attractive, articulate, academically successful, gay, and well respected. In this he was exciting to be with. He gave me a role model of success that I could believe in and the hope that I might be able to realise it for myself. He was how I wanted to be. In my transference towards him, he was the perfect older brother whom I had always wanted, who could take me under his wing and who would be like a mentor to me. What tempered this transference was that in reality I found him to be very emotionally contained, and not affirming or validating of me.

My working relationship with my supervisor felt similar to my relationship with Andrew with regard to the issues of attunement, merging, and oneness – but with the positions reversed. I was the needy one seeking empathy, validation, and affirmation. I began to wonder if there were similarities between Andrew and me that I had not realised when I had been working with him. Was it possible that I had had more than one counter-transference relationship with Andrew? A clue to this question arose out of my supervisor's response to a passage in my case study where I described taking my client to supervision:

> Interesting that you are not taking the work to supervision but the client! I had an image of you taking a small child by the hand to a consultation with an expert professional who would help you both.

I responded strongly to my tutor's image, easily relating to it and seeing Andrew and me as two lost children holding on to one another, both seeking solace and protection. I couldn't initially understand why this should be, but I had a strong empathic emotional response to it. It felt real and true.

What began to seep into my consciousness was the possibility that a further dynamic had run through this work. For the first time I was struck by how similar Andrew and I may have been. The extent of what I discovered astounded me.

- We were both gay men.
- We both had partners who were in some way emotionally not available to us.
- We both tended to form anxious/needy attachments (Bowlby, 1988).
- We both shared the experience of having strong, overbearing primary maternal caregivers.
- In managing our early experience of pain we both found the feelings and context in which that pain was experienced now comforting, because it gave us our only experience of consistency and stability in a world that appeared ever changing and threatening.
- We had both experienced homophobia directly and indirectly, which had impacted on our valuing of ourselves and our worthiness in relation to others, heightening our sense of fragility in relationships.

Another shared issue shouted at me: at the time of our working together we were both experiencing the loss of our primary maternal caregivers, in his case the death of his mother and in mine the death of my adopted mother. In becoming aware of these similarities I began to realise that perhaps the 'further dynamic' present in my work with him was indeed another counter-transference relationship.

As well as my counter-transference response to Andrew in which the dynamics of my relationship with my adopted mother played such a powerful part, I began to wonder if I had also identified with Andrew in a way that gave me an opportunity to gain a stronger sense of security by belonging to something larger than myself. What I mean by this is the idea that by joining up with a fellow lost child who possessed a felt understanding of what it was like to be abandoned and who experienced the world as being intrinsically homophobic, just as I had, I was able to feel the security and protection of a larger, shared reality.

It was at this time, in the midst of discovering the similarity of issues I shared with Andrew, that I began to understand more about the quality of melancholia I sensed in him and in my adopted mother, which also resided in me for the same reason that it oozed from them. I too was a child in search of a parent. The melancholia that I was holding was as a result of my own experience of being emotionally and psychologically neglected.

Thinking in this way, it seemed that Andrew acted like a magnet for me. Magnets attract, and they also repel objects with the same charge, just as I had internally recoiled from him. As well as providing me with an opportunity to connect with a soul-mate to fill the hole in my soul, he also provided an opportunity for me to re-experience events that I was only just coming to terms with. In this way, Andrew's intrinsic threat to me was his capacity to trigger the felt trauma of my early abandonment, especially in our first session together when he seemed most needy and demanding.

In reflecting on my work with Andrew during my dissertation studies I discovered my own child 'survival alarm' being switched on, in response to which I protected myself from my capacity to respond empathically, perhaps because to do so confronted me with the possibility and the threat of merging with a fellow lost child. In retrospect I think that this represented for me both a longing for absolution and a terror of annihilation.

This understanding was very important. Not only did it illustrate the complexity of issues I was experiencing in response to Andrew, but it also enabled me to begin to consider that he evoked in me a reaction that was a result of a combination of my counter-transference responses to him. This led me to construct the possibility that clients may evoke in therapists a range of counter-transference responses as a result of the unique meeting of both the client's and therapist's own life experience. From this thinking arose the theoretical concept of a 'counter-transference matrix' that each therapist carries with him or her, arising out of his or her own phenomenology.

As I processed these reflections and ideas over a period of time, something else began to emerge for me, which I came to recognise as a further factor in my difficulty with staying therapeutically engaged with Andrew. In him I saw my own reflection, and it was to myself that I was unable to offer a deeply compassionate response. I was ashamed of my own desire to reach out to assuage my neediness and vulnerability.

Dissociated Empathy

In relation to my own experience I would describe the empathic attunement that I believe was present in my work with Andrew not as false empathy (Mearns and Thorne, 1999) but as a genuine 'dissociated empathy', a concept I use to describe an empathy towards a client that encompasses a deep psychological connection that is beyond the conscious awareness of the therapist but in another way is actually a 'felt unknown' awareness, a kind of intuitive awareness that signals to one a need to be very careful.

In experiencing this dissociated empathy my counter-transference enabled me to pay attention to the need to be very careful. It was, in effect, an expression of my intuitive awareness signalling to me the need to take particular care. In this I believe that my counter-transference reactions acted like a defence mechanism that enabled me to remain protected against my dissociated empathic responses towards Andrew. If I had responded to them, it would have most probably led to a situation where I found myself enmeshed with him with no self-identity, a characteristic of my own relationship with my adopted mother. This would have had serious consequences in relation to my ability to nurture and maintain a therapeutic alliance and work within an ethical framework.

To return to the magnet metaphor, when I was working with Andrew I think that the tension I was experiencing arose out of my oscillation between two charges of attraction and repulsion, each of these charges correlating with a specific counter-transference response. The confluence of these charges created the counter-transference matrix I was experiencing and was expressed in the wave of internal recoiling I initially experienced in my work with Andrew. Acting as a defence mechanism, this helped me to find a neutrally charged therapeutic distance in relation to Andrew. This in turn enabled me to be neither repelled nor attracted to him in ways that would have endangered the quality of our existing psychological contact.

My learning has provided a personal validation of the thesis put forward by Heimann (1950, p. 81) that

> The analyst's emotional response to his patient within the analytic situation represents the most important tools of the work. The analyst's counter-transference is an instrument of research into the patient's unconscious.

It was also an insight into my unconscious. Heimann (1950, p. 83) goes further, suggesting that

> The analyst's counter-transference is not only part and parcel of the analytic relationship, but it is the patient's creation, it is part of the patient's personality.

On this point I disagree with Heimann in that I think that the analyst's counter-transference is the confluence of both the client's and the counsellor's psycho-phenomenology. The patient or client may attempt to create a counter-transference reaction, but whether this is actualised or not is dependent on what the counsellor brings to the therapeutic relationship in terms of his or her own issues and history (Carpy, 1989). The metaphor I would use to describe this is what occurs as a result of the intermixing of different flows of water in a river. This is dependent on the characteristics of the tributaries coming together, the intermixing of water creating the potential for a specific counter-transference response. This is a co-constructed element of counter-transference in that it recognises two components: the 'me' and 'me-in-relation-to-the-other'. Counter-transference emerges from the meeting and interaction of the client's transference with the counsellor's psychological narrative and their embodied responses to the whole situation.

In reviewing my work with Andrew for the purpose of this chapter, I'm left with the feeling that my work with him was 'reductionist' in its approach, in the sense that I maintained a focus on alleviating his presenting issues by offering him practical options for managing these issues. I was not able to help him open up the underlying dynamics of his experience. On a more positive note, however, I didn't abandon him and I didn't act out my counter-transferential reactions to him. I stayed with him to the best of my therapeutic ability, and perhaps this was the most important thing I could have done while trying to hold on to my integrity.

I think that what enabled us to have a constructive working relationship for the period in which we worked together was my ability to stay with my intention to be empathic, which took me into the challenging terrain of untangling elements within my counter-transference. I think that I also sought to honour him and our work together in my efforts to understand and resolve the dynamics that had occurred between us in the counselling room, long after our work had finished.

Perhaps an even more important awareness I have gained has been in relation to the personal issues I bring to therapeutic relationships and how strongly they can determine my quality of relating, particularly in terms of the quality of my presence and therapeutic availability. Deciphering my counter-transference matrix responses and their effect on my ability to be present for Andrew has been a revelation. Even after all these years, as I write I can still feel a settling sensation, a calmness resulting from knowing that I was not going mad. In undertaking my work with Andrew I also gained a lived experience of the importance of on-going supervision. From this I gained more confidence and trust in my ability to meet clients with empathic attunement (Greenberg, Rice, and Elliott, 1993).

It was my experience of a perceived failure of empathy and the consequent impact on my ability to express congruence in the therapeutic relationship that highlighted for me that I had issues in relating to my client. As I began to explore this experience I turned from person-centred to psychodynamic ideas. Indeed it was my struggle with empathy and congruence that provided the catalyst for my evolving comprehension of the counter-transference and my journey towards a deeper understanding of the power of counter-transference in the therapeutic relationship. In this, one psychological theoretical frame of reference became the gateway for understanding of the other. In coming full circle, it was my working through these psychodynamic concepts that enabled me not only to more authentically express empathy and congruence (Rogers, 1959) but also to develop the concepts of dissociated empathy and the counter-transference matrix.

In closing I would like to thank Andrew, because without the experience of our work together I might not have been able to hold on to, let alone express, my compassion, acceptance, and love for that little lost boy of long ago. For that I am eternally grateful.

References

Bion, W. R. (1961) *Experience in Groups and Other Papers* (London: Tavistock).

Bion, W. R. (1962a) *Learning from Experience* (London: Heinemann).

Bion, W. R. (1962b) 'A theory of thinking', *International Journal of Psycho-Analysis*, 43, 306–310. Reproduced in *Second Thoughts* (London: Heinemann, 1967).

Bowlby, J. (1988) *A Secure Base: Clinical Applications of Attachment Theory* (London: Routledge).

Bradshaw, J. (1988) *Healing the Shame That Binds You* (Florida: Health Communications).

Carpy, D. V. (1989) 'Tolerating the countertransference: A mutative process', *International Journal of Psychoanalysis*, 70, 287–294.

Freud, S. (1909) 'Analysis of a Phobia in a Five-Year-Old Boy', *The Standard Edition of the Complete Psychological Works of Sigmund Freud*, Volume X, translated and edited by James Strachey (London: Hogarth Press) pp. 1–150.

Greenberg, L. S., Rice, L. N., and Elliot, R. (1993) *Facilitating Emotional Change: The Moment-by-Moment Process* (New York: Guilford Press).

Heimann, P. (1950) 'On counter-transference', *International Journal of Psychoanalysis*, 31, 81–84.

Mearns, D., and Thorne, B. (1999) *Person-Centred Counselling in Action*, 2nd edn (London: Sage).

Money-Kyrle, R. (1956) 'Normal countertransference and some of its deviations', *International Journal of Psychoanalysis*, 37, 360–366

Pick, I. B. (1985) 'Working through in the countertransference', *International Journal of Psychoanalysis*, 66, 157–166.

Rogers, C. R. (1959) 'A theory of therapy, personality, and interpersonal relationships, as developed in the client-centred framework' in S. Koch (ed.) *Psychology: A Study of a Science*, Volume 3, *Formulations of the Person and the Social Context* (New York: McGraw-Hill) pp. 184–256.

13 Working with Mark: Gender in the Counselling Room

LYNNE ROLLO

Mark was in his mid-thirties when he came for counselling. After being depressed for several months he had been signed off from his work as an engineer, a career for which he had spent many years in training. He felt unable to cope with the responsibilities of work, the travelling, making decisions, and supervising staff. Mark was having panic attacks and episodes of low mood and was feeling very anxious and distressed about what this crisis meant for his future. Everything that was good seemed to be in the past, and the future was empty. Mark had a close and supportive relationship with his wife and with his wider family. He was getting lots of support and reassurance from people close to him, but he still felt that he was letting everyone down.

In this chapter I explore some of the gender dynamics I encountered while working therapeutically with this man. I examine how I came to make meaning from this encounter in a way that informed my sense of myself as a therapeutic practitioner. Finding a meaningful connection with Mark – as with any client – felt central to my approach to therapeutic work and my identity as a feminist female counsellor. However, from the very beginning, my work with Mark was beset with what felt like disconnections. This was troubling and made me doubt my own ability to work effectively.

My work with Mark took place early in my professional practice while I was completing my counselling training. As a student I was receiving high levels of supervision and, as I elaborate in this chapter, supervision was central to my developing understanding of this therapeutic relationship. Supervision helped me to frame and reframe this understanding so that I could gradually bring myself to the work with more insight and awareness. Starting with the first session, I describe this process of developing awareness.

Relating as a Man to a Man

The first session with Mark began and ended with my experiencing a feeling of disorientation and disconnection. After I showed Mark into the counselling room, he walked straight to 'my' chair and sat down. I made a quick decision to let this go: there was no obvious reason why sitting in my chair should pose a problem. Also Mark looked anxious, and although he had a relaxed posture I could see that there was tension in the way he held himself. His arms lay along the arms of the chair, hands gripped as though he was ready to propel himself up and out of the room. I was picking up a sense of urgency about getting started.

There was little time to complete the preliminaries of contracting, because Mark quickly launched into an account of his day-to-day struggles: feelings of depression and anxiety, fear of panic attacks, feeling unable to face work or other people. Even spending time playing with his children had become a chore. Mark broke down and cried, and it felt as if all the pain and distress he had been holding in started to overflow.

It was important for me to be as open as possible to what Mark was experiencing without trying to make sense of what was happening. In the midst of trying to take in all this emotional turmoil, my attention was suddenly distracted when I became aware of my bag sitting beside Mark's chair. This felt disorientating. I always have my bag at my side, and it is full of personal belongings as well as work items. I felt strangely separated from a part of myself but made an effort to ignore this. An uncomfortable feeling developed in me that Mark had appropriated both my chair and my bag, and this continued to intrude during this session and in others.

Notwithstanding this discomfort and disorientation, I also knew that I liked Mark. He struck me as a sensitive and serious man. He was tall and physically robust, but there was also something fragile about his presence. I was moved and concerned by Mark's apparent willingness, even eagerness, to trust me with his outpourings of distress, which had a confessional quality. He had no previous experience of counselling, but it felt as if he knew what he needed from me.

As this first session progressed, however, I became increasingly aware of a disconcerting sense of gender confusion, a feeling that I was relating to Mark as a man to a man. It is hard to find the words to describe this, but key elements included an embodied sense of masculinity, which I felt as a kind of strength in my bones, and a robust steadiness combined with a feeling of mirroring Mark's large physical presence (and weight).

I also felt as if I was holding a space open, almost as if I was pushing away psychic intrusions. Alongside feeling disconcerted by my gender confusion, I had a sense of mutuality and of being in it together with Mark. I was not overwhelmed by Mark's distress but rather curious.

Later on I noted another distinctive feature of my initial response to Mark. In first sessions with new clients I often find myself in a thoughtless and slightly entranced state and understand this as something akin to 'primary maternal preoccupation', allowing me to take in the new client without too much processing or interpretation (Winnicott, 1956). However, the fast pace and my sharp awareness of my own feelings of confusion during the first session with Mark did not allow for this, and I wondered afterwards how much of him I had really been able to take in.

After the session I felt tired and confused but managed to identify elements of Mark's emotional turmoil that seemed important. The most powerful feelings were of loss and anxiety as Mark confronted an uncertain future, unable to face a return to work and with a sense of having failed everyone in his world. I suspected that Mark was trying to protect the people close to him from his overwhelming and unmanageable feelings. It seemed that Mark had lost his sense of who he was; his sense of identity and everything that this represented was under threat. Mark's established ways of coping had finally broken down as, in Griffin's (2001, p. 419) words, 'the defences of the integrated self may fragment as they are presented with the primitive fears of a disintegrating self'.

There seemed to be a constellation of issues around Mark's changing sense of himself as a man. He talked about feelings of frustration and shame, because he was unable to live up to the expectations others had of him as a devoted and dependable husband and father and as a provider for his family. Even going to the pub felt like an ordeal, as friends could not understand what had happened to the sociable and easy-going person whose company they had previously enjoyed.

Mark was not alone; his wife and family were accepting of his emotional difficulties and were keen to offer support and reassurance. Mark was appreciative of this, even though he often felt guilty for letting everyone down when efforts to help him fell flat. For example, plans to go away for a weekend with his wife fell through at the last minute because Mark felt too tired and anxious to cope with the travelling. I wondered if Mark needed time out from normal demands and expectations, a kind of moratorium to reflect on where he was going in life. I hoped that counselling could offer him this kind of space.

As I reflected on my initial experience of responding to Mark as a man to a man, I wondered whether being separated from my bag had been significant: had I been separated from a feminine aspect of myself? This seemed far-fetched, and yet I did feel as if I had been propelled into a situation with Mark in which my grip on normal realities was somehow loosened.

In subsequent sessions Mark continued to give voice to his distress and confusion, often becoming overwhelmed and breaking down in tears. At the beginning of a session he would often report some hopeful development: a successful social event or new future plans. However, there was something in his bright manner that felt superficial and that I did not trust. As the session progressed, hope would seem to give way to hopelessness. I felt my role was to contain this and not to protect Mark from feelings of distress. I believe that the containment I was offering at this time fell somewhere between a 'holding' of the client in Winnicott's terms and a more active processing of material as described by Bion's concept of containment (Bion, 1962; Winnicott, 1960; Leiper and Maltby, 2004). My priority was to stay with Mark's experiencing of sadness and anxiety. Unlike other people in his life, I did not need Mark to feel better and he did not have to convince me that he was coping.

My containment of Mark and his emotions at this stage felt connected to my continuing experience of relating to him inter-subjectively as a man to a man. This disconcerting feature persisted, becoming an integral aspect of my experience of our relationship. We were engaged in an equal, almost businesslike, shared experience of focusing on a problem. There was no room for anything extraneous (no frills) but only a mutual resolve to tackle the problem of Mark's life crisis. Mark leaned forward with his elbows on his knees, and I felt inclined to mirror his posture. He told me that counselling was helping him and he seemed able to trust me. I felt physically very steady and emotionally capable of holding a space for him, but I also noticed the continuing sense of disconnection, a cool distance that seemed incongruent in the face of Mark's emotional struggles. I began to feel unsure about my own capacity for warmth and empathy as a counsellor.

In a supervision group I was prompted to consider whether by holding masculine qualities in the relationship I might offer Mark an opportunity to be open about his emotional vulnerability and to feel safe enough to express overwhelming feelings of loss and distress. As Maguire (1995, p. 148) suggests, 'When male patients begin to see a female therapist as having qualities they associate with the father and men, they recognise with relief that they can experiment with expressing more of their own psychic femininity'. Mark did not have to be a strong and resilient man with me but could explore other aspects of his internal emotional experience.

The concept of transference offered a framework that made some sense of my responding to Mark as a man, and I felt grateful that this might be useful to him. The possibility of a paternal transference interested and excited me. I had not considered that I might have such a capacity. Indeed Maguire (1995) suggests that female therapists may generally be disinclined to consider paternal transference in their therapeutic work with male patients. In this context, supervision group members were quick to assure me that despite my doubts, I was doing good work with Mark. I remember feeling grateful for the theoretical insight but a little irritated and unconvinced by the reassurance.

Working with the Paternal Transference

As the work progressed I was able to continue to hold a space for Mark that allowed him to talk about his emotional pain and to explore his struggles to find a meaningful way forward in life. I associated my capacity to hold a masculine presence with my coolness and steadiness in the face of his internal turmoil. However, there were two areas in the work that I was beginning to be concerned about.

First, in each session Mark took care to tell me in some detail about the support offered to him by his wife and his sisters. He expressed gratitude for their involvement, their offers of company, reassurance, and practical help. I was well aware that these women represented a vital support network for Mark; it was important that he had caring and concerned people in his life. And yet I noticed that I was increasingly experiencing the women in Mark's life as intrusive and interfering. They crowded into the counselling room and impinged on our space, breathing the same air. The stories about all their helpful and thoughtful acts of support stirred up in me feelings of frustration and something close to rage. I remember one session in which Mark told me that his sister would be waiting for him outside, and I felt a surge of anger that interrupted my concentration. I thought, 'Can't they just leave him alone!'

Second, at other times I felt drawn into seeing Mark's situation and his options from somewhat polarised and limiting perspectives, seeking black and white where there was only grey. In an attempt to be useful, I found myself drawn into a cognitive, problem-solving approach, introducing explanations or practical strategies, such as suggestions about new career options. Perhaps this reflected my response to Mark's need for solutions in a world of uncertainty. However, it also meant that we were, at times, becoming less attuned to his distress, and I was less attuned to my own feelings of confusion. This contributed to my sense of being distanced and disconnected.

Once again it was in supervision that I began to develop a deeper understanding of what may have been happening in the work with Mark. My sense of responding as a masculine presence and the feeling of emotional distance suggested that perhaps, at an unconscious level, Mark may have been at risk of being overwhelmed by the experience of working with a female counsellor. With the female counsellor as a potential mother figure in the transference, Mark might have become engulfed by feelings associated with dependent infancy and this could have been devastating when his sense of self was so fragile. Aitken and Coupe (2006, p. 76) describe this risk thus: 'The potential for regression, shame, vulnerability and humiliation is great. Gender role certainty is under threat in such an intimate relationship.' Perhaps Mark was getting what he needed from me as a masculine presence in the transference, offering containment without impingement or the threat of his being overwhelmed. I began to see that the helpful women in Mark's life may have posed a threat, preventing him from recovering a sense of an independent and strong self. From this perspective, my feelings that they should leave him alone were not so irrational.

Reflecting on this also helped me to consider the intensity of my response to the women in Mark's life in a different light. Could my angry feelings towards these women have been a projective identification of Mark's unconscious and angry feelings towards them? He took such care to express his appreciation. However, at a deeper, unconscious level their well-meaning efforts may have been overwhelming, perhaps infantilising, keeping him helpless and dependent. It was possible that he was raging against them but could not tolerate these unmanageable feelings. My strong response to the caring women in Mark's life was echoed in my irritated reaction to offers of reassurance in group supervision. I was looking for answers, not support or reassurance.

Perhaps my sense of disconnection and the tendency to be drawn into a problem-solving approach were consistent with Mark's need for a relationship with a masculine figure, rather than a maternal relationship in which there was a risk that his feelings of dependency could be stirred up. I wondered whether Mark had known at an unconscious level what he needed from me when he first entered the counselling room, claiming my chair and bag. I wondered if he needed to balance the care and support of family and friends with someone non-maternal who could contain his distress without being hurt by it, neither offering reassurance nor needing him to get better.

I began to see that my role with Mark could be understood in terms of the role of the father (Wright, 1991) or third position (Britton, 2004). A counsellor with the capacity for a paternal transference can be a bridge between the intimacy of the close relationship with mother (or primary carer) and the outside world. Perhaps this would help Mark to recognise and benefit from close, nurturing relationships and to move beyond this into a new and as yet unfamiliar external world.

Reconnecting with More of Myself

With the assistance of supervision I continued to work with Mark with a new sense of purpose and the belief that I had a meaningful role. And yet there was also a sense that the work and my relationship with Mark were somehow stuck. Mark seemed less distressed and anxious. He said that he felt better and there were incremental changes in his life that allowed a glimmer of hope: he had managed to meet up with friends on a couple of occasions and was able to talk a little to other people about his anxieties for the future. However, Mark continued to feel that if only he could get control of his mental health and return to work, life could continue as before. I felt that we were stuck in a present in which Mark was unable to move forward or reconnect to his past.

I often found myself drawn into Mark's search for explanations and solutions. This took us away from his emotional world and the difficult process of re-negotiating his identity and role in life. In responding to Mark's need to be doing something useful, I would increasingly find myself in an emotionally dead space in which only the cognitive was allowed. Sometimes I would find myself flinching, almost physically, when I talked too much or started offering explanations or interpretations.

My sense of being disconnected or emotionally distanced, which I understood as a characteristic of relating to Mark as a man to a man, began to feel debilitating. Underlying this was a feeling of being a failure because I was lacking in the sense of warmth and empathy that I considered to be the hallmarks of a good female counsellor. Later I came to understand that in identifying with a narrow stereotype of what it means to be a good female counsellor it was inevitable that I would feel inadequate. My focus had been on Mark's experience of gender and his sense of failure as a man. Awareness of how restrictive gender expectations affected my own sense of competence took longer to come into my awareness.

In supervision with a group of people who knew me well, I shared my feelings of being stuck in the work and was full of self-recriminations about being drawn into cognitive and task-centred ways of working with Mark. I also felt able to talk about my deeper concerns that I was unable to meet Mark with empathy and warmth and that this meant I was not a good enough counsellor. Within this group I was encouraged to explore and go deeper into this territory.

It became clear that I had become less attuned to my own experience of being in relationship with this client. As a new counsellor I had been grateful for a meaningful way of making sense of my response to Mark (as a man to a man) and took this up with relief as if it was a fixed role. However, it was becoming less possible for me to be authentically present with Mark because, in my eagerness to maintain a useful role, unconscious adjustments had become stuck, limiting our relationship. Perhaps responding to this client as a man to a man involved withholding essential aspects of my own self. Maybe I was losing contact with my internalised maternal object and the capacity to self-soothe and tolerate anxiety, which helps me to process difficult feelings and to move on from mistakes. I was feeling disconnected, not only in my relationship with Mark but also within my own internal world.

On reflection I came to see that I had been acting into the transference and that this was ultimately limiting: 'if the relationship is transferential through and through, what leverage can the therapist have to promote change?' (Leiper and Maltby, 2004, p. 73). I needed a foot on solid ground in order to observe the transference and to work in alliance with Mark, towards change. Part of me had been absent, and this placed limits on the work and on my resources and emotional resilience.

Following these explorations I began to feel different in the counselling room with Mark. Although I had not made any conscious decisions about using a different approach, I began to trust myself to be with Mark without overwhelming him or intruding and was able to let go of my need to provide solutions. I could see that in my eagerness to fulfil a useful role, for which I had a theoretical rationale, I had become less attuned to myself as a whole person. The work in my supervision group had a liberating effect and I was able to be present in a way that allowed for some spontaneity and challenge, although I continued to be tentative. Leiper and Maltby (2004, p. 86) discuss this process as one of 'disentanglement' from the transference, enabling an 'act of freedom' in which the therapist moves 'out of a fused state of mind into one of greater clarity'.

Over the next two sessions I was not aware of behaving differently, but the relationship felt more alive and charged with potential. My anxieties for Mark and the difficulties he had to face became sharper-edged, and I was more attuned to my own feelings of concern for him. I was less self-critical and also found I had less to say. Then in the third session there was a change in Mark. He was quiet throughout, almost sullen. I sensed that he was holding himself at a distance from me. It was an odd experience, and at one point I thought 'he's wondering what he's doing sitting here with an old woman'. There was something sorrowful in the room too. At the end of the session Mark apologised for being so quiet. I felt some confusion and sadness and wondered if this was how the women in his life felt when Mark withdrew from them.

Reflecting on this episode later on, I wondered if Mark was responding to my adjustment. I had stopped acting into the transference and had returned to a more complex and integrated self, encompassing feminine and masculine elements. Perhaps his response reflected a move towards the depressive position, a more realistic understanding of what relationships can offer and of his place in a world where there is neither a wholly good nor bad mother or father. I can see that by no longer embodying the transference unthinkingly (Leiper and Maltby, 2004, p. 77) I was presenting a new challenge for Mark.

After this Mark cancelled a session, though he returned again the next week. I felt a strong need to know why he had cancelled but resisted asking. He paid the late cancellation fee and said nothing. I sensed his need to have this space to himself and managed not to intrude. Thereafter, the work gradually began to open up. Mark talked with more acceptance about the reality that there was no way back to his former life. I felt more emotionally engaged and more attuned to feelings of loss and anxieties. At times I felt close to tears. It felt as if we were at the beginning of a longer process of change, one that included letting go of old hopes and possibilities as well as looking forward. In negotiating a new career and new ways of living, Mark needed to mourn what was lost.

There were small incremental changes, realistic adjustments, and future plans that now seemed to accumulate. We talked about how it felt for Mark to be the recipient of so much support and reassurance, and although he continued to express gratitude for this, he began to speak of needing space and more time on his own. I no longer felt the sharp edge of anger towards the women in Mark's life.

Around this time something else changed too. Mark became more able to challenge and assert himself in his relationship with me. Earlier in the relationship he would often seem surprised by my capacity to reflect back his emotional experience so accurately. Now he would more often reject my choice of words or would find his own way of framing his experience: 'No, I didn't feel anxious, anxious isn't the right word. I was a bit worried but also a bit excited.' There was an edge at times, which gave me a glimpse of Mark's aggressive energy, energy that perhaps I had been able to contain at a time when such aggressive feelings would have been too destructive for Mark to bring to consciousness.

There was something in this stage of the work that I came to understand as 'differentiation'. By Mark's making the adjustment to me as a complex, potentially disappointing, and separate person, I became real and as such a bridge to wider realities (Winnicott, 1960).

Endings

Work with Mark ended sooner than I would have liked, when he chose to finish after eight months. He had decided to embark on a new direction, working part-time in a garage and training for a different career. Mark was discovering that he needed more personal space in his life and had started hill-walking on his own. I noticed the emergence of feelings of anxiety in me. Wasn't it too soon to start a new venture? Wouldn't Mark be lonely walking on his own? Would he be safe? I recognised elements of genuine concern but also an impulse to control and protect, and possibly an impinging maternal transference. Having been attuned to what I understood as Mark's deep anxieties about being overwhelmed, I knew it was important for me to manage (and avoid acting out) these responses. I had to let Mark make his own ending and to leave counselling: this felt crucial to the integrity of the work. It meant accepting Mark's decision to end counselling, but without undermining his autonomy by making known my concern that this felt too soon. Mark knew I was still available to him, but he took his own authority and chose to finish. We talked about keeping the door open for counselling as a possible option for the future.

In one of the last sessions Mark arrived eager to talk about a weekend he had spent with friends camping and mountain biking. He had not been looking forward to this, but the physical activity and shared experience were unexpectedly enjoyable. I realised that I had not considered how important *play* might be for this client and was reassured and a little entranced by his enthusiasm. Why did I think the way forward would have to be all hard work?

During the weekend Mark had fallen into a stream and hurt his arm. He rolled up his sleeve to show me the bruise. I said nothing but raised my eyebrows a little and Mark just smiled back. I felt he was inviting me to do a little bit of 'mothering', knowing that I would not overwhelm him with concern and anxiety. Maybe there was also an element of pride in showing me what he had survived in the world 'out there'.

Reflecting on my work with Mark, I recall often feeling lost within the complexities of the relationship and the interplay of inner and outer reali-ties. As Leiper and Maltby (2004, p. 84) suggest, the transference is a 'blend, a complex alloy of the past and present, the real and fantastic, it is not a dichotomy. Everything in the therapeutic relationship is both real and transferential.' In the first session I lost my bag and my chair and with them my sense of self as woman and my bearings as a counsellor. My strong feelings towards the women in Mark's life, which I understood as a form of projective identification with denied, split-off parts of himself, were echoed in my experience of supervision. I came to think that Mark may have known at an unconscious level what he needed before he had even stepped into the counselling room. Disorientated from the beginning, I responded to his communication of need for a masculine presence. I was able to make sense of this through supervision and growing insight about transference communications. Through this work I have come to see that it is important to accept the need for 'psychic bisexuality' by drawing upon 'cross gender identifications' as described by Maguire (1995).

Towards the end of my work with Mark my capacity to be authentically present coincided with positive therapeutic change. It gradually became clearer to me that 'authenticity' is not is not an 'all or nothing' aspect of the therapeutic relationship. Rather, as Miller et al. (2004, p. 73) suggest, 'Authenticity is a process in movement – we move in and out of more or less authenticity as a consequence of the relational dynamics'. I became more authentically present towards the end of my work with Mark by bringing myself more fully to the relationship and no longer acting into the transference. If we had continued to work together for longer, no doubt this capacity for being authentically present would have continued to evolve and change.

In reflecting on my work with Mark, I was driven by a sense of the importance of making meaningful connections with clients. As this chapter has shown, I came to see that experiences of disconnection are also part of the reality and are intrinsic to therapeutic work. According to Jordan (2004, p. 62), we can 'get to know and take responsibility for our disconnections' and we should not 'become hemmed in by idealised expectations of how or who we should be'. My sense of responding to Mark as a man to a man could be understood as a connection rather than a disconnection, because it was a manifestation of what I believe Mark needed from me in the relationship. My feelings of discomfort and disorientation were not so much an obstacle to the therapeutic work but crucial clues to the complexities of the developing relationship.

References

Aitken, F., and Coupe, A. (2006) 'Female counsellor, male client: Counselling across gender' in S. Wheeler (ed.) *Difference and Diversity in Counselling* (Basingstoke: Palgrave MacMillan) pp. 74–88.

Bion, W. R. (1962) *Learning from Experience* (London: Heinemann).

Britton, R. (2004) 'Subjectivity, objectivity and triangular space', *Psychoanalytic Quarterly*, 73 (1), 47–61.

Griffin, D. (2001) 'Loss as a lifelong regenerative process', *Psychodynamic Counselling*, 7, 413–430.

Jordan, J. V. (2004) 'Relational awareness: Transforming disconnection' in J. V. Jordan, M. Walker, and L. M. Hartling (eds) *The Complexity of Connection* (New York: Guilford Press) pp. 47–63.

Leiper, R., and Maltby, M. (2004) *The Psychodynamic Approach to Therapeutic Change* (London: Sage).

Maguire, M. (1995) *Men, Women and Passion: Gender Issues in Psychotherapy* (London: Routledge).

Miller, J. B., Jordan, J. V., Stiver, I. O., Walker, M., Surrey, J. L., and Eldridge, N. S. (2004) 'Therapists' authenticity' in J. V. Jordan, M. Walker, and L. M. Hartling (eds) *The Complexity of Connection* (New York: Guilford Press) pp. 64–89.

Winnicott, D. W. (1956) 'Primary maternal preoccupation' in *Collected Papers: Through Paediatrics to Psycho-Analysis* (London: Tavistock, 1958) pp. 300–305.

Winnicott, D. W. (1960) 'The theory of the parent-infant relationship', *International Journal of Psycho-Analysis*, 41, 585–595. Reproduced in *The Maturational Processes and the Facilitating Environment* (London: Hogarth, 1965).

Wright, K. (1991) *Vision and Separation: Between Mother and Baby* (London: Free Association Books).

14 Tolerating the 'Chaos Monsters': Making Sense with Bion

DIANA SIM

Writing in the Spirit of Bion

In this chapter I explore some of the ideas of the English psychoanalyst Wilfred Bion (1897–1979), specifically those that consider the ways in which counsellor and client relate in order to deepen their understanding of the client's experience. As I undertook to familiarise myself with Bion's theories, I felt overwhelmed by the apparent complexity of his ideas. My initial response was to tenaciously chase after a rigid understanding in order to write something that was 'correct'. Then I came across the following:

> leave go of psychological comfort, venture forth into the unknown and risk the terror. (Symington and Symington, 2004, p. 184)

I began to get a sense that letting go of facts and certainty was fundamental in order to allow a different type of knowledge to evolve. This type of knowledge seemed to relate to the very thing that Bion was describing when he explored the deepening understanding that can take place in a counsellor–client relationship. Gradually, I was able to free myself of my desire to 'get it right' and allow myself to be affected by my research. What I believe I have achieved is an exploration of Bion's ideas written 'in the spirit' of Bion.

Much of Wilfred Bion's work focuses on the way in which the relationship between analyst and patient or, as I prefer to describe them, the counsellor and the client, can enable learning by a process of applying thought to an emotional experience (Bion, 1962a, 1962b, 1963, 1965, 1970; Britton, 2011; Ogden, 2003; Symington and Symington, 2004). Bion links this process to our earliest experience of relating, the relationship between mother and baby. He believes that the baby relies on the mother to help manage its emotional experiences. He suggests that

211

the mother can pick up on the emotional experience of the baby, maybe by actually experiencing some of those emotions herself. As the adult, she may then be able to make enough sense of her own experience to be able to reflect it back, meaningfully, to the baby.

Bion elaborates on this process in relation to the therapeutic relationship. He attempts to find ways to make different stages of the process available for consideration by offering terms to represent them. I will start by exploring what Bion considers to be the most primitive elements available to counsellor and client (or mother and baby) within this process. Bion believes that there are some experiences that seem to exist, for the client, in a form that is not really available for thinking about. He calls these 'beta elements' and describes them as 'undigested facts' (Bion, 1962a, p. 7). The work of other authors has helped to enrich my sense of what Bion is describing. Joan and Neville Symington (2004, p. 63) describe beta elements as 'sense impressions devoid of meaning or nameless sensations which cause frustration'. Thomas Ogden (2004, p. 1356) uses the words of Edgar Allan Poe as a way of making sense of Bion's concept of beta elements: 'Unthought-like thoughts that are the souls of thought'. I have my own understanding, based on my own experience, of what I believe Bion was describing by the term beta elements. For me, they feel like a shadowy presence, barely within my awareness but there enough for me to experience myself differently from how I would if they were not there.

Bion suggests that beta elements are made more available to awareness through a process that he terms 'alpha function' (Bion, 1962b, p. 308). He describes this process as 'that which makes available what would otherwise remain unavailable' (Bion, 1962a, p. 36). Bion links the capacity for alpha function to the infant's earliest experiences with the mother. He describes the mother's role in supporting the infant to manage beta elements by taking them in, working on them, and handing them back in a more manageable form.

Beginning to Make Sense

As I tried to deepen my understanding of alpha function, I began to realise that part of my struggle to comprehend comes from the elusiveness of the concept itself. This, in fact, seems to be the reason that Bion uses abstract terms to describe this process. 'The process by which Beta was transformed he regarded as fundamental in the production of thoughts, and, as its nature was unknown, he did not want to give the impression that it was known' (Britton, 1992, p. 105). My perception of alpha function is that it is a process that brings the shadowy presence of beta elements further into my awareness, enough so that they take a shape and a form that makes them 'something' rather than 'not quite something'. This slight transformation of beta elements through alpha function into 'something' allows me to have a relationship with them, which means that they are available for me to think about.

Bion terms those elements that have now become something, 'alpha elements' (Bion, 1963, p. 22). He describes alpha elements as 'not objects in the world of external reality but...products of work done on the sensa believed to relate to such realities' (Bion, 1963, p. 22). It seems to me that the term alpha element describes a kind of halfway house between an intangible beta element and something that is fully formed as a thought. Bion suggests that alpha elements can take the form of 'visual, auditory and olfactory impressions that are storable in memory, usable in dreaming and in unconscious waking thinking' (Symington and Symington, 2004, p. 61).

As I turn to my own experiences to help me grasp the concept of alpha elements, I find that I have less of a sense of these than I did of beta elements. Although as I write that, I am aware of a feeling of anxiety in my tummy. This reminds me that one of the ways that I 'work something out' is to focus on my bodily responses to my thoughts and to allow images and memories that relate to these responses into my awareness. Maybe this is the closest that I can come, just now, to making sense of the term alpha elements from my own experience.

It feels almost impossible to continue my description of this process in such a step-by-step way. I have reached the point of trying to outline the system that Bion suggests we use for thinking. However, I realise that as he describes the roots of this system, he is also describing the roots of alpha function. It seems that they are maybe the same thing, although up until now I have not thought of them in that way. I realise I am finding it difficult to think about something that I sense and have an emotional experience of, and even more difficult to try to communicate that in a way that will make sense to others.

Container and Contained

Central to Bion's work are his ideas about the mechanism that enables alpha elements to be worked on. He proposes a system that allows for thinking and thoughts to be brought together, in order that some kind of making sense can take place. Bion (1962a, p. 90) uses the terms 'container and contained' to describe the central elements of this system. To conceptualise these terms, Bion refers to the work of Melanie Klein and her understanding of primitive elements of the mother–infant relationship: 'Melanie Klein has described an aspect of projective identification concerned with the modification of infantile fears; the infant projects a part of its psyche, namely its bad feelings, into a good breast. Thence in due course, they are removed and reintrojected' (Bion, 1962a, p. 90).

Within this process, Bion uses the term 'container' to stand for that 'into which an object is projected' (1962a, p. 90) and the term 'contained' as 'the object that can be projected into the container' (1962a, p. 90). He then suggests that the baby can introject the container/contained system, which becomes 'installed in the infant as part of the apparatus for alpha-function' (1962a, p. 90). I also have a sense of this from my own experience of therapy; a sense of my increased capacity to do some of the work for myself that previously I would have done with my therapist.

When Bion uses the terms container and contained, he is not using them to describe fixed entities. On the contrary, they are dynamic and constantly shifting. The container has been described as 'the capacity for the unconscious psychological work of dreaming, operating in concert with the capacity for preconscious dreamlike thinking (reverie) and the capacity for more fully conscious secondary-process thinking' (Ogden, 2004, p. 1356). My understanding of the container is that it is any system that is used to gain a greater sense of meaning in relation to that which is being contained. The contained has been described as 'thoughts (in the broadest sense of the word) and feelings that are in the process of being derived from one's lived emotional experience' (ibid., p. 1356). Bion suggests that a healthy container/contained system will lead to the growth of both.

I can make sense of this dynamic relationship between container and contained through my experience of writing this chapter. At times I experience, through reading and making links, a sense of a growth of ideas. There comes a point when I feel as if I need to order those ideas and make some sense of them. For me, this usually means grouping things that I have read and then writing about them. My sense is that struggling to write down my thoughts in a coherent form is my way of containing them. In this instance the act of making my thoughts (the contained) coherent enough to be available for another person to read becomes the container. My experience fits with Bion's hypothesis that thoughts exist without a thinker and that eventually 'thinking is forced on an existing apparatus which has to be adapted to its new task of coping with thoughts' (Thorner, 1981, p. 74).

Different Ways of Knowing

Bion's work centres around his desire to develop an understanding of the nature of learning, particularly in relation to the process of psychoanalysis. Bion differentiates among different ways of knowing, one of which he terms 'K'. My understanding is that he considers the K link between counsellor and client to be the element that allows the client's emotional experience to be thought about and then framed or spoken about in a way that gives it meaning (for example through interpretation). This K link is an enabling factor that is central to the development of the thinking (container/contained) process. It also seems possible that the work of the container/contained actually carries out the process of K. It feels, to me, as if one enhances the other.

Bion is quite specific about the type of knowledge that is inherent in the K link. He argues that K does not lead to the possession of a piece of knowledge for client and counsellor but, rather, that both are 'in the state of getting to know' (1962a, p. 47). He suggests that this is made possible by bringing together 'emotion and cognition' (Malcolm, 1992, p. 122).

As with the capacity for alpha function and with the capacity for the container/contained process, Bion believes that the capacity for establishing learning in K stems from the infant's first experiences with the mother. 'The origin of the K link was in the process between mother and child based on the infant's use of projective identification and the mother's capacity to receive it and modify it' (Britton, 1992, p. 106). Within this conceptual framework the baby projects its experience onto the mother, who then hands back the experience in a way that makes sense to the baby. It seems that a successful K link relies on the mother being able to offer something back to the baby in such a way that it is neither meaningless nor overwhelming. The experience should be altered enough so that the baby can manage it but not be so altered that the baby is no longer able to recognise it as being its experience.

So far, I have explored Bion's ideas about the way in which two people, in relationship, can extend their understanding of an emotional experience.

To reach this point, I have experienced the struggle of trying to gather together ideas, structure them in some way, find words to express them, and then offer those words in a coherent form. I am uncertain about how they are experienced by the reader and whether they do actually make sense. I am proceeding with a sense of not knowing what I have achieved so far. Bion suggests that 'intolerance of the unknown and our need to snatch at something that explains it smothers the opportunity of coming to the truth' (Symington and Symington, 2004, p. 182).

Bion (1965) argues that absolute truth does exist, and he terms it O. He defines O as 'that which is the ultimate reality represented by such terms as ultimate reality, absolute truth, the godhead, the infinite, the thing-in-itself' (Bion, 1970, p. 26). Bion believes that ultimate reality is not something that we can know but rather something that we are. He states that 'The most, and the least that the individual person can do is to be it' (Bion, 1965, p. 140). In this way O (truth) differs from K (knowledge). Lipgar and Pines (2003, p. 241) suggest that O represents 'how we are alive (being)', whereas K represents 'what we know (knowledge)'.

Although O is ultimately unknowable, my understanding is that the processes that I described earlier can bring us closer to O. Symington and Symington (2004, p. 121) suggest that O is 'approached by mental growth'. So, the more we expose ourselves to the type of learning that I am exploring, the more likely we are to know more of our own O. Grinberg, Sor, and Tabak de Bianchedi (1975, p. 69) explain that O also represents an element of the learning process that I outlined previously: the contained. They state that 'it is possible to refer to the absolute truth as a "thought without a thinker"' (Grinberg, Sor, and Tabak de Bianchedi, 1975, p. 69). To help me make sense of this, I consider O specifically in the context of the counselling relationship and in the context of my own experience. According to Thorner (1981, p. 75) O 'belongs to the emotional world and not to the world of things'. In a counselling session, both the counsellor and the client are trying to find a way to make sense of the client's emotional world. As part of this process, my experience as a counsellor is that I am trying to make sense of my own emotional experience of the client. I do not know the client's ultimate reality, but I am trying to find a way 'to say something that has a quality that is true to lived experience' (Ogden, 2003, p. 597). In doing this, I am trying to find a process by which I can work on what the client is offering me, in a way that will help the client make more sense of that which he or she is offering. I am trying to contain (think about) the client's emotional truths (thoughts). In order to do this successfully, the emotional truths need to

216

be transformed into something that is available to think about. In other words, K is applied to O to produce a transformation of O.

Application to Therapy

As I write this I am aware that I am supporting my own understanding of what I am writing by using an experience in my own therapy as an example. In a recent therapy session I spent some of the time talking about an evening out during which I had felt excluded. I also talked about the extent to which I was embroiled in my dissertation and how much of an all-consuming experience it had become. For most of the session I felt distant from my therapist. I spent quite a lot of time gazing into space, not really being able to grasp my thoughts, feelings, or physical sensations. Towards the end of the session my therapist made a link between my talk of exclusion and my experience of studying in a way that seemed to revolve around an internal dialogue between my thoughts and feelings. She linked this to the way in which I was struggling to include her in my session, as if I was in a bubble and had lost the ability to make contact with anyone on the outside. For the remainder of the session I was much more able to engage with her, and I regained a sense of perspective. It was as if I could lift my head up, look around and see an 'out there' world as well as an 'in here' world.

In terms of Bion's O, I was caught up in a bubble that existed as an ultimate reality during the beginning of the session; it was a thought without a thinker. My therapist seemed to pick up on a sense of that thought. She was then able to offer this back to me in a way that was close enough to the emotional truth of my experience for her words to make sense. I believe that this was a K link between us. Through that link I experienced myself differently. Also through that link, I knew something about my O of the beginning of the session. However, I recognise that O had existed in relation to nothing. I could not know it until it was brought into my awareness, and the act of bringing it into my awareness meant that it was no longer O but a transformation of O. I had moved from a position of 'not knowing' to 'knowing about'.

My therapist brought O into my awareness by putting her experience of me into words. When she suggested that I was in a bubble and unable to really include her, I had a sense that what she said was close enough to the reality of my emotional experience for it to seem truthful. My emotional experience changed directly as a result of this new truth. Priel

(2004, p. 939) refers to this as 'the simultaneity of truth and its trans-formations'. It seems to me that this phenomenon links not only to the counselling situation but also to my experience of writing this chapter. One challenge of exploring Bion's work is that gaining new understanding simultaneously alters that understanding. Maybe I have to be content with having some knowledge (K) of the truth (O) of Bion's work.

Chaos Monsters and Negative Capability

I have explored the way in which Bion considers O to be ever-evolving. I have also given a sense of what it is like to live with the experience of something that is ever-evolving, both in my therapy and in exploring Bion's ideas. The state of constant evolution precludes the presence of certainty. This is a central theme in Bion's work: 'in positing O, Bion replaced positivistic, deterministic certainty with infinite ever-evolving, ever-transient, all too chaotically meaningful mystery and uncertainty' (Grotstein, 2004, p. 1096). In my therapy and in writing this chapter there are times when I feel unable to continue and overwhelmed by the chaos and uncertainty, so the experience of 'not knowing' seems too much. I experience a tightening in my tummy and a feeling of dizziness. This reminds me of the feelings that I experienced just before I jumped out of an aeroplane to do a free-fall sky-dive! Britton (2011) refers to the feelings evoked at these times as 'chaos monsters'.

Tolerating these 'chaos monsters', rather than fleeing from them, is central to Bion's conceptualisation of the process of learning. In the process of knowing more (K) about ultimate realties (O), he argues that a growth in K can lead to growth in O. It also seems that he considers this to be a spiralling process in which an increased knowledge of O leads to an increase in the capacity for K. In other words 'truth is essential for mental growth' (Grinberg, Sor, and Tabak de Bianchedi, 1975, p. 68). However, Bion also postulates that the transformations of O that are brought about by knowing more (K) 'are feared and arouse resistance' (Grinberg, Sor, and Tabak de Bianchedi, 1975, p. 76). At the point at which we are about to gain some understanding (K) of our emotional experience (O), we become resistant to the idea. Bion states that 'I think it is "better" to know the truth about oneself but I do not wish to imply that it is "nicer", or "pleasanter"' (Bion in Grotstein, 2004, p. 1082).

We have a choice (often unconscious) at the point of chaos or 'not knowing', 'either of evasion of the awareness of the painful emotional experience, or of choosing to accept its truth by being willing to suffer it (Bion in Grotstein, 2004, p. 1087). I think that he is saying that there is a point just before we reach a new understanding when to depart from our old understanding feels unpleasant and uncomfortable. We have a choice then: either to cling to our old understanding (or perhaps to jump to a premature new understanding), or to tolerate the experience of uncertainty and 'not knowing' for long enough to allow new understanding to evolve.

Bion offers the term 'negative capability' to suggest the state of mind in which we can cope with 'not knowing'. He borrows this term from Keats, for whom it describes 'when a man is capable of being in uncertainties, mysteries, doubts, without any irritable reaching after fact and reason' (Bion, 1970, p. 125). Bion uses this term in relation to the experience of increasing our understanding of our individual truths (O). The longer we can remain in a state of negative capability the closer we may come to knowing the real truth of our emotional experience. The alternatives may be to avoid the truth or to create a premature truth. Either of these would make us safe from the 'catastrophic anxiety that occurs at the moment of psychic change' (Symington and Symington, 2004, p. 131), but neither would honestly reflect our ultimate reality.

Bion proposes that our ability to cope with the frustration of 'not knowing' links to our earliest experiences within the mother–infant relationship. My perception is that the baby has to learn to live with the time it takes between experiencing a need and having that need met (for example time between needing the breast and finding the breast). If the baby is able to tolerate this time by having a sense of what is not there, that is 'the no-breast' (Bion 1962b, p. 307), then it is developing the capacity to think. In turn, developing the capacity to think enhances the capacity for tolerating frustration and thereby enhances negative capability.

Bion uses the term negative capability to suggest a state of mind that supports both the counsellor and the client within sessions. For the counsellor, this state is not so much about searching for knowledge about O but more about being open to whatever the client brings. Rather than searching for the truth, Priel (2004, p. 941) encourages the counsellor 'to allow oneself to be affected by it'. The more open we are, the less cluttered by preconceived ideas about what might be going on in the session, the more available we make ourselves to receive the client's experience. In that way we allow ourselves to be affected by what the client brings.

Noticing the ways in which the client material affects us may support us to make some sense of his or her emotional experience. When the time feels right, we may then offer the sense that we have made back to the client, for his or her consideration.

Over a period of time, the client is influenced by the counsellor's capacity for negative capability. The counsellor's ability to allow him- or herself to be affected by the client's emotional truth, rather than reaching for an, as yet, unavailable truth, supports the client to do the same. Bion relates this to what happens in the mother–infant relationship. He writes that 'a capacity for tolerating frustration enables the psyche to develop thought as a means by which the frustration that is tolerated is itself made more tolerable' (Bion 1962b, p. 307).

Negative capability 'is not an immediate mental discipline to be engaged with but rather a way of life' (Symington and Symington, 2004, p. 169). The capacity for negative capability and the connections Bion makes between the mother–infant relationship and that which exists between the client and counsellor are deeply significant for the system that I have been exploring in this chapter. In its simplest form, this system involves a process of experiencing beta elements, working on these through alpha function, experiencing alpha elements, thinking about these by allowing them to affect us so that we come to know more of the original emotional experience. If it is experienced over time, this capacity can be reintrojected as an internal system. This is one of the ultimate goals of the therapeutic relationship. 'The end of an analysis is not measured principally by the extent of resolutions of unconscious conflict but by the degree to which the patient is able to dream his lived emotional experience on his own' (Ogden, 2004, p. 1359).

In this chapter, I have explored some of the key ideas of Wilfred Bion. I would like to conclude by giving a brief insight into the impact of exploring Bion's work and, specifically, of exploring it 'in the spirit' of Bion. Initially, I used my investigation into Bion's ideas to deepen my understanding of an ending with a particular client. By exploring that ending in the spirit of Bion, that is, by allowing myself to be affected by the truth rather than searching for it, I learned that the client and I had avoided some of the pain of the ending of our time together. This learning has stayed with me and, I feel certain, has become part of the system that allows me to think about (contain) the emotional truths that future clients bring. I also realise that I have an increased capacity for tolerating uncertainty and 'not knowing' in my life more generally. This has helped me through some difficult periods when dwelling in uncertainty has seemed close to intolerable. I set out to explore something 'small' by focusing on something quite specific, namely the ideas of Wilfred Bion that consider how counsellor and client relate in order to deepen their understanding of the client's experience. Surprisingly, I have been affected by my learning in a way that has left me feeling altered.

References

Bion, W. R. (1962a) *Learning from Experience* (London: Heinemann).

Bion, W. R. (1962b) 'A theory of thinking', *International Journal of Psychoanalysis*, 43, 306–310.

Bion, W. R. (1963) *Elements of Psycho-Analysis* (London: Heinemann).

Bion, W. R. (1965) *Transformations* (London: Heinemann).

Bion, W. R. (1970) *Attention and Interpretation* (London: Tavistock).

Britton, R. (1992) 'Keeping things in mind' in R. Anderson (ed.) *Clinical Lectures on Klein and Bion* (London: Routledge) pp. 102–113.

Britton, R. (2011) 'The pleasure principle, the reality principle and the uncertainty principle' in C. Mawson (ed.) *Wilfred Bion Today* (Hove: Routledge) pp. 64–80.

Grinberg, L., Sor, D., and Tabak de Bianchedi, E. (1975) *Introduction to the Work of Bion* (Strathtay: Clunie Press).

Grotstein, J. (2004) 'The seventh servant: The implications of a truth drive in Bion's theory of "O"' *International Journal of Psychoanalysis*, 85 (5), 1080–1101.

Lipgar, R., and Pines, M. (2003) *Building on Bion: Roots, Origins and Context of Bion's Contributions to Theory and Practice* (London: Jessica Kingsley).

Malcolm, R. R. (1992) 'As if: The phenomenon of not learning' in R. Anderson (ed.) *Clinical Lectures on Klein and Bion* (London: Routledge) pp. 114–125.

Ogden, T. (2003) 'What's true and whose idea was it anyway?' *International Journal of Psychoanalysis*, 84, 593–606.

Ogden, T. (2004) 'On holding and containing, being and dreaming', *International Journal of Psychoanalysis*, 85 (6), 1349–1364.

Priel, B. (2004) 'Negative capability and truth in Borges's "Emma Zunz"', *International Journal of Psychoanalysis*, 85 (4), 935–949.

Symington, J., and Symington, N. (2004) *The Clinical Thinking of Wilfred Bion* (Hove: Brunner-Routledge).

Thorner, H. (1981) 'Notes on the desire for knowledge', *International Journal of Psychoanalysis*, 62, 73–80.

Index